Cruising

THE TIME-LIFE LIBRARY OF BOATING
HUMAN BEHAVIOR
THE ART OF SEWING
THE OLD WEST
THE EMERGENCE OF MAN
THE AMERICAN WILDERNESS
THE TIME-LIFE ENCYCLOPEDIA OF GARDENING
LIFE LIBRARY OF PHOTOGRAPHY
THIS FABULOUS CENTURY
FOODS OF THE WORLD
TIME-LIFE LIBRARY OF AMERICA
TIME-LIFE LIBRARY OF ART
GREAT AGES OF MAN
LIFE SCIENCE LIBRARY
THE LIFE HISTORY OF THE UNITED STATES
TIME READING PROGRAM
LIFE NATURE LIBRARY
LIFE WORLD LIBRARY
FAMILY LIBRARY:
HOW THINGS WORK IN YOUR HOME
THE TIME-LIFE BOOK OF THE FAMILY CAR
THE TIME-LIFE FAMILY LEGAL GUIDE
THE TIME-LIFE BOOK OF FAMILY FINANCE

TIME
LIFE
BOOKS ®

Cruising

By the Editors of
TIME-LIFE BOOKS

The

TIME-LIFE Library of Boating

TIME-LIFE BOOKS, NEW YORK

The TIME-LIFE Library of Boating

Editorial staff for Cruising:
Editor: George Constable
Text Editors: Bryce S. Walker, Jay Brennan, Philip W. Payne
Picture Editors: Robert G. Mason, Helen M. Hinkle
Designer: Lee Stausland
Assistant Designer: James Eisenman
Staff Writers: Lee Hassig, Wendy Buehr Murphy, James Randall, Carolyn Stallworth, John von Hartz
Chief Researcher: Nancy Shuker
Researchers: Holly Evarts, Monica O. Horne, Joan McCullough, Shirley Miller, James B. Murphy, Joyce Pelto, Kathleen Shortall
Design Assistants: Rosi Cassano, Deana Lorenz, Sanae Yamazaki
Editorial Assistant: Lisa Berger McGuirt

Editorial Production
Production Editor: Douglas B. Graham
Assistant Production Editors: Gennaro C. Esposito, Feliciano Madrid
Quality Director: Robert L. Young
Assistant Quality Director: James J. Cox
Associate: Serafino J. Cambareri
Copy Staff: Eleanore W. Karsten (chief), Edward B. Clarke, Eleanor Van Bellingham, Florence Keith, Pearl Sverdlin
Picture Department: Dolores A. Littles, Carolyn Turman
Traffic: Carmen McLellan

First printing.
Published simultaneously in Canada.
Library of Congress catalogue card number 75-27445.

The Cover: A power cruiser and an auxiliary sloop slide beneath a setting sun toward separate anchorages along Trippes Creek, on the Eastern Shore of Chesapeake Bay. The winding creeks and inlets fringing the bay offer hundreds of secluded stopover points for cruising boatmen.

The Consultants: Halsey Herreshoff, navigator for *Courageous* in her successful defense of the America's Cup in 1974, has piloted sailing craft as well as powerboats for 25 years.

John D. Atkin is a yacht designer and professional surveyor, and is the Commodore of the Huntington Cruising Club of Darien, Connecticut.

Steve Colgate is an Olympic skipper and a well-known author of books on racing and cruising techniques; he also conducts cruising seminars at his Offshore Sailing School.

G. James Lippmann, a naval architect, is the executive director of the American Boat and Yacht Council.

William Munro, a powerboatman with more than 30 years of experience, is a photographer and author of many articles for *Motorboat* magazine and other boating publications.

John Rousmaniere, a small-boat sailor and veteran ocean racer, is the West Coast editor of *Yachting* magazine.

Owen C. Torrey Jr. is chief designer of Charles Ulmer, Inc., sailmakers.

Marcia Wiley is the managing editor of *Yachting* magazine. A skipper who has cruised from Long Island to the Aegean, she writes the magazine's monthly column, "Cabin Talk."

Valuable assistance was given by the following departments and individuals of Time Inc.: Editorial Production, Norman Airey; Library, Benjamin Lightman, Lester Annenberg; Picture Collection, Doris O'Neil; Photographic Laboratory, George Karas; TIME-LIFE News Service, Murray J. Gart; Correspondents Jane Estes (Seattle), Janet Zich (Stanford).

Contents

The Wide-open World of Cruising

The Wide-open World of Cruising

by Carleton Mitchell

Many years ago, at a Cruising Club of America dinner, I found myself seated between two superb deepwater sailors, Rod Stephens and George Richards. Rod, who was then Commodore of that well-salted group, is one of the greatest of all ocean-racing skippers; George, Vice Commodore, never raced. Their boats reflected their interests: Rod's 45-foot *Mustang* was a lean blue sloop, rakish as a privateer and skittish as any wild stallion, while George's double-ended ketch, *Freya,* epitomized docile comfort.

"Rod," I asked, "what do you do when you go cruising?"

"We keep the boat moving," replied Rod. "I don't say we cruise at racing efficiency, but we come close to it—maybe 95 per cent efficiency. Cruising would be boring otherwise."

I turned to George Richards, who had not heard Rod's answer, and asked him the same question. "We throw away the clock—*and* the calendar," he said. "Keeps us from ever getting in a hurry."

As I looked out over the wake astern, I thought, "I agree with George's philosophy of cruising." I remember lazy days on the Chesapeake early one summer, aboard my 38-foot yacht, *Finisterre.* As we stole out of Annapolis harbor in a gentle little southerly, I leaned against the mizzenmast, steering with a toe. Overhead the sky seemed very blue, dappled with puffy cumulus clouds; it was warm on deck in the sun, but chilly in the shade of the mainsail. A few months earlier, my crew and I had been slogging through boisterous tradewind seas encountered during a season of southern ocean racing. Now as the hours slipped by, we gave in to the luxurious calm of these sheltered waters.

We let wind and current decide the course, avoiding beats to windward like a dread disease, and never—but never!—getting so dead before the wind that we had to set a spinnaker. The Chesapeake is such a lacy pattern of mingled water and land there is almost always a harbor to leeward. Nearing sundown each day, we would ghost along past gently rolling countryside; trees would reflect, inverted, along the shore, and our chosen creek would take on the changing colors of the sky.

After the anchor splashed down we would sit in the cockpit a while, glass in hand, then go below to a cabin warm in lamplight. Nothing so snug as the cabin of a small boat in a snug harbor. Later would come a good dinner from the galley stove, and a bottle of wine; eating well is an important ingredient in my personal cruising philosophy, abetted by good conversation and music from a hi-fi system. Then, if it came on to blow during the night, we would snuggle peacefully into our bunks and let it blow for somebody else.

But I recall moments of another kind, equally enjoyable: a dawn departure from a sea buoy, tanks full and lockers crammed with stores and spares, deck gear lashed, land astern fading into the haze and only empty ocean ahead, a thousand miles or more. For it has been my good fortune to have cruised through some of the world's best boating waters, from the skerries of the Baltic to the coral-sand beaches of the Caribbean, from the isles of Greece to the Sea of Japan. The boats I have sailed in have ranged from small knockabout sloops with an outboard hung over the stern to majestic schooners, from vest-pocket powerboats to yachts with uniformed stewards serving champagne on the afterdeck. Always, the size and type of craft, and even its destination, has seemed less important than the simple fact of being on the water, able to look ahead to a new landfall—wherever it might be—all part of a way of life whose only common denominator is wandering afloat.

Stripped to essentials, that is what cruising is all about: living aboard a boat and going places. At first it may be no farther than a favorite picnic cove for a single day's outing. But as soon as you elect to spend the night, you add a whole new dimension. No longer is a hamper of sandwiches and precooled drinks sufficient in the way of stores. The usual clutch of after-swim bath

Author Carleton Mitchell takes the helm during a brisk downwind slide off Montego Bay, Jamaica. In powerboats and under sail, Mitchell has cruised for half a century, from the Chesapeake to the Sea of Japan.

towels must be supplemented with bedding—and what's for breakfast? You quickly discover that you are very much on your own.

This sense of independence is one of the great pleasures of cruising, but it entails certain responsibilities, and a measure of foresight. Cruising boats must be self-contained; so must cruising skippers be self-reliant. The basics of seamanship become more important than ever—ability to read the weather signs, to pilot a boat through unfamiliar waters, to pick an anchorage, to handle ground tackle. Aboard *Finisterre's* successor, my 42-foot Grand Banks trawler, *Sans Terre,* I once lay in Christmas Cove near the eastern end of Saint Thomas in the Virgin Islands, alongside a yawl of about the same size. We had both set our hooks in the sandy bottom and slacked out the rode for a scope of about 7 to 1—the generally accepted ratio for normal weather. Then a small sloop nosed into the cove in the clumsy manner suggestive of an inexperienced skipper handling a strange—and perhaps chartered—boat. The sloop anchored ahead of my neighbor and promptly dragged down onto his bow. After much fending off, the sloop got underway and tried again. Same result. I called across as the anchor went down again for the third time, "Slack out more line!" The man on the bow yelled back with the fury of frustration: "Why? It's touching bottom!"

If that neophyte skipper had learned no more of other boating fundamentals, what should have been a delightful experience in one of the world's most blessed cruising grounds must have become a nightmare for all hands.

Choosing the right cruising boat can be nearly as important as knowing how to handle it. And although the variety of cruising boats is almost as great as the pleasures and destinations to be sought, to me there are certain inviolable criteria for picking the boat that's right for you: it must be one that suits the cruising ground, the size of the crew—and your pocketbook.

My own personal taste is for comfort. And to me, comfortable cruising requires basic accommodations—galley, head, true bunks, locker space. Within these minimums, it is wise for a prospective owner to think small. Around 25 feet overall provides comfort over extended periods for two people, or short-term accommodations for four. Adding another pair of bunks usually means extending the boat's length by some six feet. In projecting the true size of a boat, any increase in length increases a boat's volume exponentially. It is astonishing, therefore, how swiftly a boat gets big—and equally astonishing how cost of maintenance, difficulty of handling, and other related factors skyrocket. In these terms, a 50-footer may be literally twice as much to cope with as a 40-footer. Nor does increase in size necessarily mean greater seaworthiness, which is a function of design and construction. Big boats get into trouble just as often as small ones.

It is particularly important to remember that not every yacht that may be billed as a cruiser fits every cruising ground. Years ago I was invited by a friend to go along on his new boat during a shakedown cruise through the Bahamas. When I arrived in Miami and saw a heavy, short-rigged, double-ended ketch of the type originated for use off Norway's rugged, windy coast, I suspected that we were in for misery.

Crossing to Bimini we encountered a moderate easterly breeze and head sea—normal conditions for the area. Canvased for gales, our craft would not sail to windward. Only the motor saved us from drifting helplessly in the Gulf Stream current, away from our goal. On finally arriving at Bimini, we promptly went aground, a prelude to spending much of our vacation kedging off. The deep draft that was no handicap in fjords was completely unsuited to the shallow Bahama Bank. At the same time, we sweltered below in ventilation planned for arctic climes. When we finally struggled into the harbor at Nassau, my friend was ready to trade his dream ship for a chicken farm.

And once you have the right boat, choosing the right shipmates—even within the family—can make the difference between delight and fathomless gloom. I experienced both in the same place—Hadley Harbor, one of the most charming of the snug hideaways along the New England coast. On the first occasion, I had invited a couple casually met in Nantucket to sail with me to Newport aboard *Carib,* a 46-foot Alden-designed ketch that I owned at the time. I was shorthanded, the weather forecast was not promising and I thought an extra hand on deck might be useful. Also, as the wife had rhapsodized about her love of cooking, I anticipated a steady flow of treats from the galley. We had hardly passed through Woods Hole when a nor'easter pounced; by the time we anchored in Hadley Harbor it was blowing gale force, with driving rain. For three days it howled and poured. We could not even get ashore in the dinghy. Acute boredom swiftly set in. The husband emptied every bottle aboard; the wife didn't go near the galley; and both never stopped screaming abuse at each other, except to berate me.

The following autumn, I anchored again in Hadley Harbor, this time in company with an old shipmate, Joe McCammon, to wait out an approaching hurricane. Again for three days it rained and blew. Joe and I relaxed below, completely in tune with our surroundings and each other, reminiscing, reading, listening to music and whomping up masterpieces in the galley. From Joe I learned another facet of cruising, which added to our enjoyment and has become part of my own philosophy: "Eat and drink the best you have, then you're always having the best." We started on choice steaks and my vintage Bordeaux. By the time the storm veered out to sea, we were down to hot dogs and beer, but sorry to end our idyllic interlude.

Another simple axiom for successful cruising is to prepare in advance: do everything possible before shoving off so you can relax afterward. I remember Bobby Symonette of Nassau, who crewed aboard *Finisterre* on two of our three Bermuda race victories, lounging in the cockpit at Newport the day before a start. "Look at 'em," he laughed, nodding toward the crews of competitors rafted nearby, who were climbing the mast to inspect rigging, oiling snap shackles on deck and stopping sails. "And all we have to do is have another beer!" Such jobs on *Finisterre* had been done long before, leaving us free for an afternoon sail. Once underway, we knew that nothing was likely to go wrong no matter what conditions we might encounter—the ultimate key to the confident enjoyment of any boating.

Some cruising preparations can begin months before, while you relax in an armchair. Plan where you are going, and what you will need both when en route and when you get there. Study the charts of the area; they will give you a preview of what you will find later. If your itinerary is sure to carry you to populated ports, you can expect to replenish fresh stores as you go along, but if your route includes the byways, you will have to expand your inventory of supplies accordingly. Above all, make sure the charts in your navigator's nook cover both the waters you plan to cruise and the seas around them. If you follow the dictates of the wind and your personal inclinations—instead of doggedly adhering to a fixed schedule—you might even wind up going in the opposite direction from the one you planned, as I once did on *Carib.*

We had left Nassau for the Virgin Islands, but encountered strong head winds and big seas off Haiti. For days we tacked back and forth in sight of the same mountain peak. Then we decided to hell with it: the Virgins could wait another year. So we slacked sheets and ran down to Jamaica, having on board the necessary charts to go west as well as east, and enjoyed a wonderful winter. Ever since, I have looked upon charts as a form of insurance in case of either emergency or sheer sloth—a good investment even if never used.

Along with charts, a check list of essentials—including galley provisions and spare working parts for the boat—should be prepared at leisure. It should be broken down into departments, such as mechanical (items like spark plugs or water-pump impellers), deck (rigging and sails), and galley (including extras of whatever it takes to keep the stove going). The check list for larger vessels on long trips may go into such details as the individual duties of each crew member. On *Finisterre,* a boat best known as an ocean racer but that cruised 10 miles for every one sailed competitively, crew members coming aboard found posted a notice assigning each a bunk, a drawer for clothing, a bin in the head for toilet articles, and a regular turn at chores like cooking or dishwashing. Such predeparture organization is vital for harmonious coexistence in the limited confines of a boat.

Proper stowage of gear is essential. The importance of systematic stowage increases with size and complexity. On my vessel, *Land's End,* a 62-foot trawler built in Hong Kong, one of the ship's vital facilities was a loose-leaf notebook labeled "Location of Spares and Miscellany." In front was a foldout drawing of the belowdecks layout, with every usable cranny given a key letter and number, the letters referring to major divisions, such as forward cabin or galley, the numbers to accessible spaces. Thus A-3 might mean under the port forward bunk, C-5 behind the pilothouse settee, G-2 the lazarette locker. Everything was copiously cross-referenced. Suppose, during a gale, water began gaining below and you found that you needed a Jabsco bilge-pump impeller; would you look under J, B, P or I? Best to list all.

On either sail or power craft, stow heavy items low, in the interest of stability. If cans are stowed in lockers, be sure proper latches or hooks supplement the usual jam or magnetic catches; these can give way and release a cascade on sleepers to leeward. Plastic bags and paper towels are among the blessings of modern civilization, but make sure the former, once used, are held in a waste compartment and then disposed of ashore. The same goes for bottles and cans. Littering at sea is as reprehensible as it is ashore.

Then, after the preliminaries come the rewards. Besides the pleasures of unfamiliar scenery and new experiences, there are what I always think of as the fringe benefits of cruising—time for reading, fishing, snorkeling, learning new skills of seamanship, basking in the sun, or a little mild gluttony. No one should become an unwilling galley slave, but with imagination and a soupçon of extra effort, any cruise can be made more memorable.

You can experiment with a pinch of herbs or a dollop of sherry in a sauce, or add a hint of bourbon whiskey and some curry powder to a canned cream soup, then serve chilled instead of hot. You can bring prepared dishes from home: on a recent weekend, as we were lying behind North Carolina's Cape Lookout in a Hatteras 38-foot motor cruiser, my friend Billy Hines produced from portable ice chests such gastronomic delights as *gazpacho* and *vitello tonnato.* Aboard *Finisterre,* our first-night-at-sea dinner was, traditionally, an epic beef stew, cooked before leaving the dock.

Always, I try to live off the surrounding water and land, eating and drinking like a native. In the Baltic, the table of *Caribbee,* a 58-foot yawl I owned in the 1940s and early '50s, groaned under a daily smorgasbord ranging from several varieties of herring to smoked eel and reindeer, while we skoaled with schnapps. In the Bahamas, it would be conch salad and boiled grouper, again washed down with the wine of the country—rum punches. Along the shores of Canada's Georgian Bay, a daily hike might fill a basket with wild blueberries. In New England, clams are found on the flats and lobsters may be bought directly from fishermen hauling traps. The Chesapeake yields crabs and oysters; California, succulent abalone; the Pacific Northwest, salmon and some of the finest apples in the world. That evening at Cape Lookout it was shrimp netted the previous night, boiled in salt water and laced with celery, carrots, onions and plenty of red pepper. Sitting on the deck in the sunshine, watching the pile of shells grow on one another's plates while gulls wheeled astern begging for a share, we pitied all landsmen.

These pleasures of the galley are, for me, the gilding on the deep satisfaction of wandering afloat. I have poked into a thousand harbors and coves and gunkholes, from Granada in the Caribbean to Portofino in the Mediterranean, tied up to trees in the wooded coves of Lake Huron, or watched the moon come up over Catalina. And every passage I have taken has brought me pleasure or excitement, every landfall a sense of fulfillment. Far from telephones and shopping centers and city streets, much of my lifetime has been spent luxuriating in the sense of freedom that cruising provides. It has been a lifetime without boundaries—and no retirement age in sight.

1

IN SEARCH OF THE PERFECT VESSEL

The perfect cruising boat would be stout and steady enough to round Cape Horn, yet light and shallow enough to ghost into the tiniest cove on a calm day. While big enough to sleep eight, it would be sufficiently compact and convenient to single-hand. It would cost little to buy, nothing to maintain—yet please the most discriminating eye. No such boat exists, of course. All boats, and cruisers in particular, are a series of compromises. Each of the boats shown at left—and those described on the following pages—has its merits, and its limitations. The smaller craft combine low cost and versatility. For example, a compact outboard-powered runabout can tow a water-skier; if equipped with a cockpit cover and the kinds of seats that convert into bunks *(overleaf),* it will also serve as an inexpensive weekender. And its shallow draft allows it to poke into isolated inlets and tiny harbors far from crowds. Yet for some types of cruising, small size and shallow draft are handicaps: accommodations are limited and stowage areas insufficient for all but the hardiest crews and shortest cruises—and then strictly in sheltered waters.

A cruising skipper can extend his range and comfort—at considerable expense, and loss of versatility—by embarking in a larger boat. But here, too, he must compromise between his cruising style, his skills and the waters he plans to cruise—unless he is a master mariner like Joshua Slocum who, from 1895 to 1898, took the 37-foot sloop *Spray* singlehanded around the world. However, Slocum was not only an accomplished seaman, but also a skilled amateur shipwright who was able to convert his boat from a sloop to a yawl partway through the voyage when he found that a yawl rig made his particular boat more suitable for deep-sea sailing. Few modern sailors possess Slocum's considerable talents, and not all boats lend themselves to easy conversion for different waters.

In general, weekend harbor-hopping is most easily done with a simple sloop rig; extended deepwater passages are generally undertaken with the more balanced rig of a ketch or yawl. The shoals of the Chesapeake dictate a shallow draft; off California, a deep-keeled sailboat or trawler-type power cruiser will provide stability and ample capacity for fuel and stores—in an area where sheltered ports and supplies are far between. For comfort on hot days, a Gulf Coast boat should be reasonably open and airy, qualities that are frequently undesirable when cruising in September off the New England coast or on the northern Great Lakes. In those areas, small, tight hatches and a coal-burning stove would be more in order.

The most stringent limitation on a skipper's choice remains the size of his pocketbook. But the more he spends, the greater his cruising range and comfort are likely to be. Stock boats, even in the larger sizes, tend to have standardized accommodations, but in the more expensive vessels accommodations can be custom designed to suit the skipper's taste. Sailing auxiliaries, while less spacious belowdecks than are powerboats of comparable size, allow great flexibility in the arrangement of berths, facilities in the galley, multiple heads and areas for stowage.

The following pages contain a sampling of cruising boats that are shown underway, with their living accommodations detailed in cutaway drawings. For easy identification, the main elements are color-coded. The bunks are blue, the heads green and the galley equipment red. Each boat, with its living arrangements, is a representative example of a size and type. But the boatman should keep in mind that the possible variations are endless, and his own ideal vessel may be the ultimate compromise, with elements taken from every one of the samples shown.

Three yachts off California present a study in cruising tastes. At bottom is a comfortable power cruiser, at top a sleek auxiliary sloop, between them a ketch for long sea passages.

A Compact Cruiser-Camper

This 16-foot outboard provides spartan quarters for waterborne family camping. The two aft-facing cockpit seats (blue tint) fold down to make five-and-one-half-foot bunks, with the collapsible cockpit cover handy as a rain protector. Larger crewmen can use the six-foot seat forward. A tent ashore provides alternate accommodations. A camp stove carried ashore serves as a galley. With its six-foot-five-inch beam, the boat carrying its full gear can be conveniently trailered.

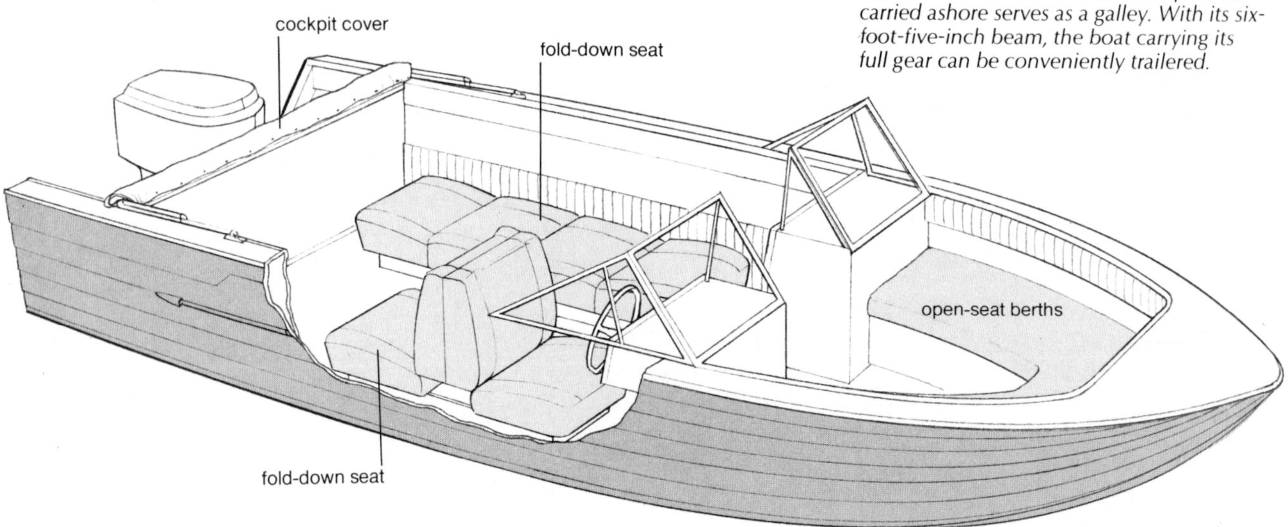

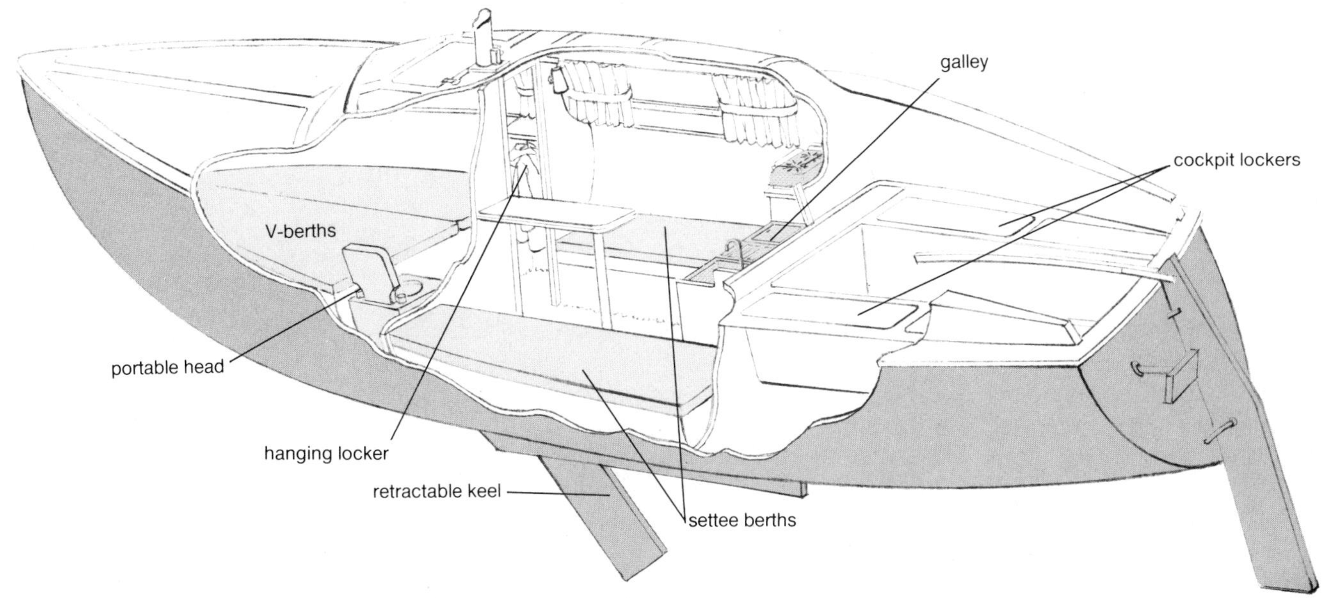

A Snug Weekender

A cruising yacht in miniature, this 23-foot sloop can accommodate a young family for a weekend or short week's vacation. There are four bunks: a pair of V-berths under the foredeck and two settees in the cabin. The head, shown in green, is closed off from the main cabin by a sliding door; and the galley, in red, is just under the hatch for maximum headroom. A retractable keel permits exploring in shoal waters–and also makes for easy launching from a trailer.

A Versatile Runabout

The 23-foot inboard-outboard runabout below doubles as an overnighter and a water-ski boat. Twin berths forward may be supplemented by two folding-seat bunks in the cockpit and a convertible bunk across the stern—all protected at night by a removable awning. The head is between the berths. A galley can go amidships, replacing one seat; an 80-gallon fuel tank gives ample range to secluded cruising grounds.

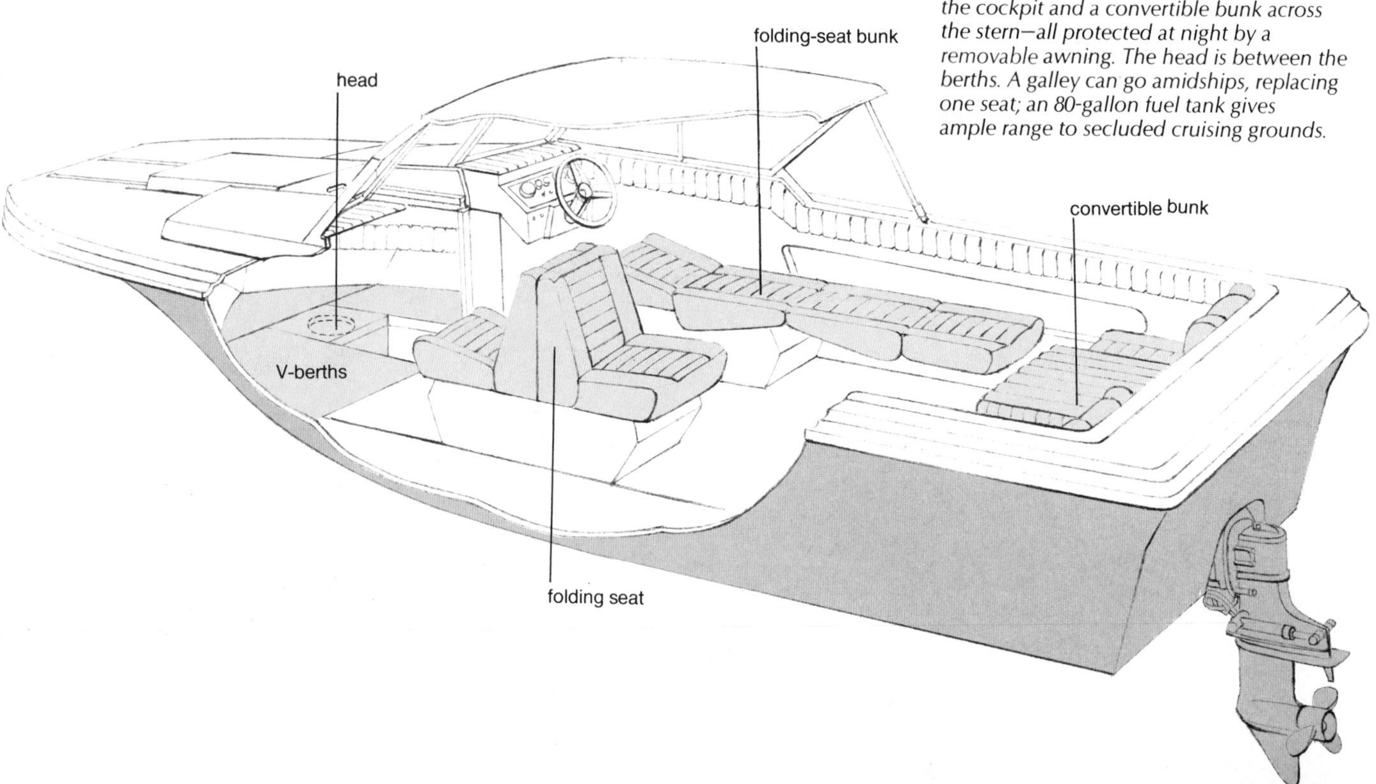

A Family-sized Sloop

Stout enough for fairly heavy weather, roomy enough to live on, this 27-foot sloop has accommodations for medium-range cruising. Two separate cabins, standing headroom amidships and a fully enclosed head with sink provide essential comfort and privacy. A stove, icebox and 12-gallon water tank allow temporary self-sufficiency. The vessel's full-ballast keel gives stability in a blow. An inboard or outboard engine can be installed.

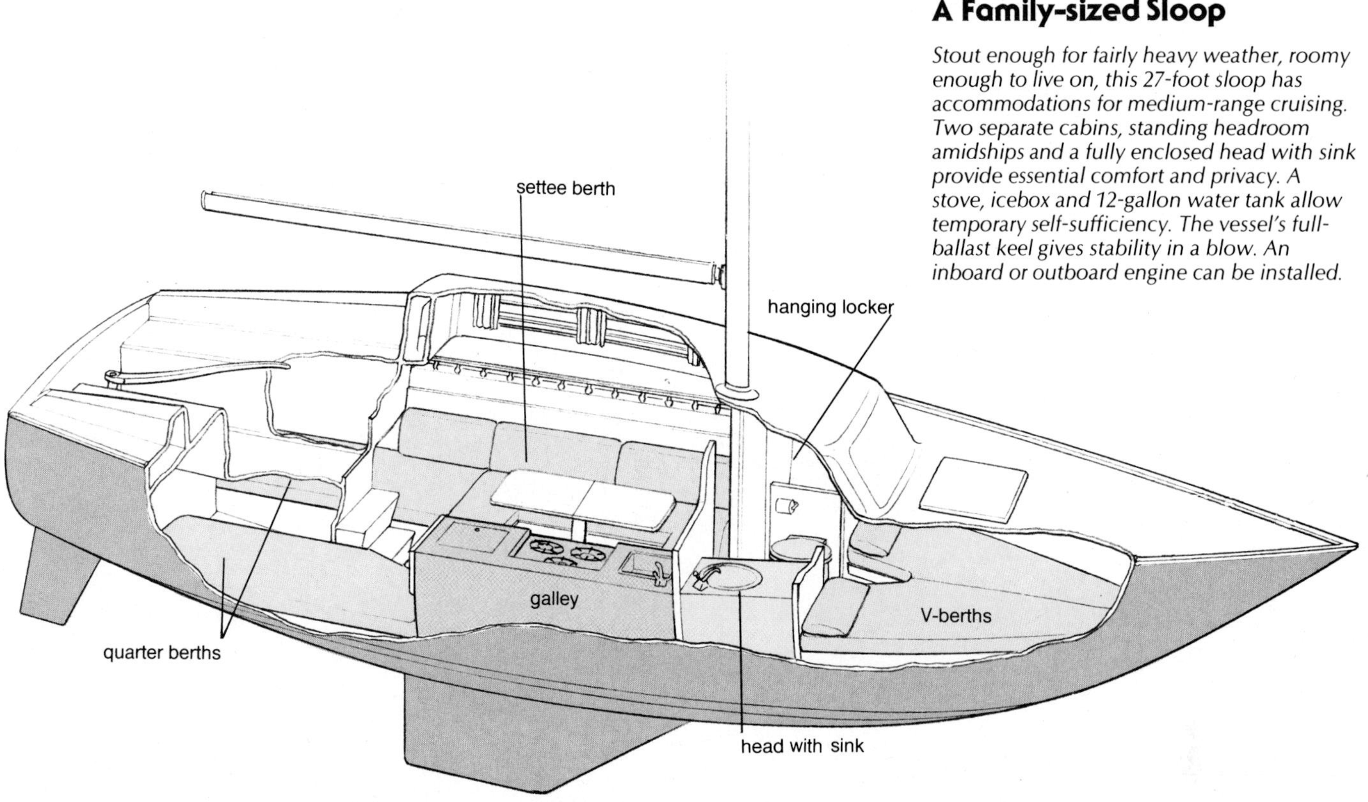

A Fast Sport Fisherman

This speedy utility inboard combines the open cockpit and unobstructed bridge of a sport fisherman with cozy accommodations for a weekend cruise. Two bunks, enclosed head and a small galley fit below. The 31-foot deep-V hull handles well in offshore swells; and with twin 233-hp engines generating speeds of more than 30 miles an hour, the boat can quickly get to where the fish are—and back, if a storm should arise.

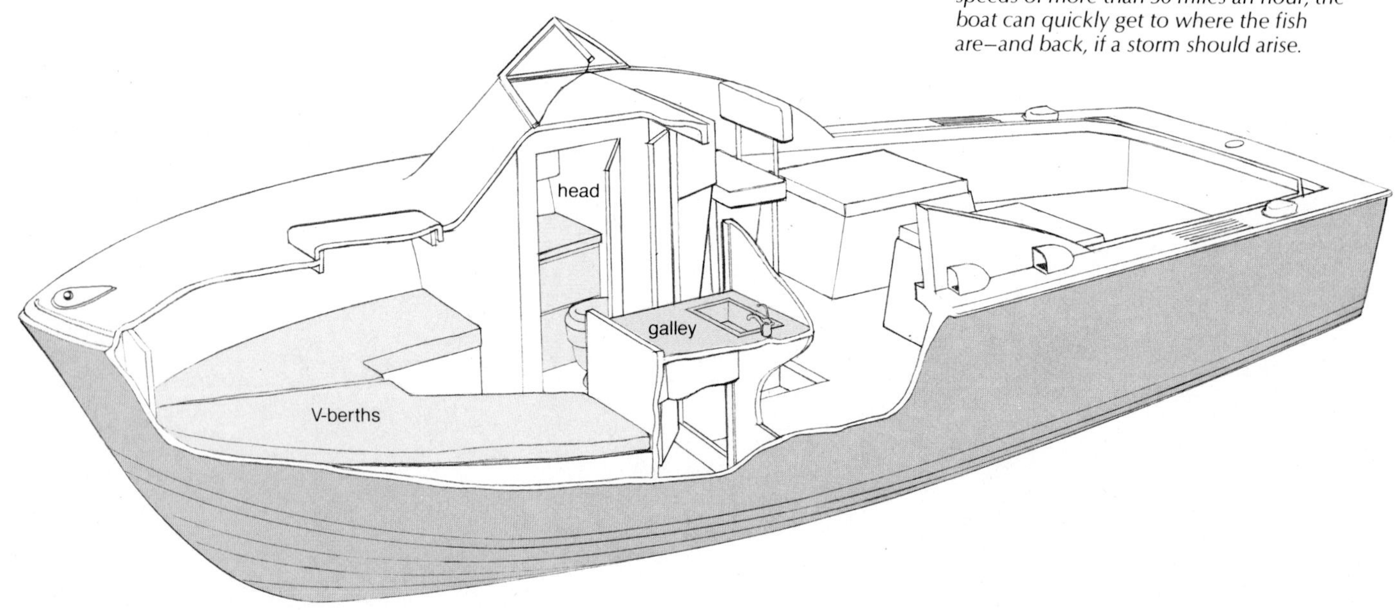

The Comfort of a Houseboat

For sheltered lakes or tidal waters, few craft can match the comfort of a well-planned houseboat. This 34-footer has double bunks for six, headroom of six and a half feet in all the cabins, house-sized windows, and a sun deck on top. The boat's 12-inch draft gives it almost unlimited freedom of movement in the shallow protected waters where it operates best, and a 225-hp engine provides a surprising top speed of 25 mph. But the flat bottom and high-profile deckhouse would make offshore cruising hazardous.

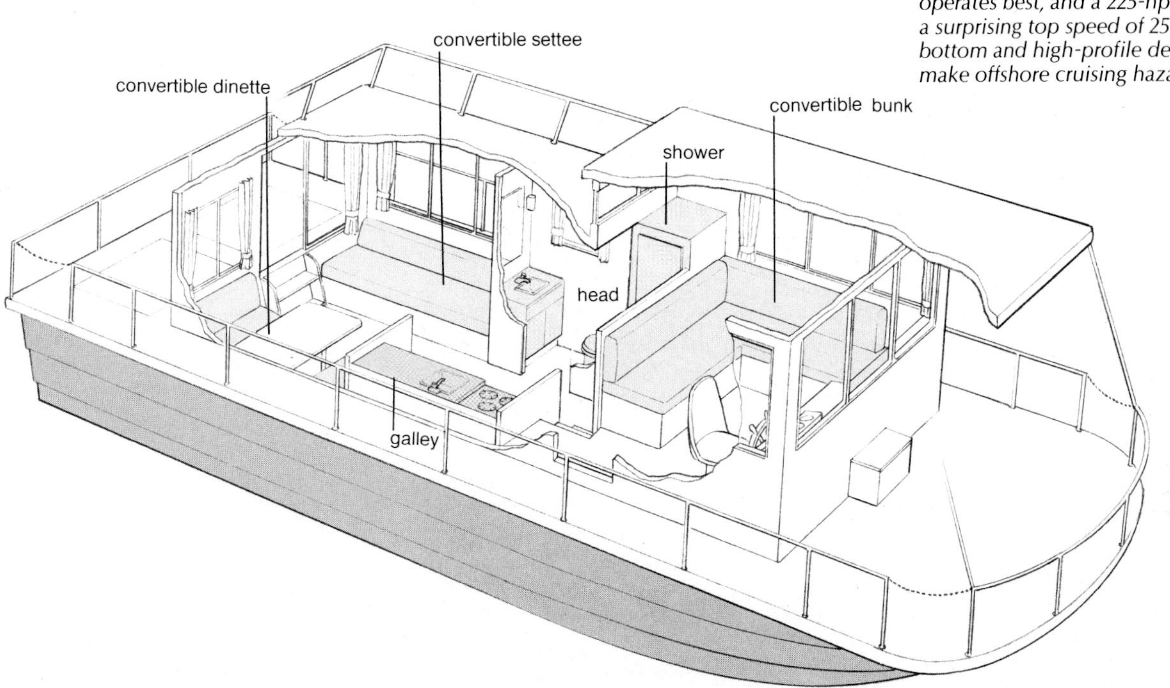

The Far-ranging Ketch

Designed for extended coastwise cruising, this 31-foot ketch has a full galley, enclosed head with sink, and bunks for six—including a dinette that converts into a double berth. The high cabin trunk gives six-foot headroom below. The ketch rig, though somewhat sluggish to windward, is easy to balance; in a storm the mainsail can be dropped, leaving the vessel under control with shortened sail.

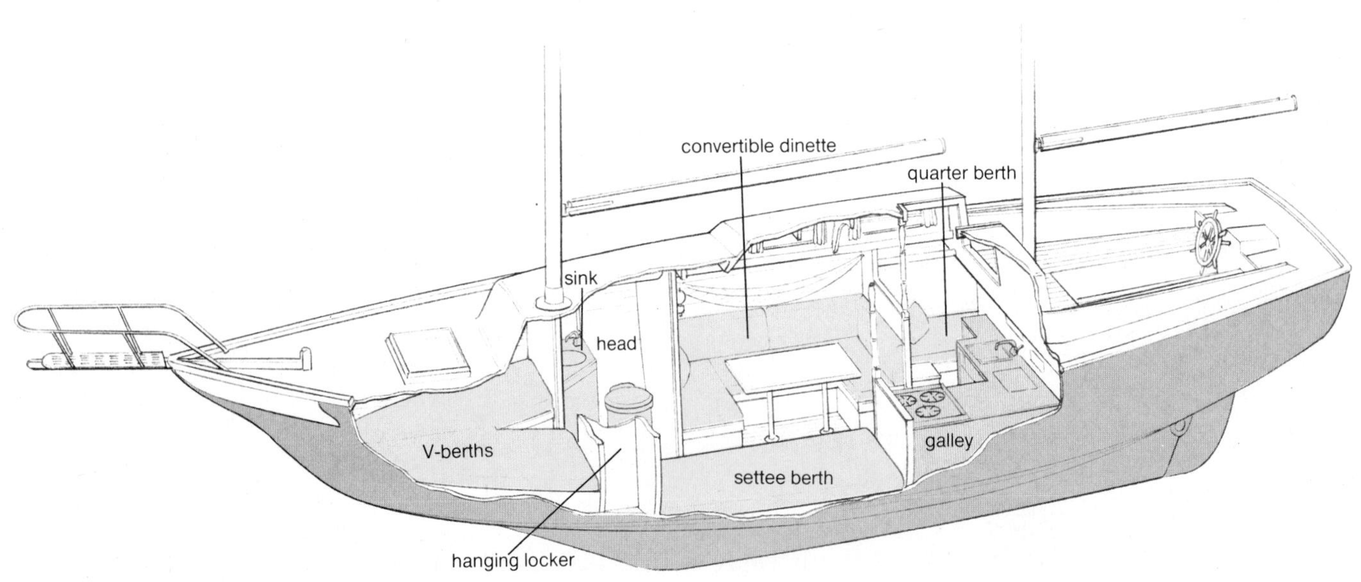

A Fast-footing Yawl

A yawl like the 32-footer shown here is perhaps the most versatile of rigs. Like the ketch, it balances easily, but the yawl's relatively larger mainsail and smaller mizzen allow it to sail faster to windward. For ease in handling with a reduced crew, the mizzen can be struck altogether and the boat sailed like a sloop—or, if the hands aboard are able, they can slide downwind under a mizzen staysail and spinnaker, as here.

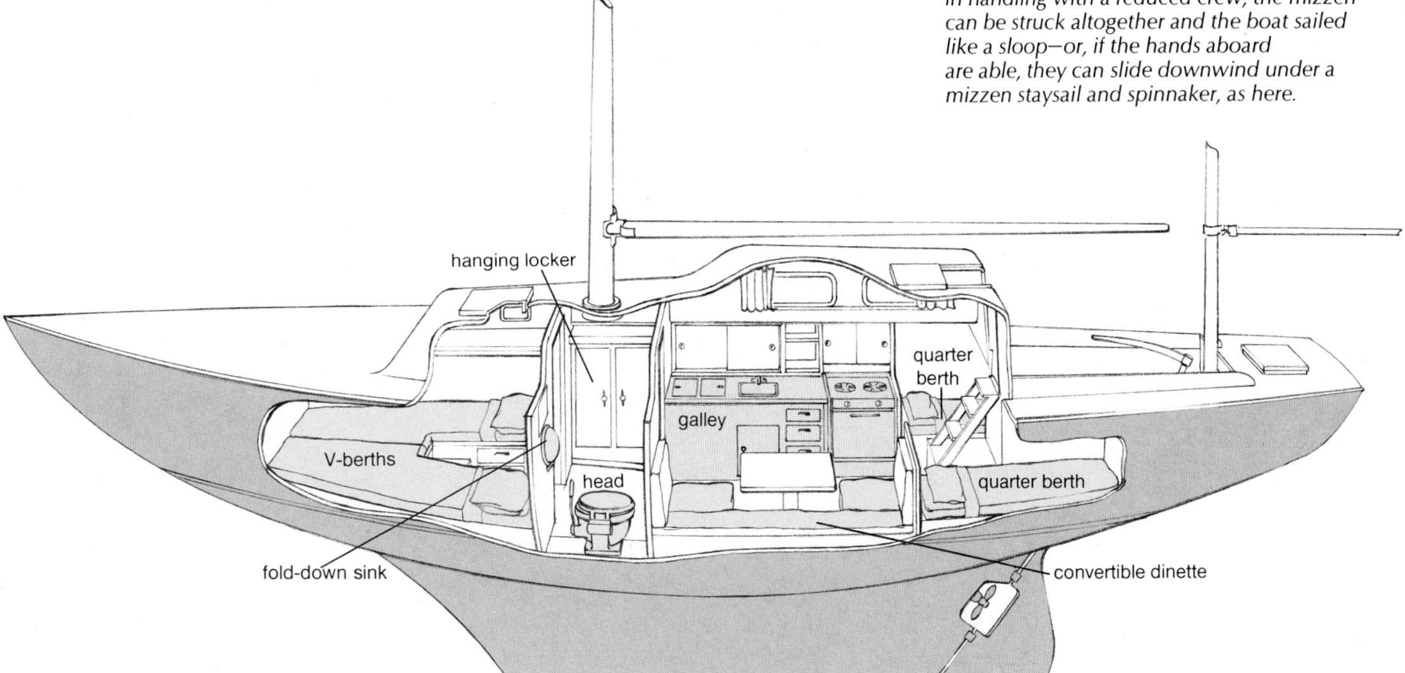

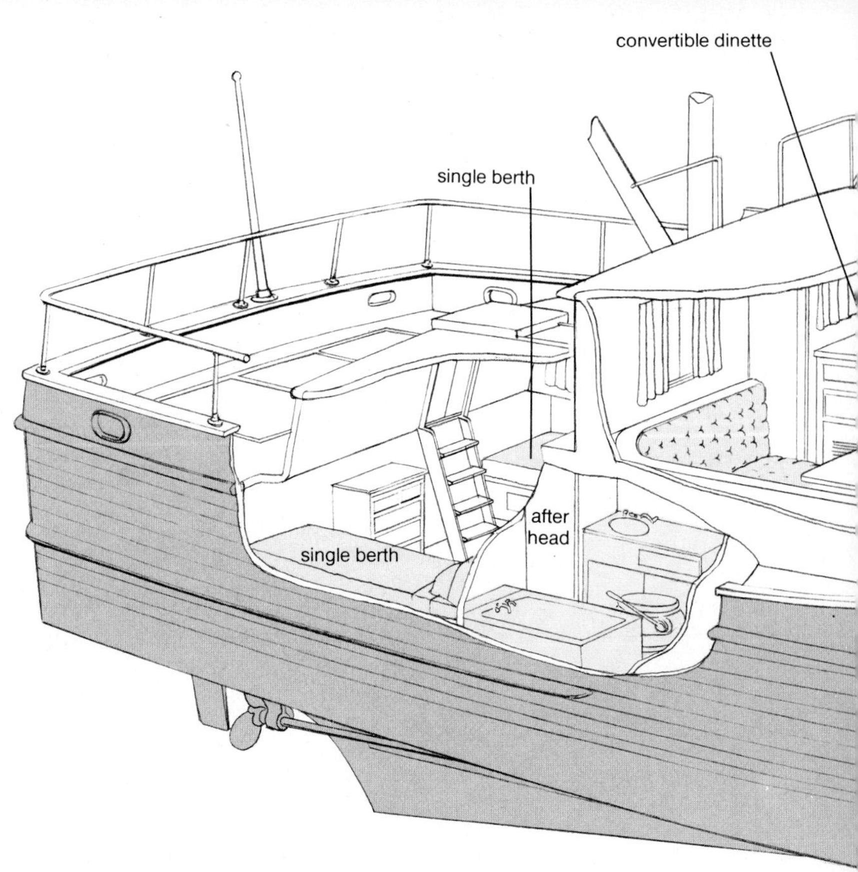
convertible dinette
single berth
after
head
single berth

A Luxury Trawler

Designed for oceangoing comfort and stability, this 42-foot luxury motor yacht has the long-range sea capability of a commercial fishing trawler—after which it was modeled—and posh accommodations for extended living aboard. A double stateroom aft and a spacious forecastle contain a head and shower each—with a sit-in bathtub in the after head. The boat's AC generator supplies current for lights, TV and galley, and also provides for a 250-gallon hot-and-cold-water system. The twin 130-hp diesels and 640-gallon fuel tanks can keep the vessel moving at 10 knots for nearly 1,000 miles.

The interior of the main cabin, custom finished in teak, shows a wheelhouse console forward, with radar screen and ship-to-shore telephone. The galley, to port, has a four-burner electric stove with oven, a freezer and plenty of stowage bins. A companionway between the galley and helm leads to the forward stateroom, and the dinette in the foreground converts into a double berth.

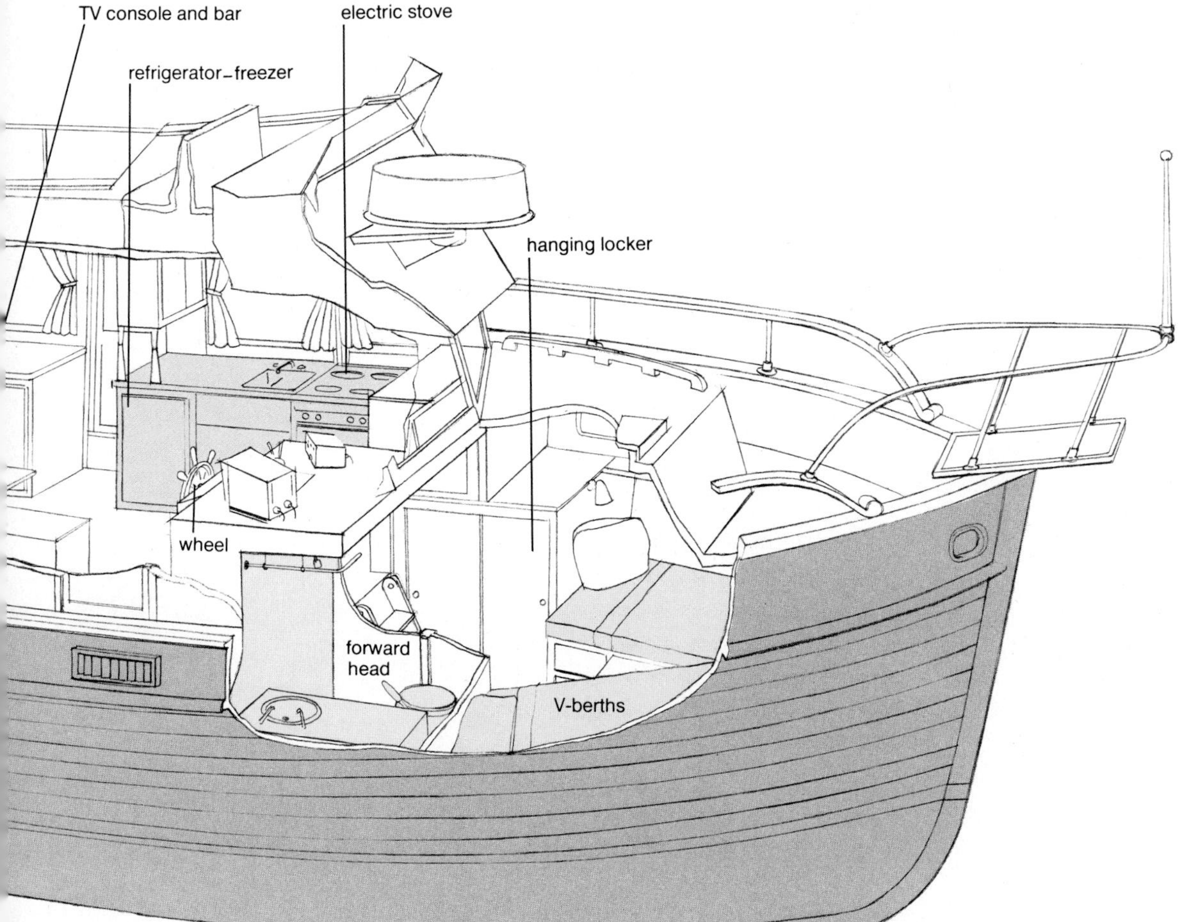

TV console and bar
electric stove
refrigerator–freezer
hanging locker
wheel
forward head
V-berths

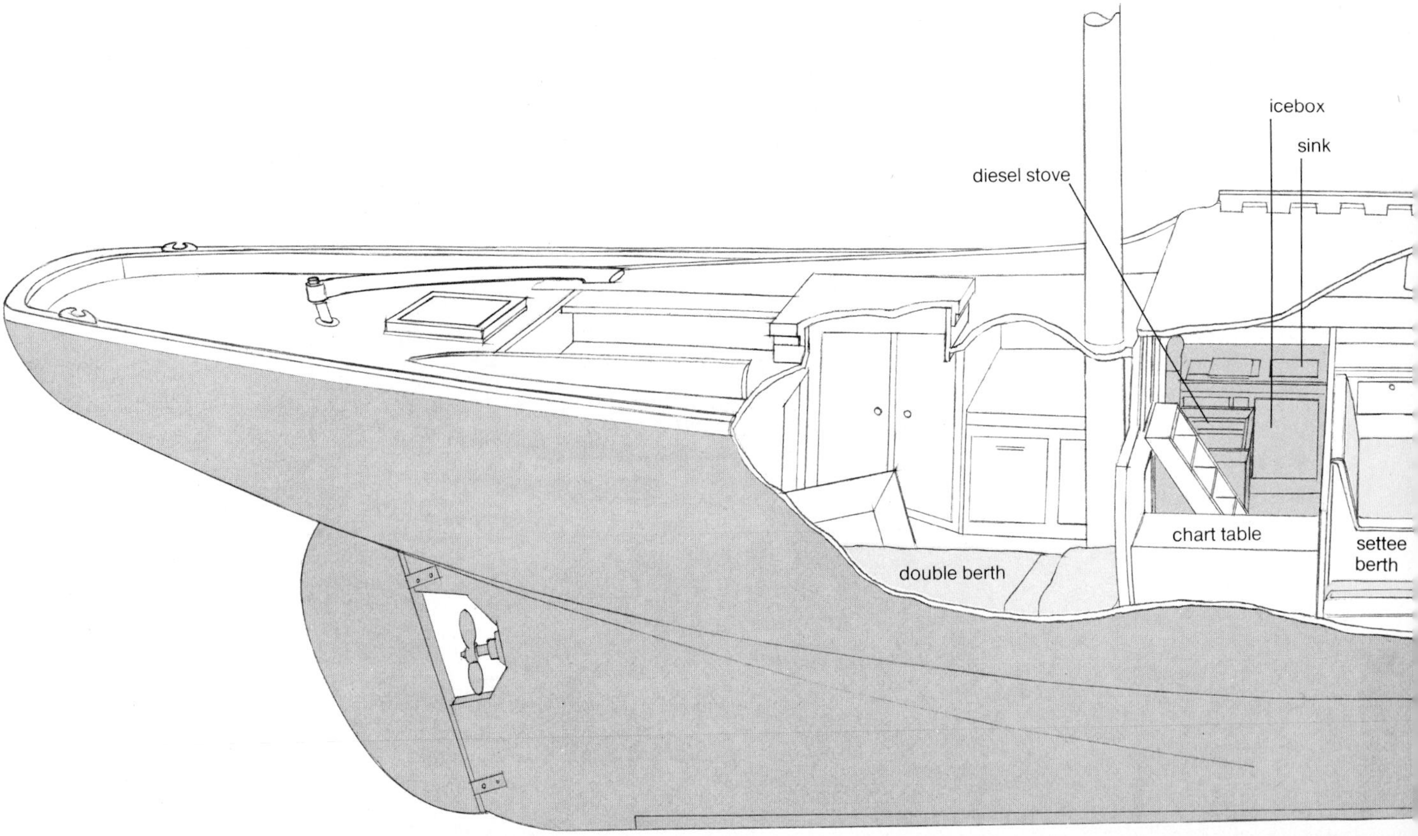

icebox
sink
diesel stove
chart table
settee berth
double berth

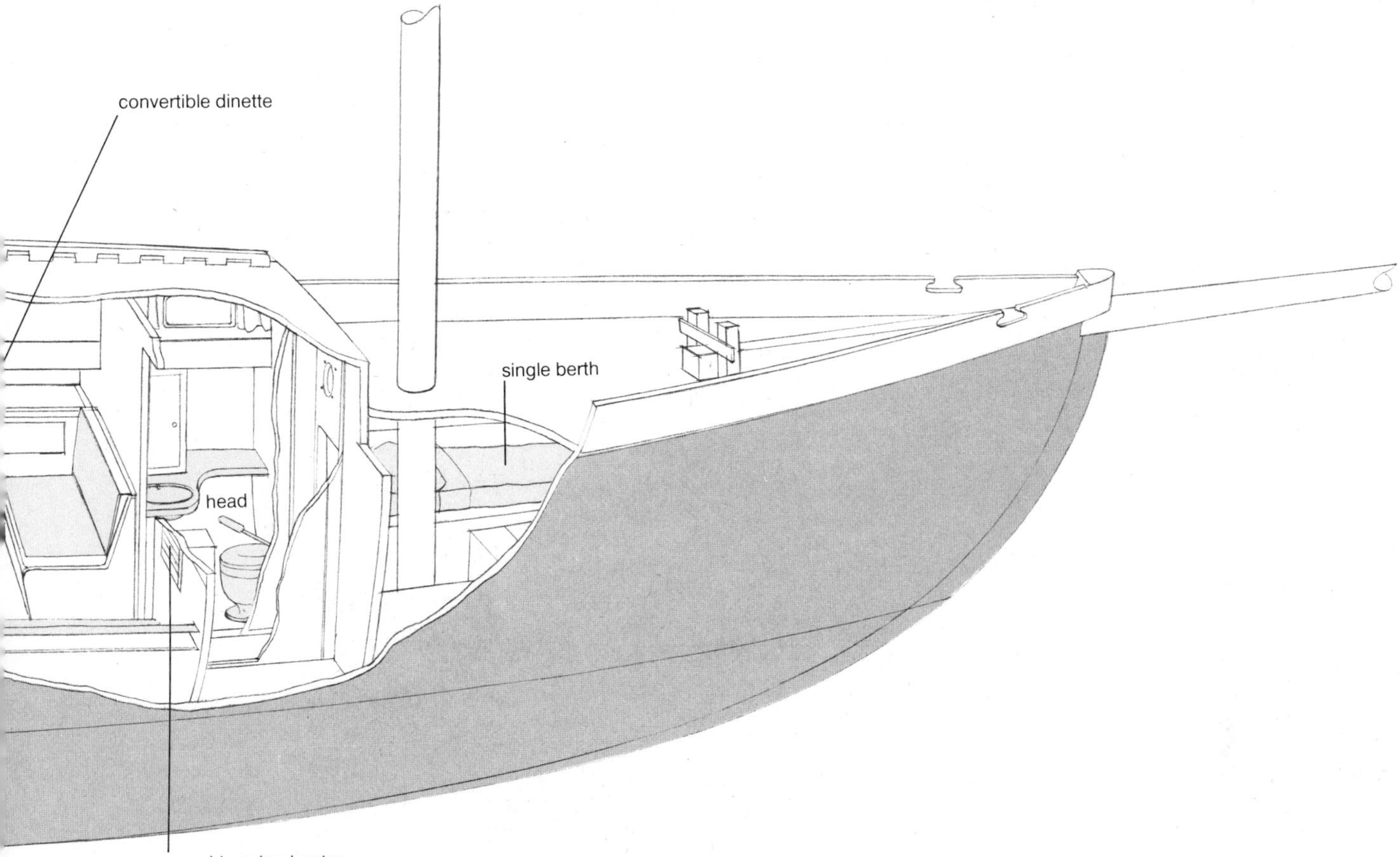

convertible dinette

single berth

head

wood-burning heater

The Traditional Schooner

Thrusting its bow into a rising sea, this handsome schooner typifies the traditional designs that still appeal to many cruising sailors. With hull and rig patterned on fishing schooners of the last century, this 41-footer is safe, roomy and comfortable enough for extended offshore sailing with six passengers. A small wood-burning heater warms the main cabin in cold weather. Comparatively low masts and gaff-headed sails make for stability in heavy winds—and easy handling on long reaches between distant landfalls.

The after section of the main cabin has a galley with sink, icebox and counter space (left), and a diesel-burning range (center). In hot weather, a kerosene stove is used. The navigator has space (right) for charts, radios, direction-finding gear and books.

Richly trimmed in teak, the motor sailer's galley has a sink and electric refrigerator in a counter running athwartships, storage opposite, and receives supplemental light and ventilation from a skylight. The companionway leads to the cockpit; and the passageway at right gives access to the engine and a double stateroom aft.

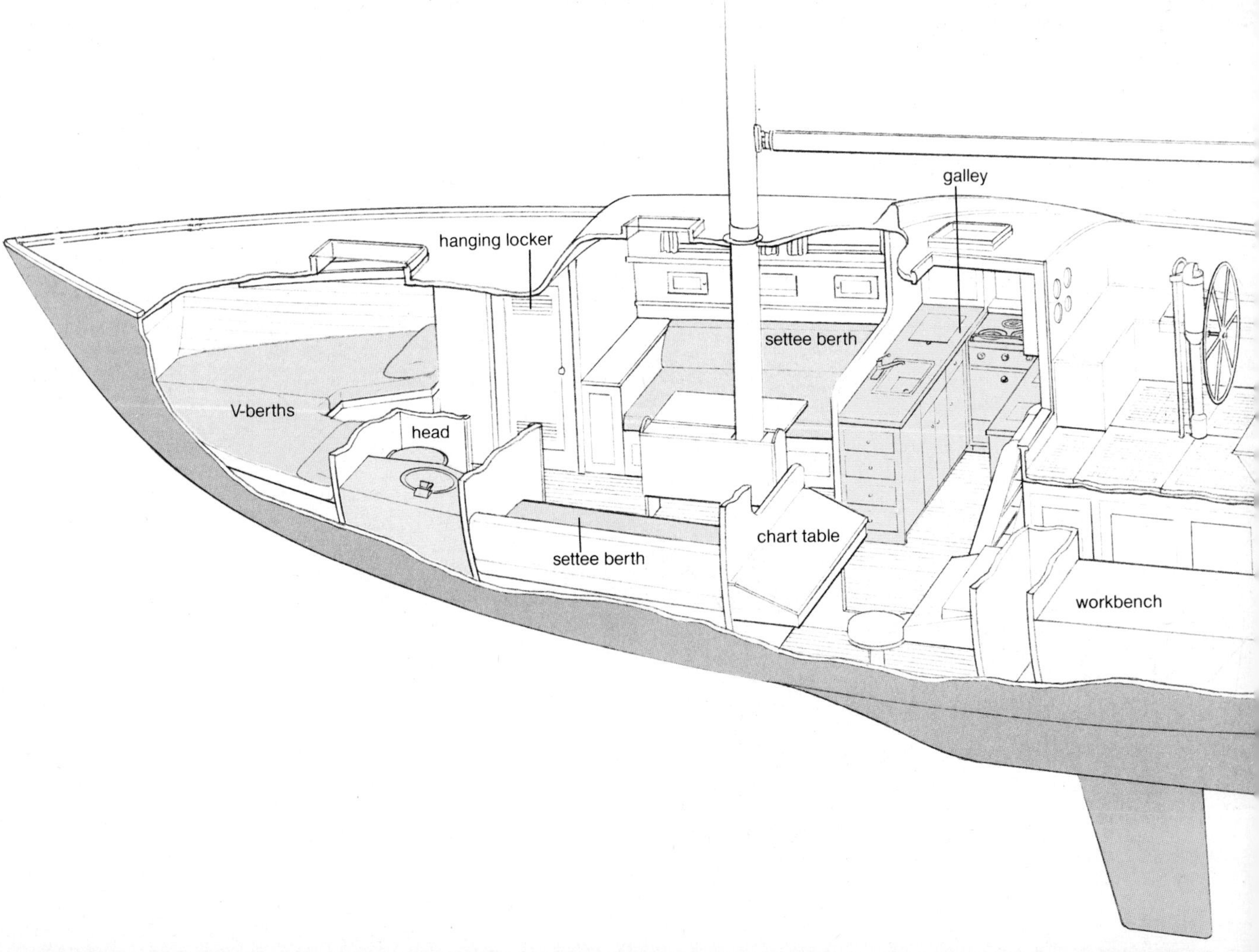

A Handsome Hybrid

The stately 45-footer above represents the ultimate cruising combination: a ketch-rigged motor sailer designed to perform equally well under power or sail. An 80-hp diesel tucked under the amidships cockpit delivers a cruising speed of 8 mph and a range of 700 miles. Nine hundred square feet of sail extend the cruising radius almost indefinitely. The vessel's 13-foot beam and high superstructure provide more space belowdecks than exists in most straight sailing craft of similar length; its deep hull and plenty of outside ballast lend a degree of stability and seaworthiness impossible in a regular motor yacht.

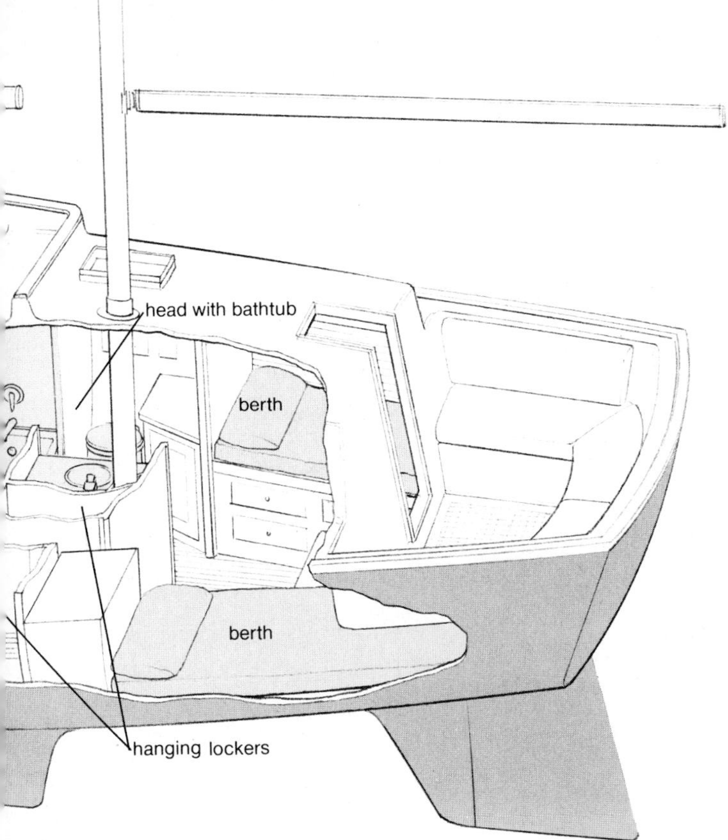

PRIVATE NAVY OF THE MERCHANT PRINCES

Built in 1908 with a fortune made in coke manufacturing, the 287-foot Cassandra provided posh transport for her owners, Roy and Paul Rainey. She took them on extended trips to Africa for big-game hunting.

The merchant princes of America's Gilded Age, casting about for ways to spend their fortunes, were not long in arriving at yachting as a suitably conspicuous outlet. But not just any kind of yachting. They wanted to acquire the kind of boat that would match their hard-driving life style. The solution was a sumptuous steam yacht, like the 551-ton *Cassandra* above.

Steam yachts were fast, showy, expensive, reliable—and therefore they were much more suitable than an elegant but poky sailing craft. As Edward Jaffray, owner of the 189-foot steamer *Stranger,* explained it, "Steam yachtsmen can go where they please and when they please, and what is more important, *they know when they will get back.*"

Cornelius Vanderbilt, a parvenu shipping magnate, inaugurated steam yachting in America when he launched the $500,000 *North Star* *(page 30)* in 1853. Yachting society was slow to follow, calling the steamers teakettles and golden cockleshells. For a time the New York Yacht Club refused membership to any of their owners. But not for long: too many influential men were riding about in them. By 1875 the steam yacht had become the new status symbol, and competition for the biggest, fastest and most expensive had become a sport in itself.

C. D. Borden, a textile manufacturer, demanded speed at any cost. While trying out his brand-new 24-knot, 137-foot *Little Sovereign,* he found himself being passed by the 25-knot, 165-foot *Winchester II,* owned by industrialist Peter Rouss. Furious, Borden steamed back to the shipyard to order work begun on the 166-foot *Sovereign,* which would make 38 knots.

Costs of owning such vessels only began with building and staffing. When Elbridge Gerry, Commodore of the New York Yacht Club, went on a two-week cruise aboard his 173-foot *Electra* in 1890, his champagne bills reportedly exceeded those for coal, crew's wages and ship upkeep. In an acquisitive and flamboyant age, this kind of spending was admired as a kind of visible reward for success. One contemporary commentator wrote, "Those who possess wealth and will not spend it are the thieves and robbers of society"; the spending habits of steam-yacht owners must have delighted him.

Cassandra's regular crew numbered 42. These included a chef, cooks, stewards (in white); nine officers (in brass buttons); and 22 seamen, firemen, greasers and other able-bodied hands (in middies). In many steam yachts, when the owners' families were aboard, the number was swelled as ladies' maids, nannies and valets were added.

First of the great steam yachts, the 270-foot side-wheeler North Star took Commodore Vanderbilt on a grand tour of Europe in 1853. At fashionable ports he would invite upward of 400 guests aboard for a day trip.

Cornelius Vanderbilt III, great-grandson of the original Commodore, poses circa 1907 aboard his own steam yacht, also called North Star. He is wearing the three-star insignia of Commodore of the New York Yacht Club. Eccentric and crotchety, Vanderbilt owned a succession of steam yachts, to which he fled in order to escape his large and contentious family; finally, he took up permanent residence afloat.

The floating home of Cornelius Vanderbilt III during his last years was the destroyer-like Winchester. Built in 1915, in the final days of the steam-yacht era, she sacrificed grace and grandeur for speed: to achieve a top velocity of 32 knots, a vast amount of belowdecks space had to be given over to machinery, with very little room left over for private accommodations. Vanderbilt was hardly discomfited —he much preferred his own company to that of anyone else.

Niagara, owned by Howard Gould, a son of the fabulously rich Jay Gould, contained this lavish 30-foot drawing room. Craftsmen imported from Europe decorated the room in a style called Renaissance Revival, which in this case featured coffered ceilings, a stained-glass skylight, porcelain paneling and a marble fireplace.

Niagara's library, abaft the drawing room, was stocked with yards of handsomely bound classics, all safely kept behind the glass doors of oak-framed bookcases. Like other showy reading rooms of the industrial era, this one, with its ornate but dim chandeliers, was probably little used—though cruises to places as remote as Queensland, Australia, left Gould and friends ample time for browsing.

Bark-rigged and capable of sailing moderately well in case of engine failure, the 272-foot Niagara was as seaworthy as she was opulent. Gould had her built at Wilmington, Delaware, in 1898 at a cost of one million dollars.

The handsome steam vessel Privateer began life as a commercial craft in 1902 and caught the fancy of R. A. C. Smith, a New York utilities tycoon, who had her converted to his own elegant purposes. Accommodations aboard the 177-foot yacht included 12 staterooms and a late-Victorian style parlor, as well as a 17-foot dining room.

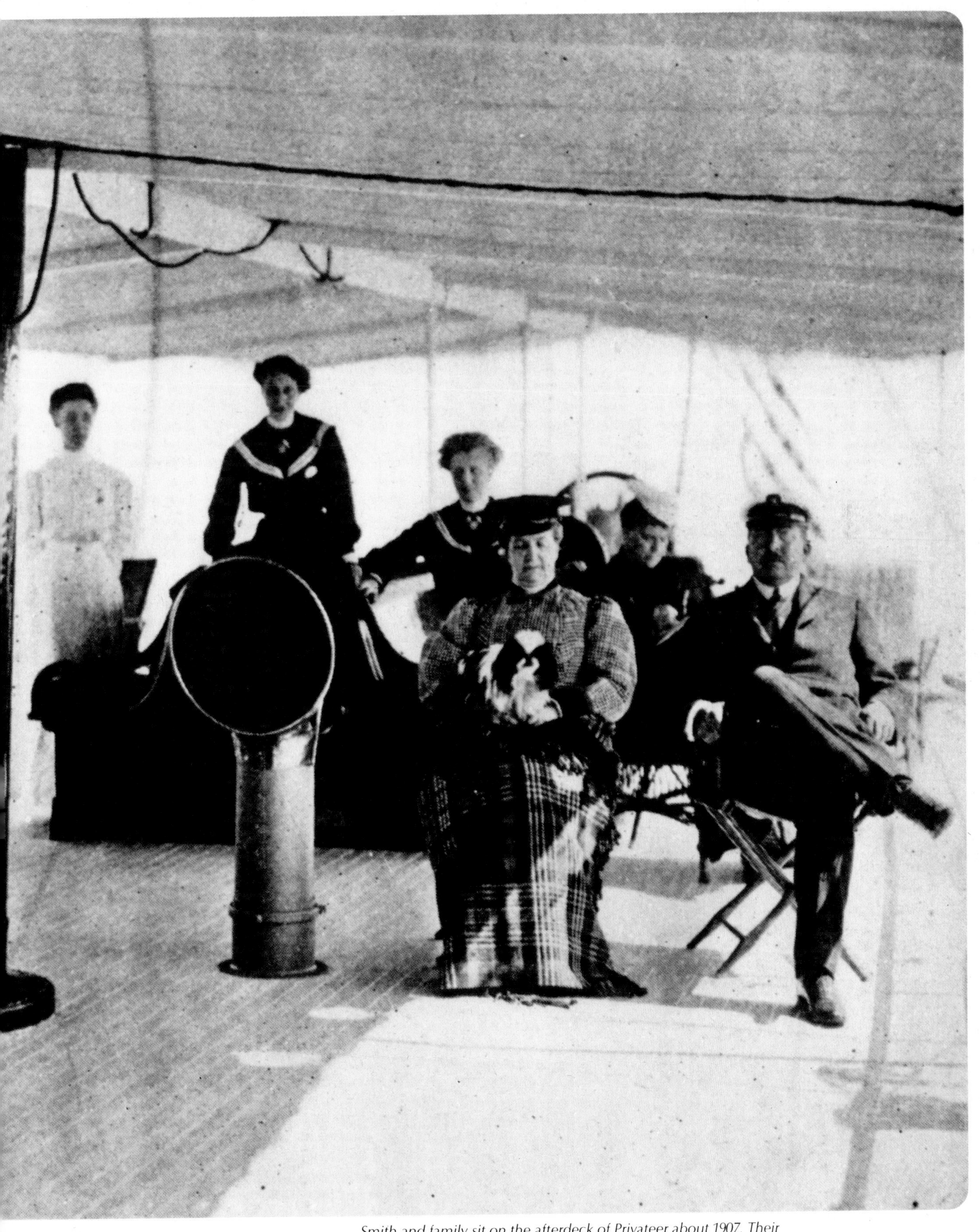

Smith and family sit on the afterdeck of Privateer about 1907. Their costumes reflect the code of dress observed by well-bred yachting people of the time: jacket, vest and tie for gentlemen; long-sleeved, high-necked dresses for ladies. Lest vulgar suntans mar fair complexions, Smith had the decks shaded by a stem-to-stern awning.

J. P. Morgan (in yachting whites) was a frequent visitor at London's Royal Yacht Club, where this rare photograph of the camera-shy tycoon, here in the company of an unidentified fellow yachtsman, was taken. Morgan's usual practice was to cross the Atlantic by commercial steamer, sending ahead whichever one of his Corsairs was in commission (he owned three in succession), and to make up parties of social and business acquaintances for cruises when he arrived. Morgan's Corsairs were always the most admired ships in any harbor, outstanding for their clipper bows and sleek lines.

The third Corsair, launched in 1899, rides at anchor off Piazza San Marco in Venice. With a top speed of 19 knots, a 304-foot steel hull and twin screws, she was one of the most powerful American civilian ships afloat. In 1917, Morgan's son reluctantly turned her over to the United States Navy for use during World War I as a patrol boat.

2

Any successful cruise takes shape long before the skipper casts off from the dock. Just as no experienced outdoorsman sets out on a canoe trip or a backpacking trek without first plotting his route, checking over his equipment and stocking provisions, so veteran yachtsmen plan each detail ahead of time. The first order of business is to figure out where to go and how to get there, as the family at left is doing. If the skipper and crew intend to voyage in an area outside their home waters—the Bahamas at Christmastime, say, or August in Nova Scotia—they must prepare either to sail or to trailer their boat to the cruising ground. Or, as more and more boatmen are doing, they can make

MAKING PLANS FOR A VOYAGE

prior arrangements to charter a boat at a location that is near the planned cruising area *(pages 58-71)*.

When mapping out a cruise, the skipper should heed the basic seaman's maxim to have two ways of doing everything, in case one way fails. Thus it makes good sense to plot an alternate set of bad-weather routes and stopovers, and to mark all important harbors of refuge on the chart in advance. Note all ports where the cruising boat can put in to replenish galley supplies, gas and water. Whenever possible, plan each leg to coincide as closely as possible with an area's prevailing winds and currents; many boatmen calculate tidal conditions in advance, and set their schedules accordingly. Before leaving, the skipper should have on hand all the necessary navigational material for the main cruising area—and for short trips to outlying sectors as well. Nothing but the most detailed—and up-to-date—versions of marine charts and tables will do. Recently, one skipper, while riding at anchor in a morning fog in Rockland, Maine, was startled by a frenzied hail from the owner of a brand-new power cruiser, who was asking directions to Bar Harbor. The neophyte powerboatman had ventured—fortunately without mishap—all the way east from Massachusetts using only the map on a railroad timetable. Such beginner's luck is rare indeed.

The same principle of total preparedness applies to the second stage of cruise planning: checking over the boat and its inventory of equipment. A carefully equipped cruising vessel can be self-sufficient for days on end, serving as a floating restaurant, first-aid station, repair shop and recreation center. Well before departure, inspect all fittings, lines and other working parts, and replace any that are worn out. Be sure the boat carries a judicious inventory of spare parts, for the sea is hard on equipment, and on any cruise of a week or more, the skipper can expect to spend at least some of his time changing spark plugs, replacing a battery, sewing up ripped genoa jib or fitting the dinghy's outboard with a new shear pin. Sometimes, too, a skipper will find himself in urgent need of a spare part due to an absolutely unpredictable action by someone on board—as one powerboatman learned to his dismay when his toddler son flung the only set of ignition keys overboard into 15 fathoms of water.

Galley provisions, both staple and fresh, must be stocked in sufficient quantity so that the voyagers will not be forced to subsist on canned beans and soggy bread during the last days of the cruise. Personal clothing and gear must be chosen for comfort, for compactness in stowage, and with due regard for sudden changes in weather. The contents of the boat's game locker should also be selected with the weather in mind. A rainy day in a battened-down boat can be infinitely more tedious than one at home, if no good books, games or other diversions have been brought along. And all of this cruising gear should be itemized on a set of lists, like the ones on pages 45-57, to be checked off at dockside before the voyage begins.

Skipper Joseph Lucarelli and his family crew gather at their Rumson, New Jersey, library table to study charts and plan an itinerary for a week-long summer cruise on Lake Champlain.

Proposed Passages

The first step in planning a cruise is to map out a sensible itinerary indicating the harbors to be visited, the best routes for reaching them, the distance to be traveled each day—and establishing a timetable that brings the skipper home on schedule. Two such itineraries are plotted on the chart at right—a three-day trip for a power cruiser *(red lines)* and a nine-day voyage for a sailboat *(blue lines)*. The area of the cruises, straddling the border between Washington and British Columbia, is one of narrow channels, swift currents, varying winds and exceptional physical beauty. Both trips take into account all these natural features. Both skippers have built in plenty of flexibility for swimming, digging clams and fishing, and have included stops to fill up on water, fuel and ice.

Each skipper has avoided the common cruising pitfall of trying to go too far. He has calculated the distances so that no day's passage should take more than four or five hours. Unless held back by the weather, he should reach his evening landfall by midafternoon, with plenty of time to go ashore and take a look around before dinner.

The powerboat skipper has chosen to weave through the San Juan Islands; because of their generally light winds and protected waters, they are well suited to small power craft. He will spend the first night at anchor in a wooded harbor, then motor the next day to a lunch stop at a secluded outisland before doubling back to his second overnight landfall at a marina. On his last day he has an easy 22-mile leg home—or he can take a side trip *(dotted line)* on his way back.

The itinerary for the sailboat skipper cuts through the San Juans and leads up the coast of Vancouver Island, where the winds tend to be stronger and steadier. While this cruise covers far more territory than the powerboatman's, each day's passage is shorter—about 20 miles. Not only is the skipper's vessel slower than the power craft, but he must take more account of the weather, allowing for possible head winds and calms, as well as for an unpredictable storm that could confine him in port for a day.

To ensure getting home on time, some sailors prefer to make long, outbound leaps early in the trip and shorter hops on the inbound run. This sailboat skipper has another plan in case of delay; he can skip three home-coming landfalls and spend the last day riding the prevailing northwesterlies in a long, hard sail down the open waters of the Strait of Georgia.

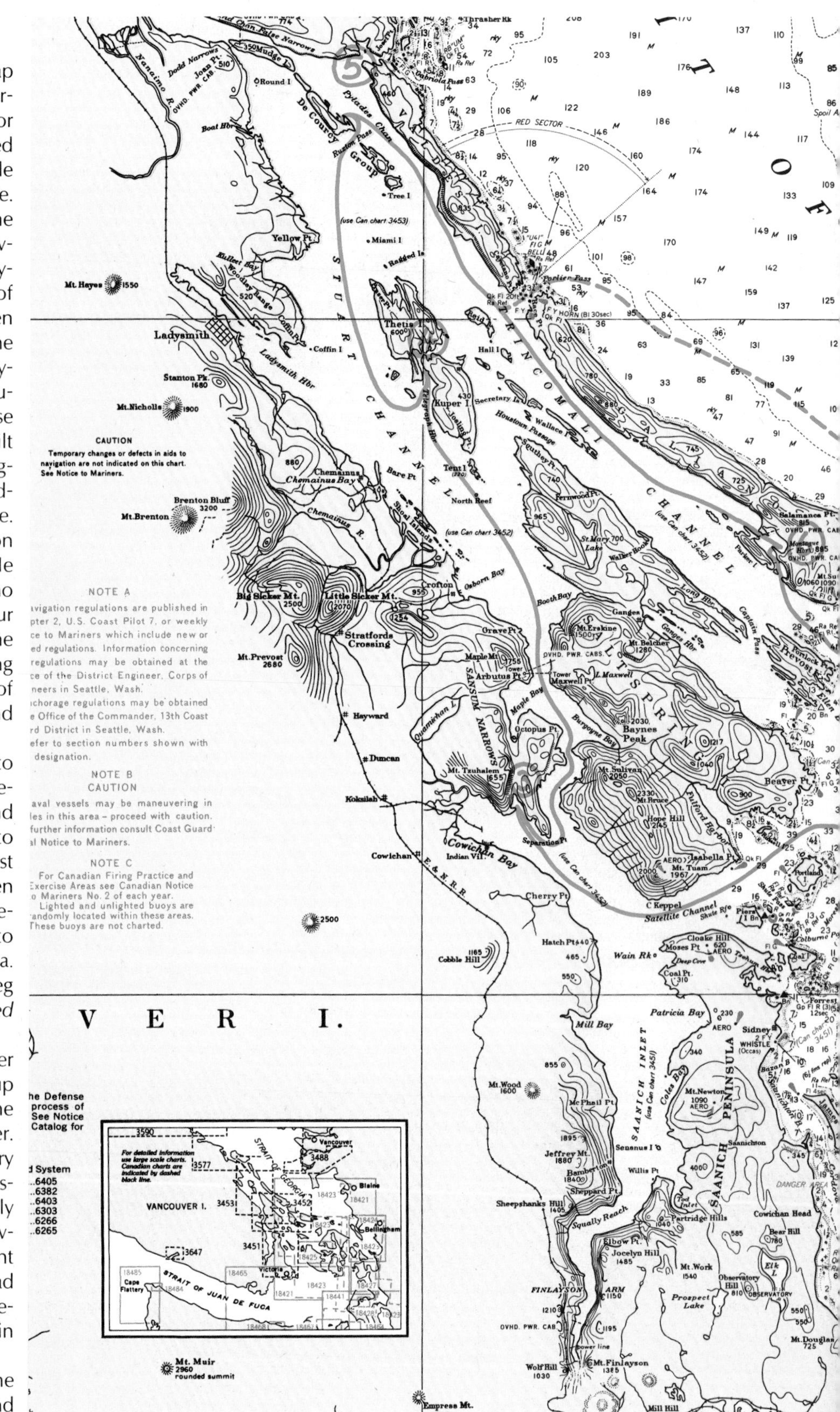

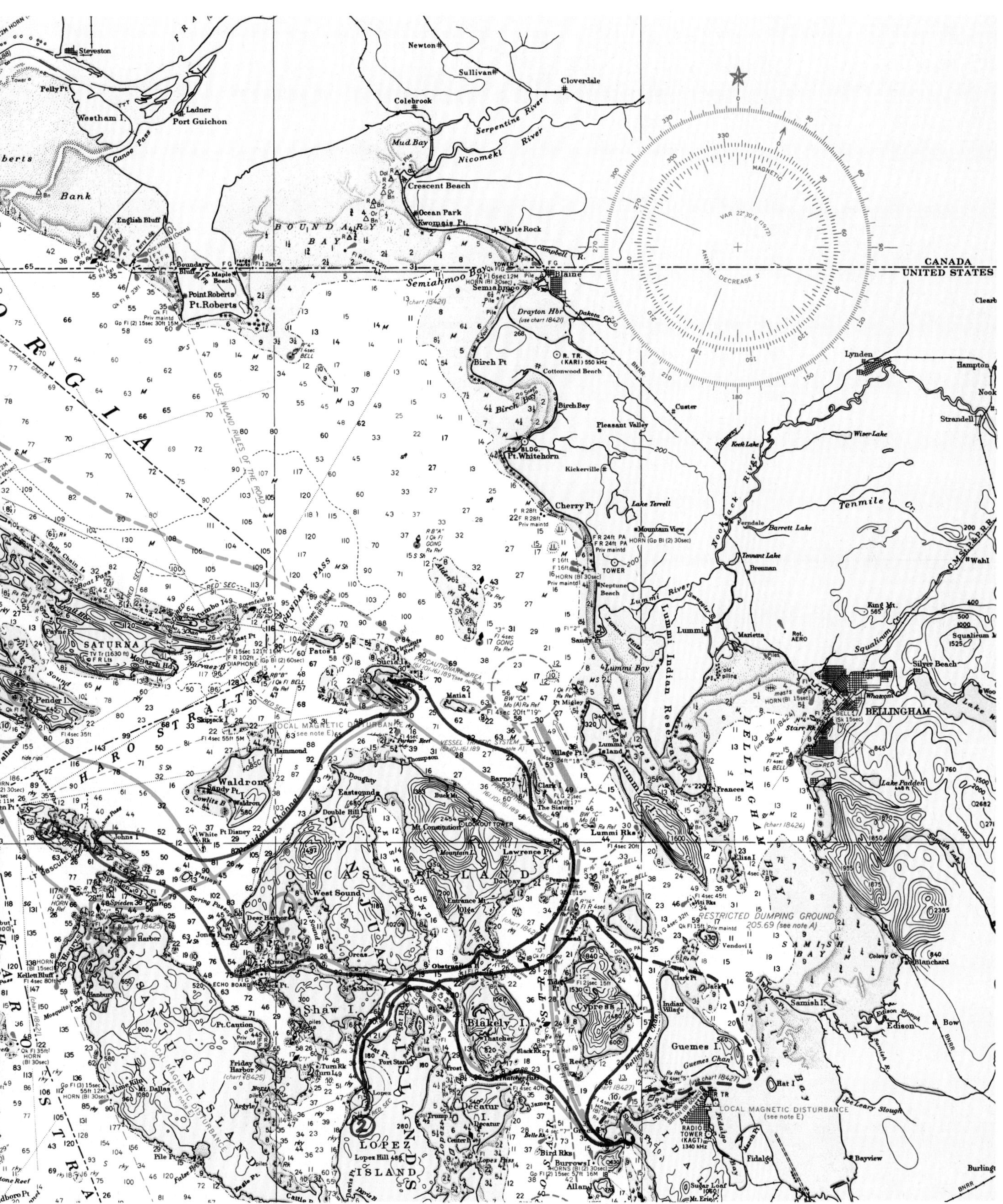

The routes for two cruises are plotted on this chart of the waters off Vancouver Island, British Columbia. Both start at a marina near Anacortes, Washington, seen here as a green cross. The three-day cruise is marked as a solid red line, the numbers indicating the sequence of overnight stops. The nine-day sailing trip is shown as a solid blue line and is similarly numbered at the layovers. For each of the cruises, alternate routes are represented by dotted lines.

BASIC REFERENCES

For a cruise in the New Orleans area, a skipper would use Coast Pilot 5 to help him in selecting harbors to visit, and also the Atlantic and Gulf Coast light list for a summary of aids to navigation along his chosen route. In negotiating tidal channels such as the canal from the city's inner harbor to Lake Pontchartrain, he would consult tide and tidal current tables. Copies of the Rules of the Road and Chart No. 1 would refresh his memory of marine traffic regulations and of the symbols used on nautical charts.

THE PROPER CHARTS

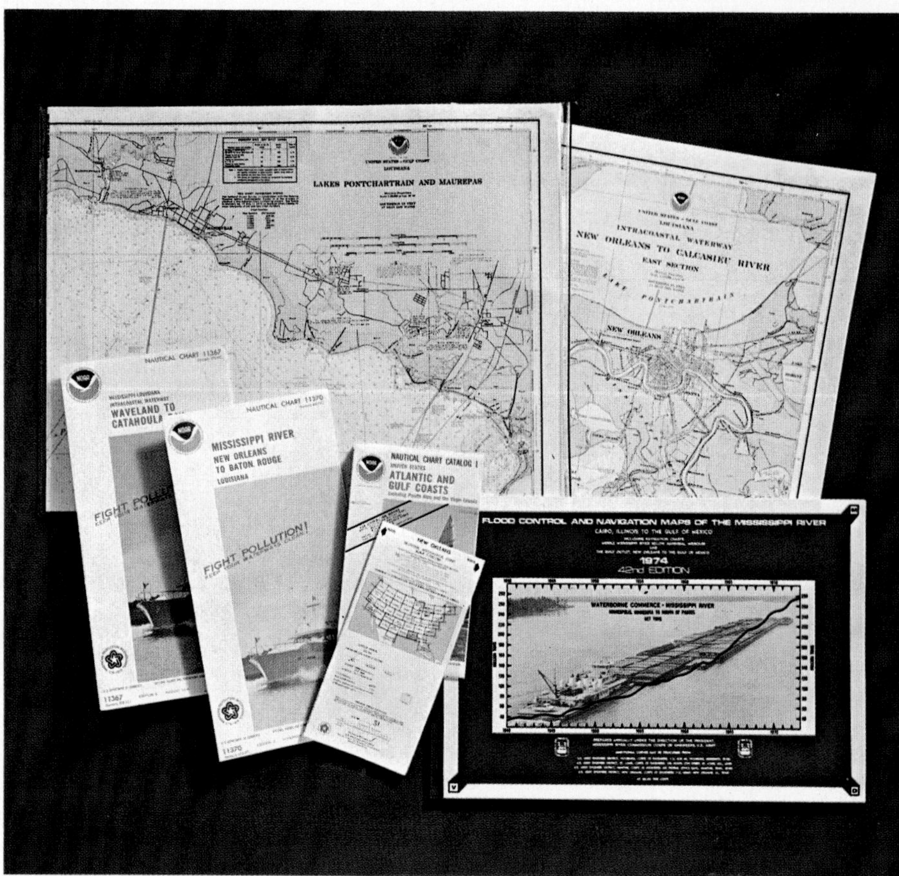

Besides the items above, a skipper cruising the New Orleans-Lake Pontchartrain area needs the maps and charts at right, most of which are listed in the National Ocean Survey catalogue for this locale (bottom center). A small-scale coastal chart of the whole area and a larger-scale harbor chart are both shown here in a waterproof case. Two other charts (bottom left), designed for use by pleasure craft, pinpoint channels convenient for cruising. An aeronautical chart locates aircraft beacons—helpful to navigators—and an Army Corps of Engineers book contains maps delineating the Mississippi's channels.

The Pilot's Library

Before embarking on any cruise, the skipper should have the latest editions of all necessary charts, tables, booklets, lists and guides that apply to his intended sailing area. The federal government's National Ocean Survey (NOS), which is headquartered in Rockville, Maryland, puts out the bulk of all such cartographic and written data. Its charts and maps offer overall views of every coastal-United States cruising ground, as well as closer perspectives on individual passages and harbors. Both kinds are essential for safe piloting. NOS tide and tidal current tables, published annually, are vital for calculating the movements of local waters.

Many skippers also carry an NOS Marine Weather Services Chart indicating the whereabouts, call letters and frequencies of the radio stations that broadcast weather reports, and also the locations of Coast Guard stations, which display storm warnings. And any skipper should stock an updated version of the *Coast Pilot* volume covering his area; these excellent booklets describe in detail the characteristics of coastal waters and harbors.

In addition to the appropriate publications of the NOS, the cruising skipper should carry the most recent edition of the Coast Guard light list for his locale—which contains descriptions of beacons, lighthouses, fog signals, buoys, loran stations and other navigation aids. Light lists are available from most marine-supply stores, or from the Superintendent of Documents in Washington, D.C.

Most cruising boatmen also depend on commercial cruising guides, sold at most major book, map and nautical stores. These guides include some of the same data as the government publications, plus detailed information on the locations of marinas, yacht clubs, restaurants and shops. In addition, the best guides offer historical sketches of the areas covered, list points of interest ashore, describe normal weather conditions and provide tips on snorkeling, beachcombing and fishing—including suggestions on the best baits, lures and tackle.

The commercial cruising guides above, for areas from New England to the Bahamas, give general directions for getting from place to place and also throw in a bonus of helpful tips and fascinating information. A skipper may be advised, for example, to watch out for submarines when entering New London, Connecticut, and to expect heavy traffic in the lock between Lake Pontchartrain and the Mississippi. He will also discover that near Greenville, Mississippi, he can visit burial mounds of the Natchez Indians, and that Montauk, New York, boasts a lighthouse built by order of George Washington.

HOT-WEATHER WARDROBE

In this wardrobe for warm-weather cruising, the individual garments are loose-fitting, lightweight and generally light in color in order to reflect the heat. Clothes that protect the wearer from overexposure to sun are important, too. On hot nights, sheets and a light blanket are used in place of the lightweight, quick-drying nylon sleeping bag.

COOL-WEATHER WARDROBE

Proper clothing for a cruise in northern waters should include several changes of heavy slacks and shirts, and at least two heavy wool sweaters. Wool, unlike synthetic materials, holds in body heat even when wet. Extra hats will help to keep the skipper's head warm and dry, and for warm, sunny days there are swim trunks and sunglasses.

What to Pack

The trick to packing for a cruise is to take all the clothing necessary for comfort and still fit most of the items into a single duffel bag. The two lists below, one for a cruise in a warm climate, the other for cold-weather sailing, suggest wardrobes that meet these criteria. Each list includes foul-weather gear and a set of dress-up shore clothes (including shoes that will not mar the deck), which are stowed separately in hanging lockers.

GEAR FOR WARM CLIMATES

1 Wide-brimmed sun hat
2 Duffel bag
3 Nylon sleeping bag
4 Sheets, pillowcase and light blanket
5 Lightweight muslin slacks
6 Nonskid sneakers
7 Dress clothes for shore
8 Foul-weather boots
9 Foul-weather parka and pants
10 Nonskid deck shoes
11 Beach and bath towels
12 Shoregoing sandals
13 Fingerless work gloves
14 Waterproof ditty bag for personal gear
15 Dark-tinted sunglasses
16 Lightweight sweaters
17 Lightweight wind-breaker
18 Sunsuit and shorts
19 Lightweight cotton blouses
20 Cotton head scarf
21 Underwear in plastic bag
22 Cotton nightshirt
23 Extra swimsuit

GEAR FOR COOL CLIMATES

1 Water-resistant garment bag
2 Dress clothes for shore
3 Pea jacket
4 Foul-weather parka and chest-high pants
5 Cap with brim
6 Foul-weather boots
7 Synthetic-filled sleeping bag
8 Sheets, pillowcase, towels and heavy wool blanket
9 Duffel bag
10 Thermal underwear
11 Cotton underwear in plastic bags
12 Light cotton socks
13 Nonskid sneakers
14 Shoregoing shoes
15 Fingerless work gloves
16 Swim trunks and shorts
17 Soft-brimmed sun hat
18 Waterproof ditty bag
19 Sunglasses with elastic headband
20 Sport shirts
21 Cotton T-shirts, long- and short-sleeved
22 Heavy sailcloth and wool slacks
23 Heavy wool socks
24 Wool hat
25 Heavy wool sweaters
26 Wool mittens and gloves
27 Heavy wool shirt

STAPLES AND CONDIMENTS

IRON RATIONS

Basic Galley Supplies

Before any cruise, a boat's galley should be fully stocked with a variety of nonperishable staples and also with a supply of stowage bags and cleaning materials. These basic stores, shown here assembled in a kitchen ashore and keyed by number to the listings below, are generally laid in at the beginning of the season and replenished as they give out.

The provisions should include not only such items as flour, salt and sugar, necessary for day-to-day cooking, but enough canned food to provide emergency meals if the boat's fresh provisions should give out. The morale of many a crew, their cruise delayed by bad weather or equipment failure, has been saved because the cook was able to break out these rations to feed them during the layover.

DRIED AND BOTTLED STORES

1 Flour, salt, sugar
2 Breakfast foods and packaged mixes
3 Spaghetti, noodles, rice, instant mashed potatoes
4 Regular and instant coffee, tea and iced-tea mix, powdered fruit drink, hot chocolate, powdered milk, instant soup
5 Dried fruits, peanut butter, jelly, crackers
6 Syrup and honey
7 Oil, vinegar, chili sauce, ketchup, soy sauce, mustard and mayonnaise
8 Artificial lemon and lime juice
9 Dried sauce mixes and salad dressings
10 Herbs, spices, grated cheese, dried bacon, bouillon cubes, Tabasco sauce, Worcestershire sauce
11 Relish and olives
12 Hard salami, dried beef sticks

CANNED GOODS

1 Potato sticks, nuts
2 Bread
3 Fruit
4 Fruit juices
5 Soups
6 Assorted vegetables
7 Condensed and evaporated milk
8 Tuna, salmon, minced clams
9 Preserved ham
10 Beef stew, roast beef hash

HOUSEKEEPING INVENTORY

1 Spray disinfectant
2 Window cleaner
3 Whisk broom and dustpan
4 Scrub brush and sponge
5 Dishwashing detergent
6 Powdered cleanser
7 Plastic garbage bags
8 Towels, napkins and toilet tissues
9 Plastic bucket
10 Assorted sponges
11 Dish towels and nonrusting pot scrubbers
12 Plastic food bags, aluminum foil and plastic wrap

PROVISIONS FOR CLEANING AND STOWAGE

In this first-aid kit, designed for a season's cruising, the assembled items are stowed first in a strong, compact box like the plastic toolbox shown here, and the entire package is enclosed in a waterproof plastic bag. At the start of each season, each item should be checked to be sure it is fresh and usable.

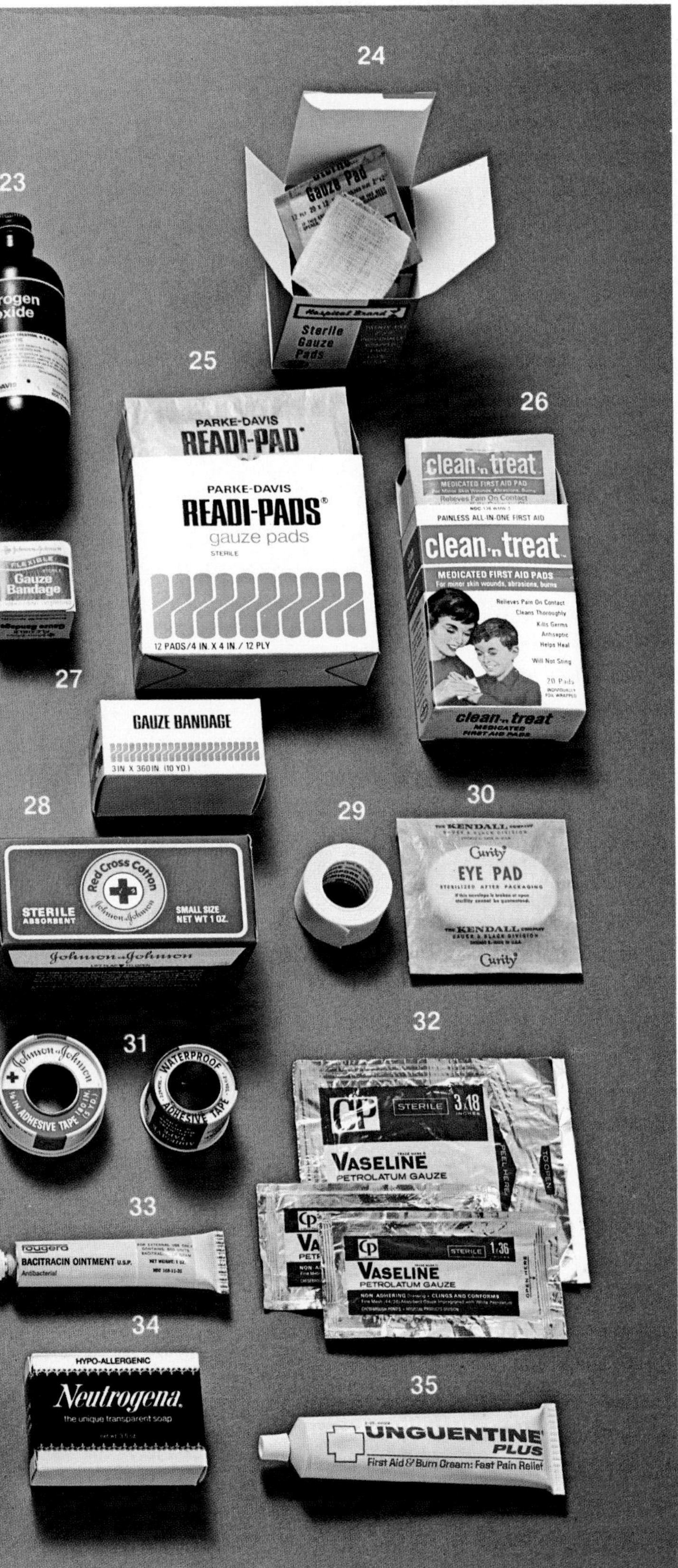

A Full First-Aid Kit

1 Plastic first-aid box
2 Waterproof plastic bag
3 Hot-water bottle
4 Antidiarrhea medicine
5 Laxative tablets
6 Antacid tablets
7 Eye lotion and plastic eyecup
8 Toothache drops
9 Lotion for skin irritations
10 Thermometer
11 Tweezers
12 Scissors
13 Smelling salts
14 Petroleum jelly
15 Pain-relief tablets
16 Seasickness pills
17 Decongestant nasal spray
18 Sun-screen cream
19 Suntan lotion
20 Astringent wet dressing
21 Elastic bandages
22 Adhesive bandages
23 Hydrogen peroxide antiseptic
24 Gauze pads, 2" by 2"
25 Gauze pads, 4" by 4"
26 Antiseptic pads
27 Gauze bandage
28 Absorbent cotton
29 Surgical tape
30 Eye pad
31 Adhesive tape
32 Vaseline-treated gauze
33 Antibacterial ointment
34 Nonallergenic soap
35 Burn cream

Rx for Seasickness

While seasickness most frequently attacks novices, it can also bring down even the most experienced skipper. Its warning symptoms are lethargy and drowsiness, followed by loss of appetite, and finally chills and nausea, often severe. Antimotion pills, when taken before departure, usually help ward off the malady; if they do not, these procedures can help bring relief:

- Keep busy. Do not lie down.
- Get fresh air—but keep warm. Stay on deck, and put on extra sweaters.
- Try to eat something. Warm tea, dry crackers and carbonated beverages may help to stave off queasiness.
- Stay on the leeward side of the boat, in case vomiting occurs.

FOR HULLS AND ENGINES

A comprehensive tool kit like the one shown here should provide a remedy for any common affliction to hull or engine on either a sailing craft or a powerboat. There are tools for accomplishing dozens of different jobs, from fixing a crack in a fiberglass hull to giving a balky engine a tune-up. All the items fit into a plastic toolbox; the box itself is stored in a plastic bag when not in use, to keep out dampness, which would rust the tools. As further antirust protection, all of the metal tools should periodically be rubbed with light machine oil.

FOR SAILS AND RIGGING

The tools and materials required for repairing ripped sails and faulty rigging on a sailboat are stashed together in the vessel's ditty bag. Sail patches of nylon and Dacron are selected to match the weight, color and material of the boat's sails; ripstop tape permits quick, temporary sail repairs; jib hanks, sail slides, turnbuckle and shackles with extra clevis pins conform in size and material to the boat's fittings. The marlinespike, pusher and fids are used for splicing line.

Kits for Repairs

THE COMPLEAT TOOL CHEST

1 Plastic toolbox *(opposite, top left)*
2 Plastic bag
3 Assorted screws and nails
4 Inboard and outboard motor oil
5 Silicone spray lubricant
6 Ether spray for cold engine starts
7 Oil spray lubricant
8 Assorted cork plugs
9 Sandpaper
10 Fiberglass repair kit
11 Epoxy glue
12 Socket-wrench set
13 Spark-plug wrench and handle
14 Allen-wrench set
15 Screwdrivers with insulated handles
16 Test light
17 Plastic electrical tape
18 Assorted nuts and bolts
19 Seizing and electrical wire
20 Portable vise and C-clamp
21 Pipe wrench
22 Adjustable wrench
23 Locking-grip pliers
24 Open-end-wrench set
25 Conventional and side-cutting pliers
26 Cable cutters
27 Needle-nose pliers
28 Spark-plug gauge
29 Knife
30 Drill bits
31 Battery-powered drill and recharging cord
32 Hacksaw
33 Ignition file
34 Multipurpose file
35 Rat-tailed file
36 Hammer

THE SAILOR'S HANDY BAG

1 Sail patches
2 Ditty bag
3 Tape measure
4 Waxed twine
5 Ripstop tape
6 Whipping cord
7 Plastic sealant for whipping rope
8 Heavy and light thread
9 Sail needles
10 Waterproof sail tape
11 Marline
12 Seizing wire
13 Beeswax
14 Palm
15 Rigging knife with marlinespike
16 Nylon tubing
17 Elkhide chafing gear
18 Rings and thimbles
19 Sail slides
20 Jib hanks
21 Sail shackles
22 Assorted shackles
23 Turnbuckle toggle
24 Cotter pins
25 Clevis pins
26 Turnbuckle
27 Pusher for splicing
28 Assorted fids

EXTRA PARTS FOR GENERAL USE

EXTRA PARTS FOR LIGHT AND POWER

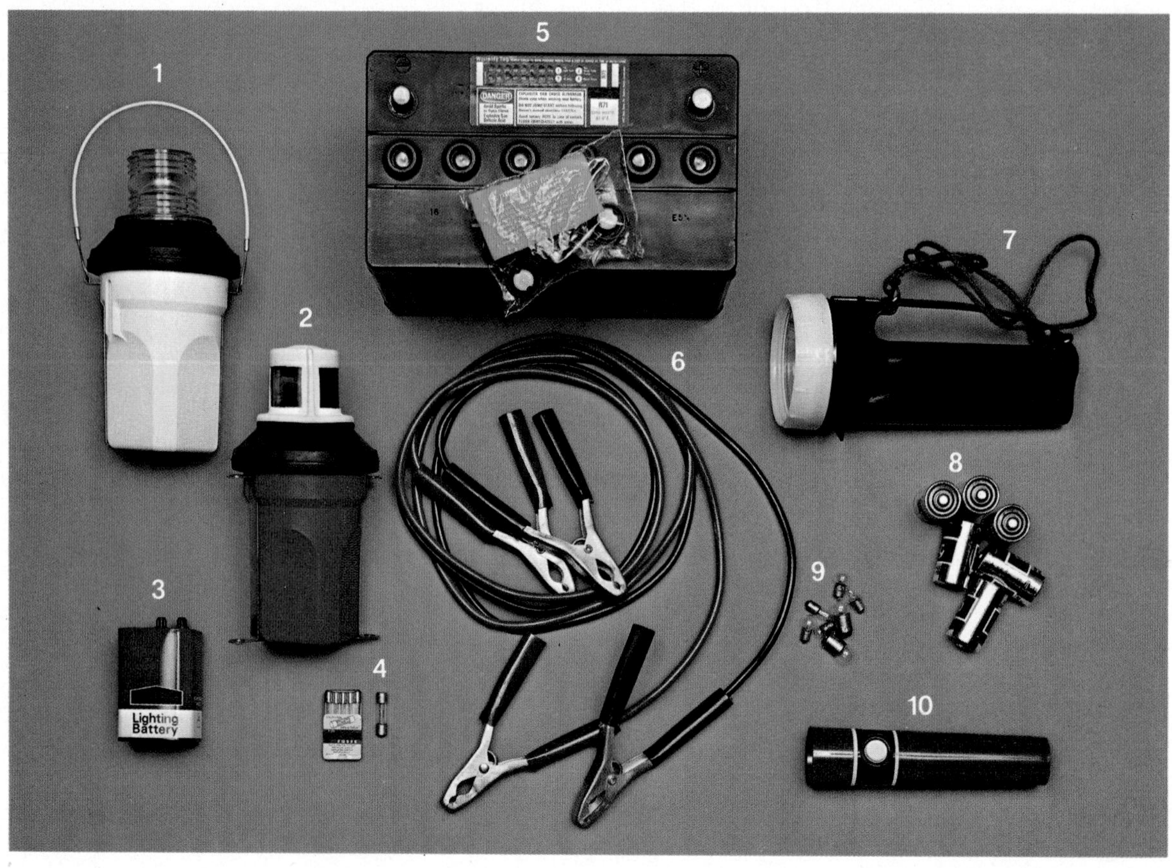

Key Replacements

Every cruising boat should carry a supply of replacements for vital equipment that may become lost, damaged or worn out during a voyage. General spares usually should include a propeller, an anchor, flexible plastic hose for making plumbing repairs or for use with the emergency hand-operated bilge pump, an extra can of compressed gas for the foghorn, and —since a foghorn can be a critical item —an old-fashioned mouth-powered horn.

Stand-by electrical gear should include a reserve battery for the engine, batteries for waterproof flashlights, extra light bulbs and fuses, and a battery-powered anchor and running lights in case the boat's electrical system fails.

A sailboat's backup equipment should include a spare safety harness, additional line, battens and blocks, an alternate anchor shackle, a spare tiller and a winch handle to replace the one that inevitably gets dropped on deck and is forgotten until it slides overboard.

ASSORTED SPARES

1 Propeller
2 Marked lead line
3 Lead
4 Docking lines
5 Flexible plastic hose
6 Stainless-steel hose clamps
7 Hand-operated bilge pump
8 Parts for sink pump
9 Parts for toilet
10 Can of compressed gas
11 Foghorn
12 Anchor
13 Shock cord
14 Burner for stove

ELECTRICAL SPARES

1 Anchor light
2 Combination running light
3 Battery for anchor and running lights
4 Fuses
5 12-volt battery (with cell caps in plastic bag)
6 Jumper cable
7 Waterproof searchlight
8 Flashlight batteries
9 Assorted bulbs
10 Waterproof flashlight

SAILBOAT SPARES

1 Tiller
2 Block
3 Snatch blocks
4 Anchor shackle
5 Winch handle
6 Safety-harness line
7 Safety harness
8 Battens
9 Extra line

EXTRA PARTS FOR SAILBOATS

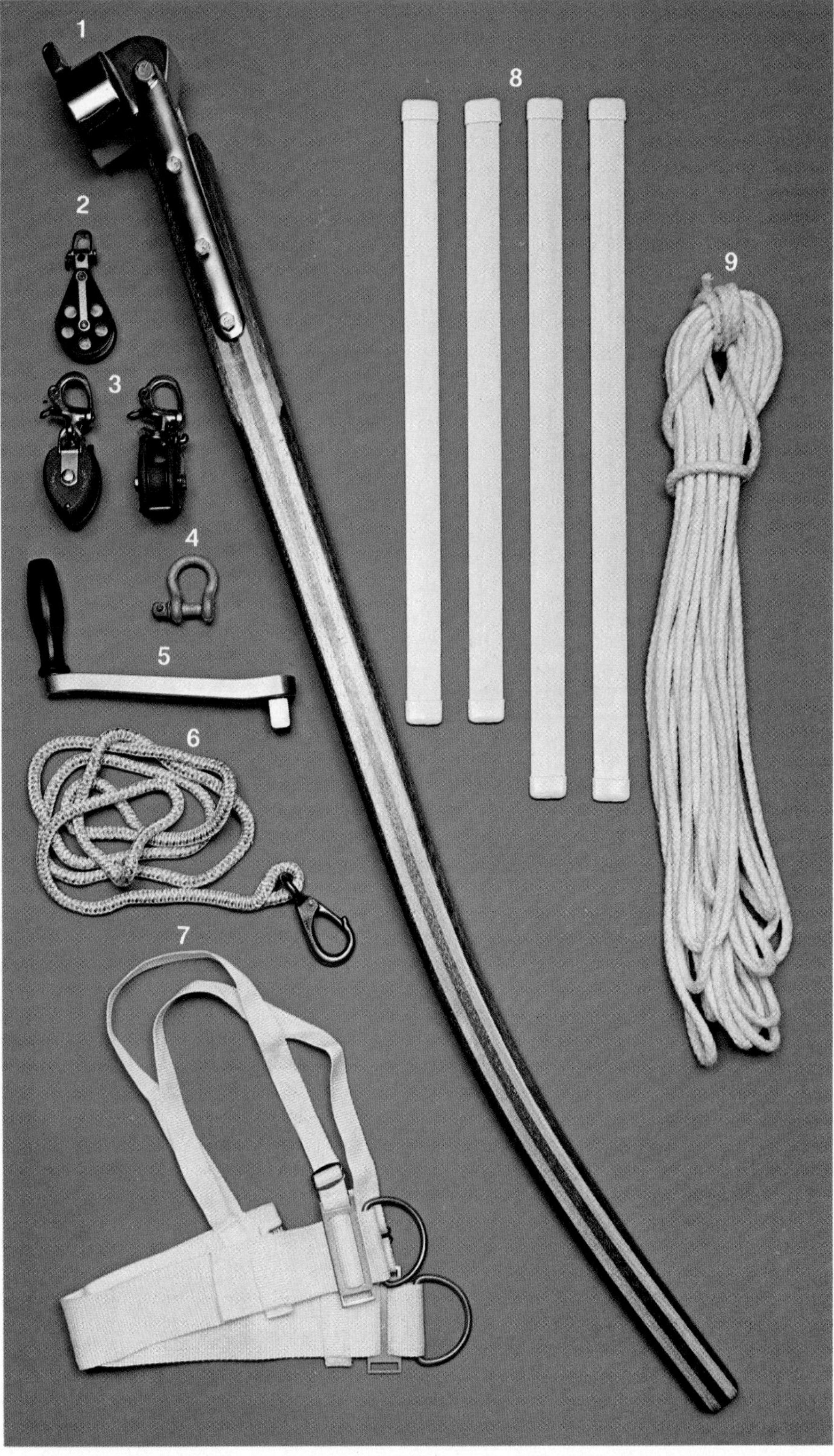

INBOARD PARTS

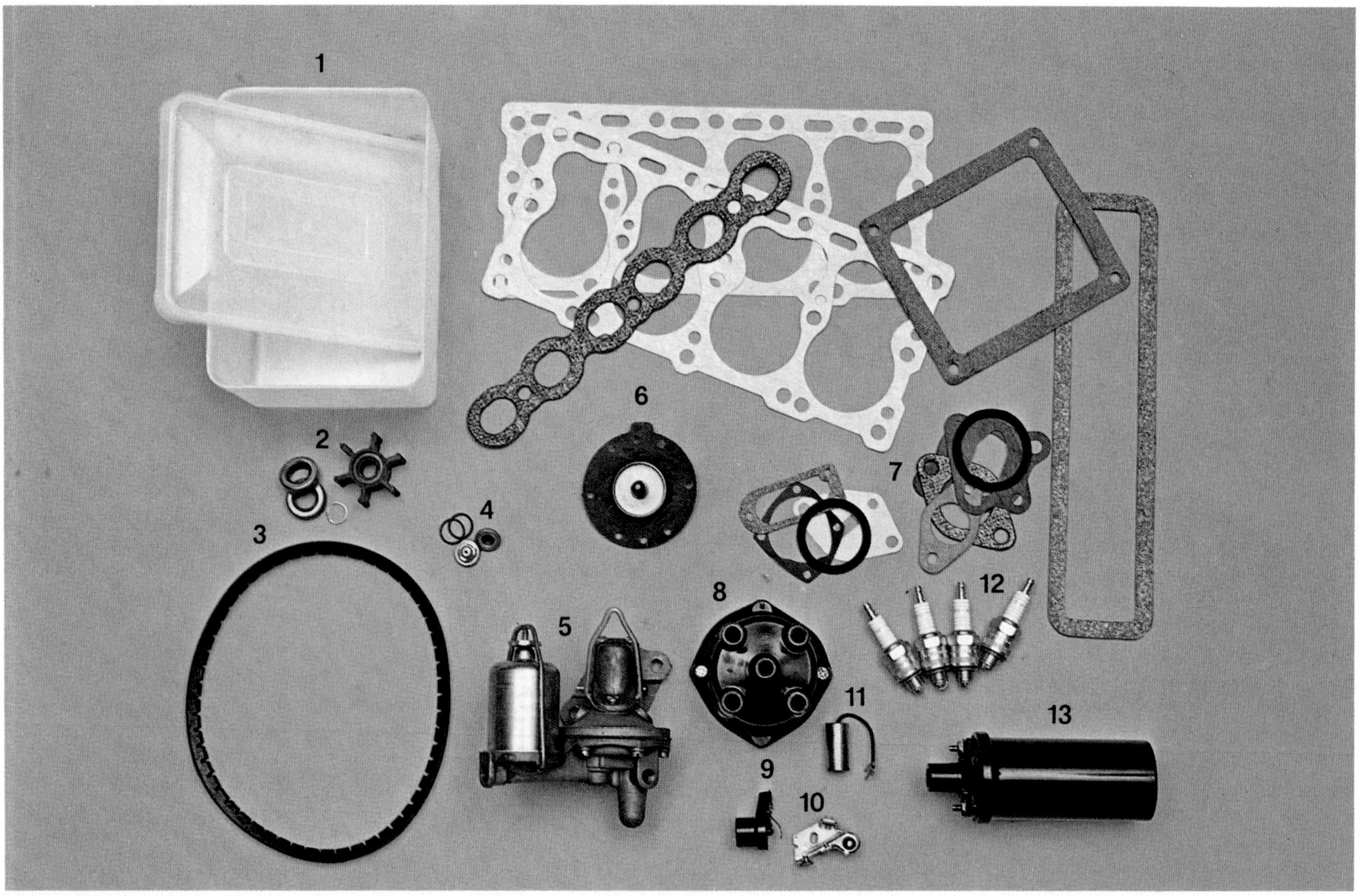

DIESEL PARTS

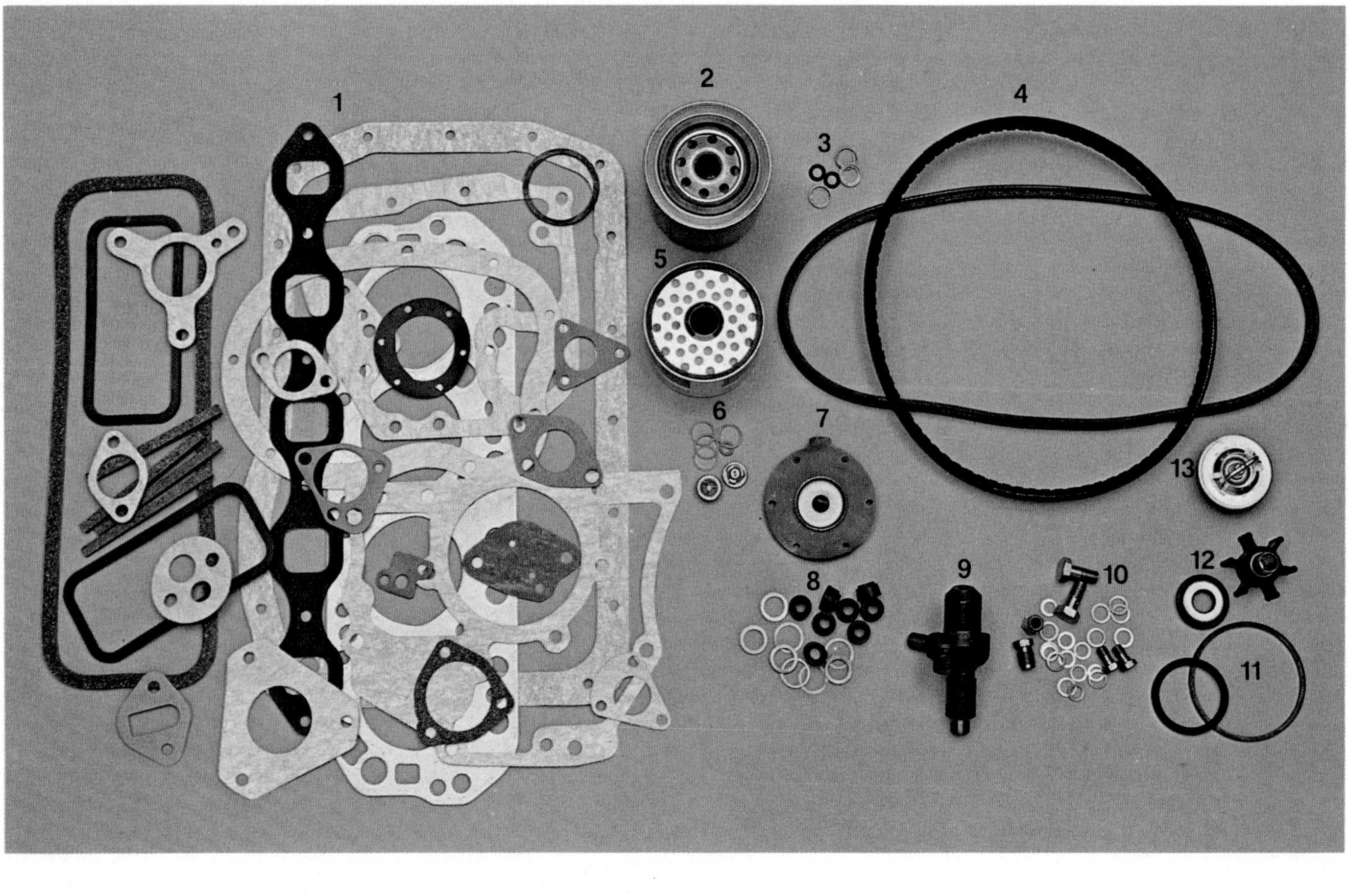

Engine Spare Parts

A complement of spare engine parts is a vital form of insurance for a cruise of any length. Often these parts are available in manufacturer's repair kits like the ones shown here. For gasoline engines there should be extra distributor components such as breaker points, condenser and rotor. A diesel kit should contain a spare fuel injector and its attendant bolts, washers and gaskets. An outboard kit may include a propeller assembly with exhaust hub, locknut and washers; for some models a plentiful supply of shear pins is crucial, especially in shallow waters.

Installation of some spares will be beyond the average skipper's skill—but at least he will have the requisite parts at hand wherever a breakdown occurs. He should also take along an engine service manual—available from the appropriate dealer—to guide a professional mechanic in making complex repairs.

GASOLINE INBOARD

1 Watertight container for components
2 Water-pump repair parts
3 Generator belt
4 Fuel-pump check valves and gaskets
5 Fuel-pump assembly
6 Fuel-pump diaphragm
7 Assorted gaskets
8 Distributor cap
9 Rotor
10 Breaker points
11 Condenser
12 Spark plugs
13 Distributor coil

DIESEL

1 Assorted gaskets
2 Oil filter
3 General-purpose washers and sealing rings
4 Alternator and water-pump belts
5 Fuel filter
6 Gaskets and fuel-pump check valves
7 Fuel-pump diaphragm
8 Fuel-injector gaskets and engine-valve seals
9 Fuel injector
10 Fuel-injector bolts with washers
11 Fuel-pump and oil-filter gaskets
12 Water-pump repair parts
13 Thermostat

OUTBOARD

1 Propeller
2 Trim tab
3 Exhaust hub
4 Lock and tab washers
5 Locknut
6 Shear pins and cotter pins
7 Fuel line
8 Lubricants
9 Water-pump impeller
10 Spark plugs

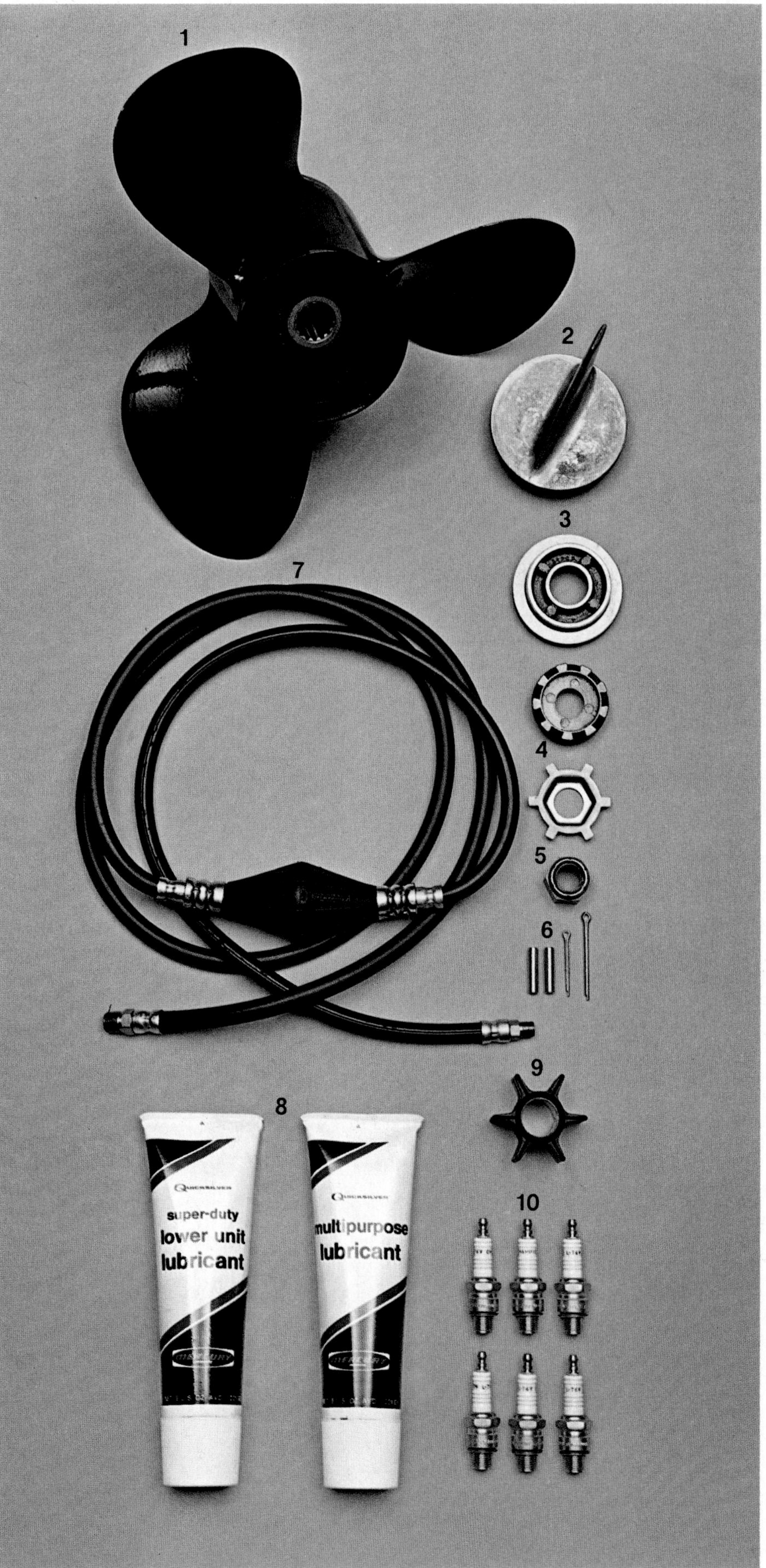

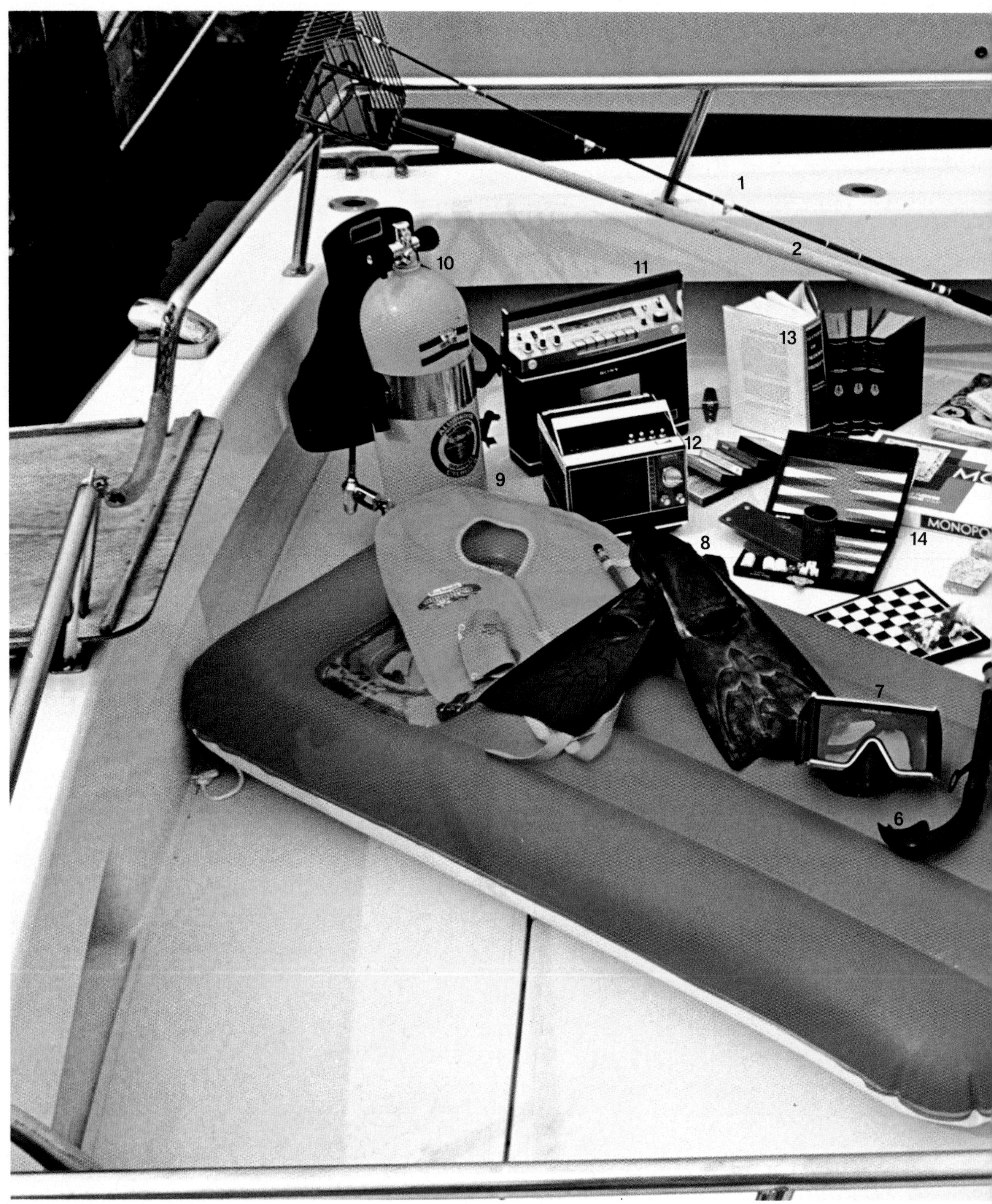

An assortment of sports gear, games and radio equipment help fill idle moments while cruising. The fishing rod can be rigged for trolling, while the scuba gear allows underwater fish watching—as well as facilitating hull maintenance. Books include a field guide to local birds, cookbooks and classics. Magnetic board games hold pieces in place when the boat rolls. The TV and radio run on batteries to save power, and the tape deck can be used to record the ship's log.

The Sport Locker

1 Fishing tackle
2 Clam rake
3 Tent
4 Camera
5 Inflatable raft with underwater window
6 Snorkel tube
7 Underwater face mask
8 Flippers
9 Emergency life vest for scuba diving
10 Oxygen tank and regulator for scuba diving
11 Battery-powered stereo radio/tape recorder
12 Television with battery pack
13 Selection of books
14 Cards and games

The swimming ladder, here being rigged on the port rail of an auxiliary ketch, is invaluable for both recreation and safety. Not only does it assist swimmers in clambering aboard after a dip, but if a crewman should fall overboard while the boat is underway, it will prove essential for helping him climb up and over the side. In the folding type shown here, fittings at the upper ends of the two risers secure into sockets in the rail. By untying a strap that holds the top and bottom rungs together, the hinged lower section of the ladder can be dropped into the water.

Awaiting charter at their home marina in Tortola, British Virgin Islands, these auxiliary sloops—and their would-be renters—will be thoroughly checked out before any vessel is signed over. They are operated by Caribbean Sailing Yachts, Ltd., which, like most of the new charter companies, does most of its business in bareboating, that is, without supplying a professional crew for cruising.

CHARTERING: ADVENTURE FOR RENT

For budget yachtsmen who yearn to venture beyond familiar horizons, chartering offers a bounty of new experiences—the chance to explore new waters, to try a larger vessel than the boatman handles at home or simply to enjoy the leisure of cruising without the worries of ownership.

Though charters have existed for centuries in some form—usually as private arrangements between individuals—the range of charter possibilities has grown enormously in recent years, both in terms of boat types and cruising locales.

Nowadays the great bulk of the boat-rental business is handled by commercial firms who advertise widely in the pages of yachting magazines, big-city newspapers, and through chambers of commerce and mailing brochures. Some offer their own fleet of boats, chosen specifically for ease of handling and stability. Other firms act as agents for selected boats belonging to individual yachtsmen but available for charter part time. A third source is the traditional private rental by yacht owners who choose to handle their own arrangements. Private listings also appear in the classified sections of boating periodicals and in some local newspapers.

From most of these sources, a charterer may hire a boat, complete with professional skipper and uniformed crew; even an experienced yachtsman may opt for a crewed vessel if he wants to sail with a minimum of fuss and plenty of feet-up relaxation. Or he may contract for a do-it-yourself vacation aboard a bareboat, one that leaves the charter skipper and his party entirely on their own.

Whatever the source, any charter arrangement should be conducted in crisp, shipshape fashion from the first contacts to the day the boat returns to home port. What to expect when negotiating a charter, including the application forms, contracts and check-out rituals, is described on the following pages.

Selecting a Charter Boat

Despite the efficiency of chartering companies, arranging any charter still remains something of an art, as anyone who has tried it knows. The charterer agrees to take command of an unfamiliar boat, which will become both his transportation and his living quarters for the extent of his cruise. So, good sense dictates that he choose the boat carefully, making sure that it comes fully found, that is, with all its gear in prime working order and with whatever comforts and conveniences he requires fitted or stowed aboard.

The simplest kind of charter to arrange is one involving a cruise in nearby waters: the charterer lines up a list of local prospects and checks them out firsthand, just as though he were renting a house. But for vacationing at distant cruising areas —Christmas in the Caribbean, say, or March off Baja California—the charterer will probably have to select his vessel, sight unseen, through the mail.

Most long-distance chartering is arranged through companies, which on request send detailed brochures like the ones at right, depicting the boats available, and often including schematic diagrams *(opposite)* of interior layouts.

A careful study of these brochures will reveal the suitability of each type of vessel —its size and sleeping accommodations; the amount of headroom in the cabin; whether or not the craft affords such luxuries as hot water, a shower, an electric refrigerator or a gas oven. The brochures will also give the rate schedule for each boat, and describe any special services the company may offer. For example, some agencies will, as part of the charter agreement, deliver the boat fully provisioned for the duration of the cruise.

Before chartering any boat, whether from a commercial agency or from a private yacht owner, the charterer should ask for a thorough inventory of the equipment carried aboard, so he can tell how much, if any, of his own gear he may need to bring. The list at right is typical for a charter agreement with a commercial agency. It is a good idea, when taking possession of a newly chartered boat to arrive at the dock with the list in hand, and mark off each item during the final check-out *(page 65)* before setting out on the cruise.

Most charter companies have illustrated brochures for prospective clients—though some make do with only a mimeographed letter. The important specifications to look for are the vessel's length, beam, water-storage capacity, sleeping accommodations, headroom and horsepower. Any of this information not included in the brochures can usually be found in the company's supplemental literature —which also should include a list of equipment like that at bottom.

What the Owner Normally Provides

Any boat offered for charter presumably comes equipped with all the basics necessary for safe operation—engine, sails, docking lines, anchors and so on—and also such vital emergency gear as life jackets, signal flares and fire extinguishers; when taking over an unfamiliar boat, check thoroughly to make sure these items are aboard. In addition, most charter vessels carry the following equipment and supplies, necessary for comfortable cruising.

Charts of the cruising area
Navigational equipment
Radiotelephone
Dinghy with oars
Tool kit
First-aid kit
Pots and pans
Dishes and cutlery
Stove fuel
Ice
Bedding and linens
Cleaning supplies

What the Charterer Brings Himself

Food, clothing and entertainment are, with few exceptions, the responsibility of the client. To help him plan ahead, brochures often include a reminder list like the following.

Camera and film
Portable radio
Games and cards
Fishing tackle
Ice chest for bait
Food and liquor
Paper towels
Plastic bags
Sun lotion
Insect repellant
Soap
Personal gear

Other Items to Have Aboard

Besides the standard inventory listed above, many charter boats come with a variety of important extras that contribute to comfort, enjoyment of the waters and safety. Some of these items—such as flashlight and rain gear—are truly indispensable, and they should be part of the charterer's baggage if the company does not provide them.

Outboard for dinghy
RDF
Binoculars
Flashlight
Foul-weather gear
Swim ladder
Snorkeling gear
Awnings
Dodger
Screens for hatches
Charcoal grill
Clothes hangers

Belowdecks accommodations, as shown in this typical schematic diagram from a charter company brochure, are illustrated by a standardized art technique, and may or may not be labeled. Thus bunks are often depicted as made up for sleeping; pot lockers and water tanks are indicated by rectangles with crossing diagonal lines; hanging lockers are shown by a series of parallel lines. This plan for a 41-foot sloop reveals a galley, two heads, plenty of locker space and sleeping quarters for eight—two in the forward cabin, four in the main cabin, and two in an aftercabin that has its own companionway.

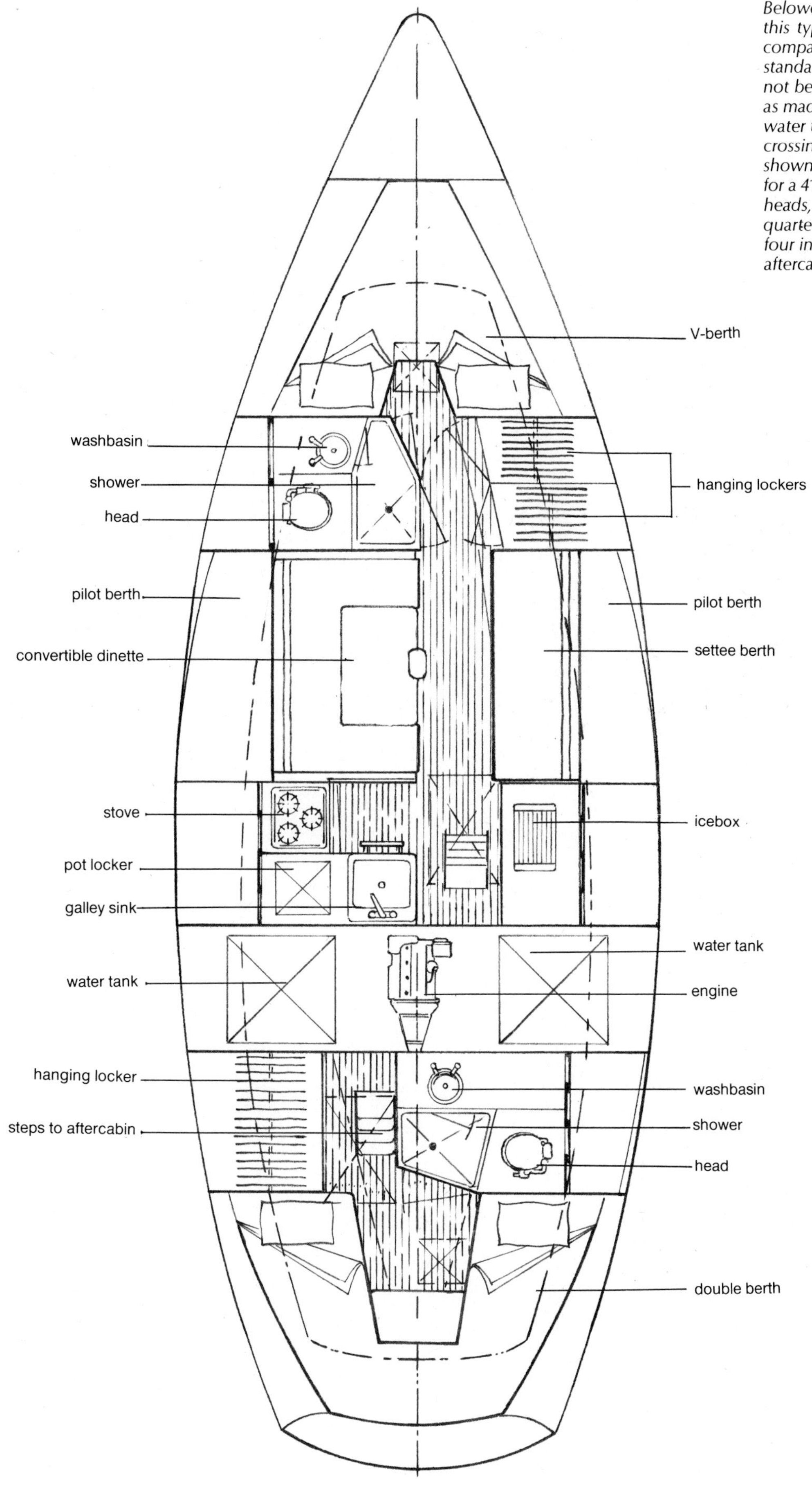

A Watertight Contract

As the number of private individuals and commercial agencies offering boat rentals has grown, charter arrangements have become increasingly formalized. Renters and owners alike realize that there is no substitute for knowing just which party is responsible for what—and for having the watertight documents to prove it.

In any chartering agreement, the boatowner orchestrates the proceedings, and he sees to it that the boat's best interests are served first. Before filling out the formal contract, the owner can demand that the client testify to his nautical skills by filling out a questionnaire like the one at right. And he can turn away any person he thinks unsuitable to take out his valuable, vulnerable property. He can have the contract itself written entirely to his specifications, and he can set not only the fee but also the timing of payment. In addition, he can require a security deposit and designate the terms under which it is to be repaid—or forfeited.

Since a charter agreement comprises a set of enforceable legal documents, the prospective client should read the agreement with the same thoroughness he would apply to any contract. And, if possible, he should peruse it long before his vacation begins, providing himself ample time to renegotiate any terms he finds too difficult—or to look for another charter more to his liking.

SEAMANSHIP RESUME

The following information pertains to the charter skipper.
Have you ever:

Handled a heavy-displacement boat? Describe: Cal 40 sloop

Raced a heavy-displacement boat? Describe: crewed on a 68' yawl

Chartered before? Company: private charter Boat: Cal 40

Owned a boat? Describe: Thistle daysailer, Columbia 26 sloop

Do you understand:

Basic navigation? yes Charts? yes Compass? yes

Anchoring procedures? yes Rules of the road? yes

Radiotelephone procedures? yes

In what boat have you had the most experience? Columbia 26

Your sailing experience is mostly on which bodies of water?
Puget Sound

Do you belong to a sailing or yacht club? yes Please give name and address:
Juan de Fuca Yacht Club

Have you any friends who have sailed with this company?
Please give names. George Robbins, in 1979

Please give two sailing references (name, address and telephone number):

1. Edward van Nessen, Catalina Island, Calif. (407) 432-5202
2. Francis Prince, Mercer Island, Washington (625) 691-0613

Brian L. Drake — Witness to skipper's signature
Hancock Walker — Skipper
12/15/75 — Date

The résumé above is patterned after one used by a firm that offers sailboats for charter in the British Virgin Islands. Questions relating to heavy-displacement boats are intended to sort out small-craft sailors with little experience in handling the sizable boats that the company provides. Inquiries about navigational know-how and the bodies of water on which the client has sailed will give the company a sense of how he will fare in Caribbean waters. If the company has doubts about the client's skills, it may reject him. Alternatively, it may offer him the option of taking an on-board test with the understanding that, should he fail, he can charter only with a paid crewman aboard.

The Informal Private Charter

Boat Charters —802

36' GRAND BANKS TRAWLER
Annapolis Area
Fully eqpd. Qualified people only (407) 253-8290 or (407) 253-5556

46' AFT CABIN KETCH
Fiberglass, Perkins Diesel, Good condition. $600/wk. (625) 556-2007

NARRAGANSETT CHARTER Morgan 37' Sloop, sleeps 6. Wheel, full electronics, sailing dinghy. $450/wk. E.J. O'Day, 312 W. Village Drive, Henderson, R.I. 32500 or CH 2-3587

1974 BRISTOL 33
South Conn. $350/wk. Sun. thru Sat. Fully eqpd. galley. Linens avail. Call eves. betw. 6 & 10 M-F. (226) 691-7363

CHARTER my 37 ft. power cruiser. Sleeps four to six. Fully eqpd. $450 per wk. J.V. Davenport, P.O. Box 230, Seal Cove, Maine 19250

CHARTER-MARINER 36, new, fully equipped for safe, comftble cruising, by day, week or month. Dennis Greer, Greenpoint, L.I. (112) 526-1113

Individual boatowners like the ones offering their vessels for charter in these sample newspaper advertisements seldom conduct the sort of detailed investigation of prospective clients' sailing skills that charter companies undertake. For example, of the six ads shown here, one states that only "qualified people" need apply. However, an owner will usually talk with a prospective client to assure himself that his boat will be properly handled, and may even suggest a short sail with the client at the helm.

The Basic Chartering Agreement

Although a typical charter contract may at first seem like a cold, frightening and overly complex document, it is no more than a sensible setting forth of the fundamental things that the owner and client agree to do—and not to do. Basically it should say that the owner will deliver a certain boat for hire, ready for sea, at a given place at a given time, and that the client will return it in good condition at some specified place and time. Beyond that, the terms may be—and often are—negotiable.

Essential Terms of Charter	A charter contract normally starts off with the length, design and name of the yacht, and any other data by which it can be identified. Its draft, beam and type of engine, if any, should also be given. Other basic data that should be included are dates of the charter, the fee, the amount of the security deposit, whether a paid skipper or crew will come along, the schedule of payments, and the pickup and return locations.
Delivery of the Boat	The contract should guarantee that the boat is fully equipped and ready for service at the specified delivery point on the agreed-upon date. Some contracts reserve the owner the right to a 24-hour grace period should there be an unavoidable delay in the delivery.
Running Expenses	The cost of engine fuel, stove fuel, food and drink, ice, docking fees and the like may or may not be included in the basic charter fee. If nothing is specified, these necessities will have to be purchased by the client.
Breakdowns	The contract should spell out who is liable in case of damage to the boat. The best contracts distinguish damages caused by unavoidable accidents from those by the owner's negligence and by the client's faulty seamanship. The charter company will often give itself a 24-hour grace period for making repairs or replacements due to its own error. Typically, if damage is extensive and the boat must remain in port, the owner will refund the charter fee.
Insurance	Charter companies carry blanket insurance policies that cover any damage to the boat—whether caused by the client or not—exceeding the amount of the security deposit. Most companies also have coverage for the death or injury of any person on board. The client can invalidate the policy by sailing beyond the boundaries that have been specified, sailing at night, exceeding a given speed limit, engaging in a race or subchartering the boat. In private charter arrangements, the owner may require the client to take out his own short-term policy to cover the boat and its passengers.
Defaults and Security Deposits	The contract will commonly state a number of circumstances under which the security deposit will not be returned. The default terms include damage charged against the client and failure to comply with the terms of the insurance policy. The contract should state that under all other circumstances the deposit will be returned within a specified time limit.
Redelivery	The conditions for return of the vessel should be stated. Some charter companies require that the boat be brought back to port in precisely the condition in which the client found it. More often, contracts specify that the boat be returned in "good condition . . . with normal wear and tear." How much the client will be penalized if he is unable to return the boat to home port on time should also be detailed. Sometimes a distinction is drawn between lateness due to negligence and lateness due to acts of nature—but not always.

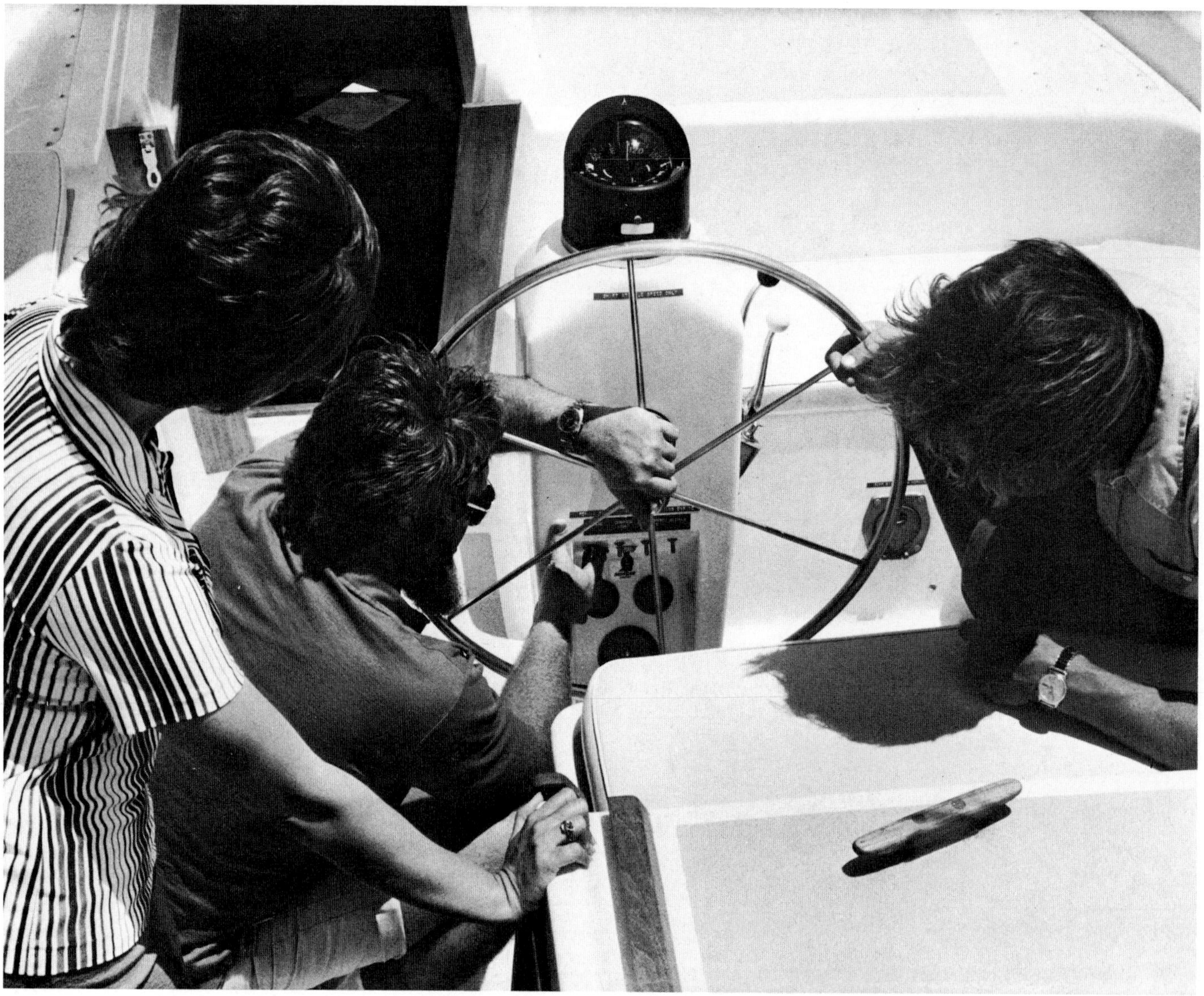

A Florida charter representative begins his orientation tour of a 41-foot sloop by demonstrating the vessel's engine-control panel to a pair of clients. Although six people will share the charter, this representative —like many others—briefs just two of them on details of operation and stowage, and will require only one to prove his sailing skill.

Conversion of the dinette into sleeping space starts with dismantling the table. The top is temporarily propped against the seat cushions while the legs are slipped out of their sockets. The top will be lowered to fit flush with the benches; a foam cushion will be placed over it to form a double berth.

Sailing through the Test

Prior to closing any charter agreement, both client and owner should insist on a check-out, aboard and underway. This brief shakedown, which can be painstaking on a sophisticated auxiliary sailboat like the one shown here and overleaf, serves two purposes: it allows the client to familiarize himself with his new vessel, and gives the owner a good look at the client's boating skill.

The check-out usually takes place on the day before—or the morning of—the scheduled departure and takes up to three hours, depending upon the complexity of the vessel and the degree of seamanship required. It begins with a detailed tour of the boat. Among other things, the charterer must know where safety gear is stowed, how the engine, toilet, stove, radiotelephone and other devices operate, and how to master such miracles of marine inventiveness as the fold-up bunk, drop-down table, inflatable dinghy and collapsible oar. The charterer should also locate halyards and sheets, test all electrical switches, and see that fuel and water tanks are full.

Once the dockside tour is over, the boat drops her dock lines for a test spin in the harbor with the would-be skipper in charge, as described overleaf. If all goes well, this part may take only a few minutes; but some charter company representatives, like the one pictured here, will run clients through a variety of maneuvers if there is any doubt about their capabilities.

Up on deck the representative shows how to control the chain feed when raising and lowering the anchor, and how to snub the anchor to the roller chock in the bow. At the same time he informs the charterers where spare ground tackle is stowed, and recommends the correct scope for setting the unfamiliar plow anchor on local bottoms.

Down below, the representative calls attention to two key items: life vests, which he and the charterer count to be sure there are enough, and the inflatable dinghy, shown here in its bag and with the bellows used to blow it up. Many charterers use such dinghys for exploring; it should be kept inflated and securely lashed to the deck.

The dockside check-out over, the company representative takes his clients through Florida's Intracoastal Waterway and into the Gulf of Mexico for a sail. Setting a jib from roller-furling gear, as above, is a new experience for the pair, as is running the shallow and often narrow channels in these waters. The representative cautions them to expect crosscurrents and to watch markers both ahead and astern to see that they are not being carried into the shallows.

Approaching a drawbridge, the charterers have signaled the bridge tender with three blasts of the air horn. Clearing a tight opening like this is a tricky bit of boat handling that sailors are likely to face in this area. The helmsman has correctly taken the starboard side of the channel to give his mast maximum clearance under the bridge. Satisfied the boat was in good hands, the representative soon after ordered the boat returned to the marina so that the charter could begin.

A flotilla of 34- and 36-foot houseboats for rent nestles at a marina in Flamingo, Florida, awaiting vacationers who will charter them for anything from a weekend outing to an extended cruise through the Everglades. Moored among the houseboats is a fast service launch that brings supplies—or help—to charterers who get into trouble.

The owner of the houseboat rental company whose craft are shown above begins the orientation of two prospective charterers by going over a chart of the Everglades, where they intend to cruise. Having learned that they want to do some fishing, he suggests some promising areas, points out interesting side trips and firmly outlines the boundaries inside which they must operate the boat under their charter and insurance agreements.

Floating Cottages

Taking a cruise on a river, a lake or a lagoon aboard a houseboat like those shown here and on the following pages is more like renting a summer cottage than chartering a conventional boat. Rental arrangements tend to be more relaxed than for a standard sailboat or powerboat, because the risks to life and property are considerably less in the sheltered waters where these homey craft tend to operate.

Nevertheless, owners still provide prospectuses for clients to study and contracts for them to sign. And there is a quick check-out aboard the premises, in which the working of engines is demonstrated, unfamiliar stoves and toilets explained, safety equipment pointed out and navigational tips given.

But the houseboat owner need be only minimally concerned about the renter's boating expertise aboard one of these stable steel or fiberglass boxes, which drive almost as easily as cars. Many companies will even charter to a client with no previous experience. If, after an hour or less of practice, the novice *(overleaf)* can learn to steer forward and in reverse, to turn within a reasonably tight radius, and to dock without too much speed—all relatively easy skills for a candidate to acquire or demonstrate—he is pronounced a fit skipper.

Despite simplicity of handling, houseboats provide a mobile livability for a special kind of waterborne adventure. With their shallow draft they make it possible for charterers to mosey up a blind creek for a little angling, poke into a saw-grass marsh to watch the birds or nose up to an inviting riverbank to explore a shore on foot. And all this is done from a floating home that is hardly less comfortable than the place the renter left behind.

A short lesson in the care of the houseboat's 250-horsepower motor begins with a look into the engine compartment under the afterdeck. The owner pulls out the dipstick and asks that the clients check it daily for any drop in the level, replenishing the oil if necessary from the spare cans stowed nearby. The adjacent hatch (foreground) opens onto the space used for garbage storage.

Under the owner's knowledgeable direction, a tense novice starts his practice run up a bay in southern Florida. The most important lesson to be learned is that houseboats are slow to respond to any steering changes, and the helmsman must consistently give other boats a wide berth when passing. The skipper also must expect even moderate wind to influence handling markedly, as the boat's high, broad sides tend to act as a sail.

Their test passed, two newly accredited houseboat skippers take a final look at the charter contract and sign it. The owner will send them off with an engine instruction sheet and some final bits of counsel—such as to choose the leeward side of an anchorage to escape the mosquitoes; to hold the boat's speed under eight knots; and to keep a watch out for mangrove roots that may lie submerged in brackish rivers.

Snugged for the night in the backwaters of Everglades National Park, a chartered houseboat rides at anchor on the reflection path of a full moon.

Lipton
TREET

3

On a cruise, the combination of fresh air and exercise breeds ravenous appetites. And the need to see that all hands are fed has always been among any skipper's most pressing preoccupations. In the earliest days of sail, on the better-appointed vessels, seamen might dine on salt fish cooked in olive oil over a wood fire set in a sandbox on deck. (Hong Kong sampans and Arab dhows on the Indian Ocean are still using these simple, practical sand stoves.) On many ships, weevil-ridden biscuits might have been the staple fare—and more than one mutiny had its roots in bad food. Later, as ships got bigger and owners became more generous, passenger packets carried live cows, pigs,

THE SEA COOK'S BAILIWICK

chickens and sheep on deck for a provision of fresh meat, milk and eggs, which were cooked up on heavy iron stoves below.

Today, though virtually all sailing voyages are for pleasure, and most of them last less than a week, the heart of any cruising boat, and the secret of a contented crew, is still the galley. Thus, anyone who is considering buying, outfitting or improving a boat for cruising should devote as much time and forethought to the layout and equipping of the galley as he would to the selection of an engine or a suit of sails. Good planning will allow adequate space on most boats for a galley that is equal to the eating requirements of as many people as the boat can carry.

The skipper should first consider the galley in relation to its principal occupant, the cook. A galley in which the same person will repeatedly do most of the cooking should be fitted to that particular cook's taste. A short cook may want a built-in step for reaching high shelves. A tall cook in a galley with a low ceiling will appreciate a well-anchored stool *(page 87)*. If various people take turns cooking, the galley appointments should be standard and uncomplicated, and the contents well organized—for example, canned goods should be grouped according to the meals for which they will be used.

Though most skippers prefer to stock a practical minimum of kitchenware , no cruising cook should be denied room for a favorite seagoing tool—whose educated use can make life better for all hands aboard. For one East Coast cook, this means the inclusion of at least one large cast-iron frying pan with a tight-fitting lid for making anything from chicken paprika to beef Stroganoff. The Mississippi-born wife of a Los Angeles lawyer who cruises on the West Coast refuses to put to sea without a large, flat pan for jambalaya. And a supply of paper plates will certainly brighten the life of any cook—a breed that tends to dislike dishwashing.

The galley must be so arranged and equipped that it can be used not only when the boat is lying at anchor in a flat calm, but under far less favorable conditions. When a boat is underway, a cruising cook, like the one at left, seldom works in a vertical position. In fact, a lot of cruise cooking is done at a constantly changing series of angles. The stove must be gimbaled to keep it level when the boat heels. The contents of shelves, bins and lockers must be adequately restrained *(pages 88-89)*. And the galley must be laid out *(page 74)* so that all vital equipment is within arm's reach even when the cook is confined to the limits of a galley strap.

The addition of a simple but secure drawer lock *(page 88)*, the handy placement of a garbage can or a bottle opener, can be important to cook and crew. So, too, is the very location of the galley. Most galleys are located amidships or at the after end of the main cabin, not only for convenience in serving crewmen on deck, but also to permit a cook at work to be part of the boat's social life—one more reflection of the fact that a contented cook is a crucial factor in ensuring a happy cruise.

In the galley of a heeled cruising boat, a seasoned sea cook tends the gimbaled stove. Her tools are within easy reach and a galley strap contributes to her safety and stability.

Galley Layouts

The perfect galley is compact but not overly cramped, tucked out of the way of traffic but easily accessible, brightly lighted, fully ventilated and conveniently arranged. In practical fact, galleys are always a compromise between these goals and the boat's capacities—although careful arrangement and ingenious devices *(pages 86-87)* can greatly increase even the smallest galley's utility. The basic necessities can be crammed into a small sailboat, as at right, while a larger sailboat can accommodate more lavish equipment, like that shown below, and a big power cruiser may flaunt a fully equipped kitchen *(opposite)*.

A galley set near the companionway enjoys the blessings of direct ventilation and is handy to both the cabin table and the cockpit—the two places where most of the meals will be served.

A sailboat's galley, especially, must be compact, not only because space tends to be limited but because all supplies and utensils will be within arm's reach, an important advantage if any cooking is to be done while the boat is underway and heeling. In a U-shaped galley like the one at right the cook can brace himself between the counters when the boat pitches in heavy weather or when it heels on a windward leg. On powerboats, usually roomier than sailboats and designed to ride on an essentially even keel, galley arrangements can be more flexible.

On any type of craft, a stove should be put where it is least likely to set curtains or wooden fittings afire if its burners flare up suddenly. The sink and icebox should be so positioned that the cook need not reach across a hot stove to get at them. All galley countertops should be at a height convenient for the cook, just above waist level in a cabin with full headroom, or lower on small boats with less overhead, where much of the cooking is done sitting down.

The amount of working surface can be greatly increased by the use of hinged or folding covers that fit over stove, sink and icebox when they are not in use.

The counter of the galley below, in the after end of a 23-foot sloop's cabin, forms a step in the companionway. To use the two-burner alcohol stove that swings into position on a pivoted shelf, the cook sits on the icebox lid between the stove and the step. The sink at right has a hand-operated fresh-water pump and can be covered, as here, with a cutting board to increase counter space.

The expansive design of this galley on a 36-foot power cruiser reflects an abundance of cabin space and a ready supply of electric power from the boat's generator. A full-sized electric stove and refrigerator flank a sink supplied with hot and cold water that flow on a pressure system. A hinged cover can be lowered over the stove to increase the ample counter area. There is also voltage enough to operate a small head-height fan for the cook's comfort, and an electric percolator.

The U-shaped galley at left, on the port side of a 36-foot sloop, is near the companionway and the dining area but out of the way of crewmen going to and from the cockpit. Under the generous countertop (right) is a top-loading icebox. A removable lid covers the three-burner alcohol stove-oven unit. The sink has both pressurized fresh water and foot-pumped salt water. Staples and dishes are stowed above the sink, pots in the sliding-door cupboards behind the stove.

A typical two-burner alcohol stove, complete with oven under the range, runs on fuel stored in the airtight container mounted on the left of the stove. Pressure built up by rapid strokes with the brass pump handle (top left, on the fuel container) forces fuel to the burners. A railing prevents pots and pans from sliding off whenever the boat heels.

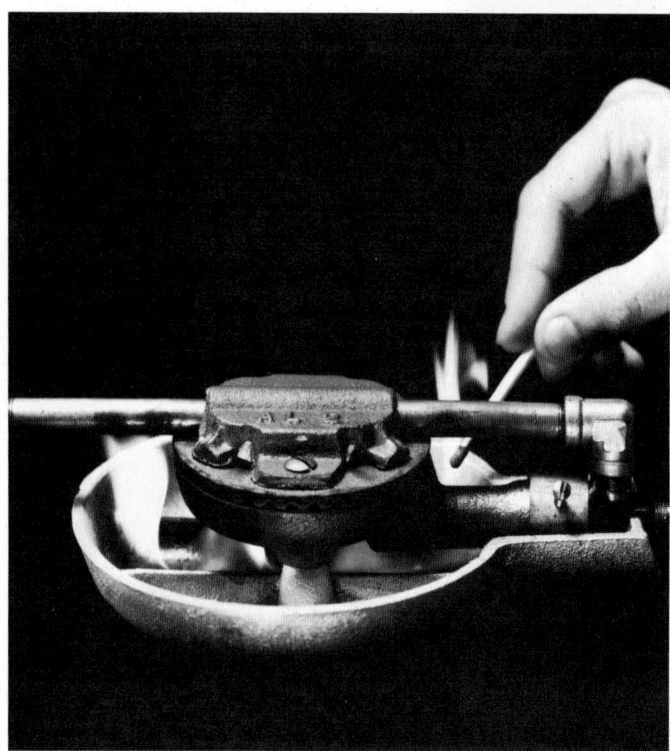

To prime an alcohol stove, pump the fuel tank up to its recommended operating pressure. Open the burner knob long enough to permit a teaspoon of alcohol to seep into the trough beneath the burner. Close the knob, and using a kitchen match, ignite the liquid and let its flame heat the burner.

When the primer fire dies out, turn the burner knob on a second time and light with a match. The burner should now be hot enough to vaporize the alcohol as it reaches the burner ring, producing an even circle of flame. If not, shut off the stove for a moment or two; then repeat the priming and reignite.

The Most Common Stove

The stove most frequently found aboard cruising vessels is the type fueled by ethyl alcohol—for a variety of excellent reasons. Electric stoves are expensive to install and, unless the boat carries its own alternating-current source, can be operated only with dockside power. The gasoline stoves favored by many campers ashore are too dangerous aboard, for their heavier-than-air fumes, settling into the bilge, can be exploded by any wayward spark. The use of a gasoline stove on board, in fact, may cancel an owner's insurance policy. Kerosene stoves, also popular with campers, can be problems in a confined galley: they produce a strong smell and leave oily soot deposits.

Alcohol stoves, by contrast, are relatively odorless. They are also compact, inexpensive and, used with the proper precautions, reasonably safe. Flare-ups may occur, but an alcohol fire can be easily doused with water *(bottom right)*. Moreover, ethyl alcohol is readily obtainable at marinas and drugstores.

Alcohol stoves do, however, pose some inconveniences. They must be primed *(far left)* before they can be started. Also, ethyl alcohol does not generate much heat, and boiling even a cup of soup may take 10 minutes or more.

A more efficient alternative to the alcohol stove is the type fueled by propane or butane, petroleum gases that permit cooking aboard with no more difficulty than is required for meals prepared on a gas stove ashore. However, propane is a potentially explosive fuel, and requires special installation and extra precautions, as explained on the following pages.

A small flare-up like the one shown here often occurs when an alcohol stove is being lighted—either because too much alcohol spills into the trough during priming, or because the cook turns the burner back on before it is hot enough to vaporize the fresh dose of alcohol. A flare-up of this size is no cause for alarm, and can be allowed to burn itself out. However, should the flames become too high—eight inches or so —emergency action (left) must be taken.

When a flare-up threatens to get out of hand, the cook should instantly douse the flames —which can be done with a pot of water, as shown at left. Because alcohol has the unique property among liquid stove fuels of mixing readily with water, the alcohol becomes diluted to the point where it will no longer burn. To be prepared for just such an emergency, therefore, the cook should always keep a saucepan of water close at hand when priming and lighting an alcohol stove.

Gimbals for Stability

To keep pots on an even keel when the vessel is not, marine stoves, like the one above, are frequently slung in gimbals —pivoted mountings that permit the burners to stay level as the ship rolls.

The Most Efficient Fuel

The most convenient and satisfactory of shipboard stoves to operate are those that burn liquefied petroleum gas (LPG), commonly propane or butane. Each of these LPG fuels burns with a hot, steady flame that heats a frying pan evenly and can boil a six-cup pot of coffee in 10 minutes. Better yet, LPG stoves require none of the complex circuitry of their electric counterparts; the fuel is stored in tanks that are connected to the stove by copper and rubber hosing. Moreover, unlike alcohol stoves, LPG models need no priming. They are simply turned on and ignited with a kitchen match.

However, LPG does demand certain precautions. The fumes of propane and butane, like those of gasoline, are heavier than air and will settle into the bilge, where they too can be exploded by a spark. Common sense therefore dictates that fuel containers be carried on deck, in vented lockers that allow any stray fumes to dissipate. In addition, propane and butane tanks are installed with three separate valves: a cutoff valve on the fuel tank; a pressure-regulating valve—usually next to the fuel tank—that should be adjusted by a professional before the stove is first used; and another cutoff where the fuel line enters the stove.

Both cutoff valves should be turned off whenever the stove is not in use, or when a fresh tank of fuel is being installed—as demonstrated on these pages. During tank changes, all valves and other fuel-line connections should be checked for possible leaks.

Having removed an empty stove fuel tank from its well, a skipper puts in a freshly filled tank. It holds four pounds of liquefied propane—enough for 20 stove-burning hours. The well has a vent at the bottom to allow any leaking gas to dissipate, and a cover that is kept unlatched—so that, in case of an explosion, the blast's force will shoot upward, rather than downward through the hull.

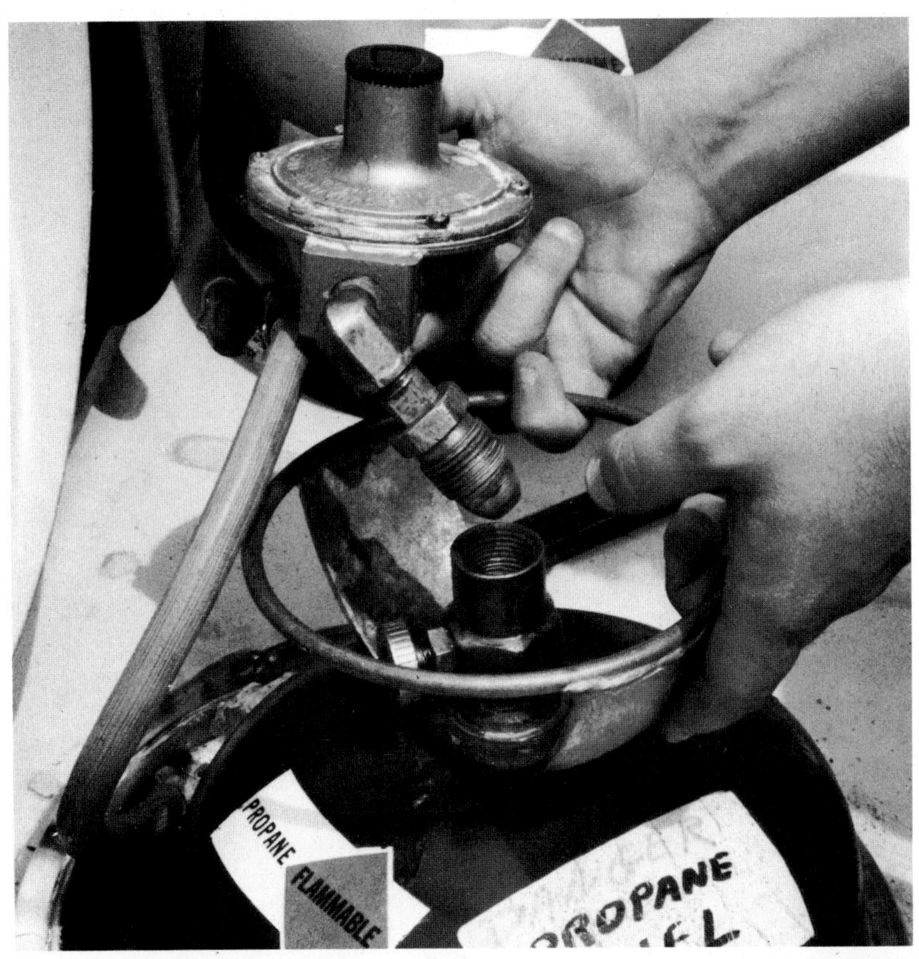

The skipper starts to attach the fuel line to the full tank after unscrewing the line from the empty one. The fitting in his right hand is the pressure-regulator valve, which sits directly atop the tank. After inserting the metal nipple in the opening, he will screw down the nut just above the nipple, securing the line to the tank. The thumbscrew on the side of the tank's neck is a cutoff valve.

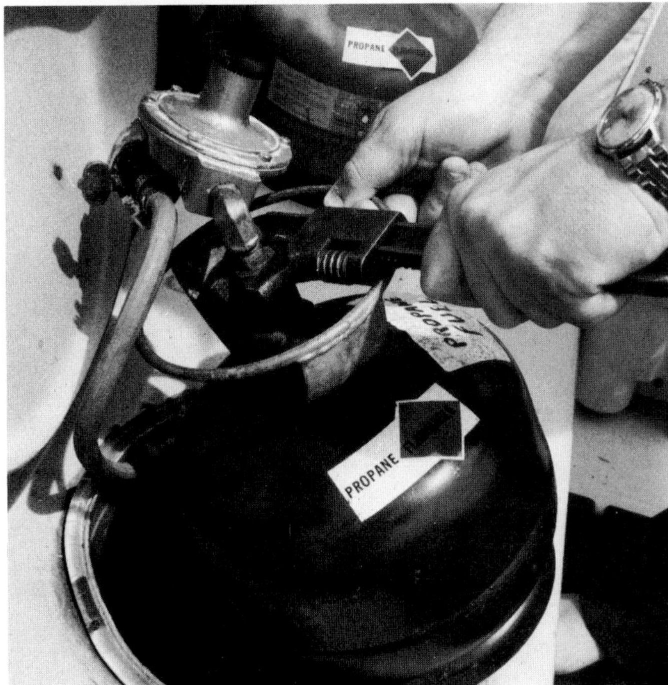

After hand-tightening the nut on the regulator pipe, the boatowner clinches the nut with a wrench to ensure a leakproof seal. The nut should be checked on regularly to see that the engine's vibration has not loosened it.

Liquid detergent smeared on the joint between the regulator and tank will reveal whether gas is escaping: a leak will cause the detergent to bubble, as shown. If further tightening does not stop the leak, then the tank or the regulator is faulty and should be replaced at once. All connections from which gas might escape should be similarly tested for leakage on a regular basis.

To preserve its interior cold, a marine icebox needs adequate insulation—such as four inches of polyurethane—and a snugly fitting door. In the top-opening box at left, provisions are stowed directly atop the ice. Most boatowners prefer this design: it increases the life of the ice block because cold air tends to sink and only a small amount of coolness escapes when the lid is swung up. As the ice melts, water drains out through a plastic hose, either into a container or else directly overboard, so that no meltwater spills into the bilge. An elbow in the hose keeps cold air from escaping along with the water.

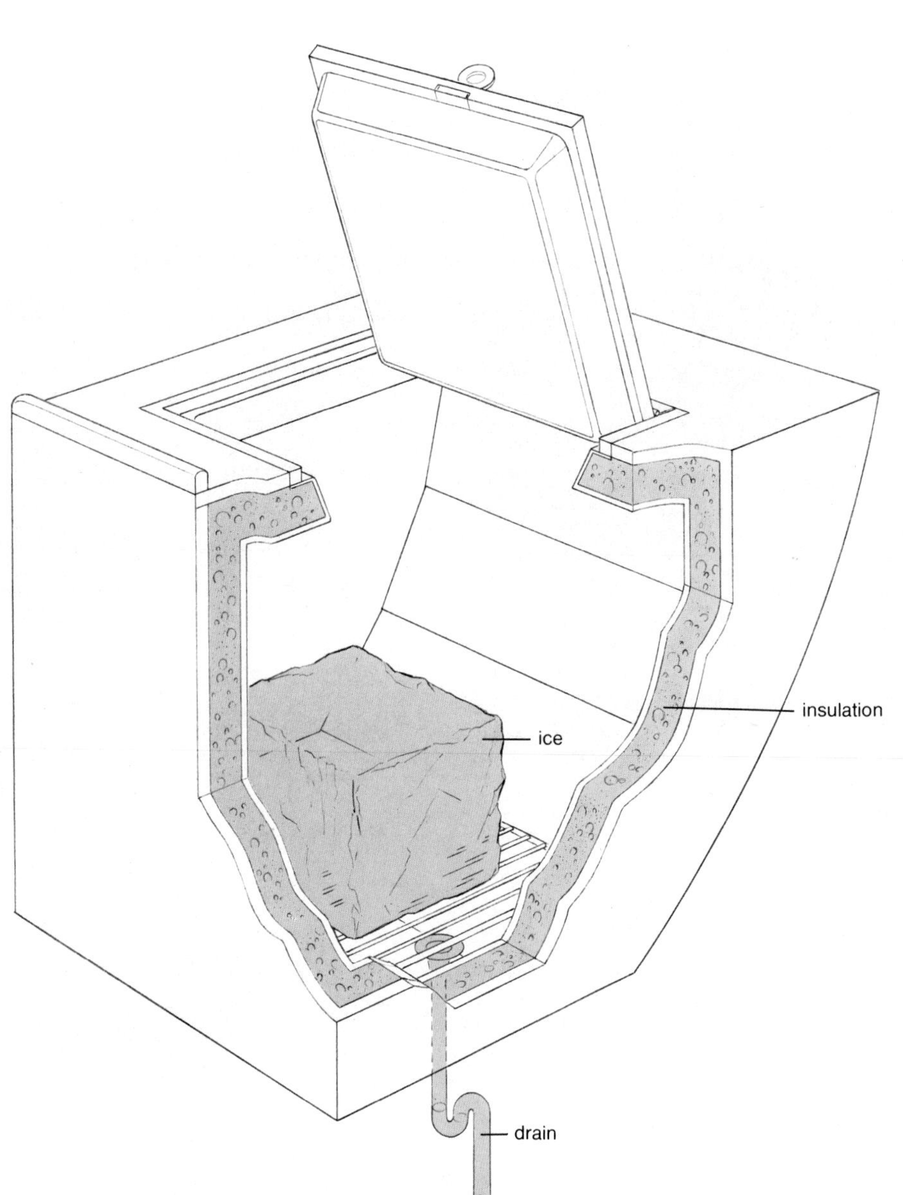

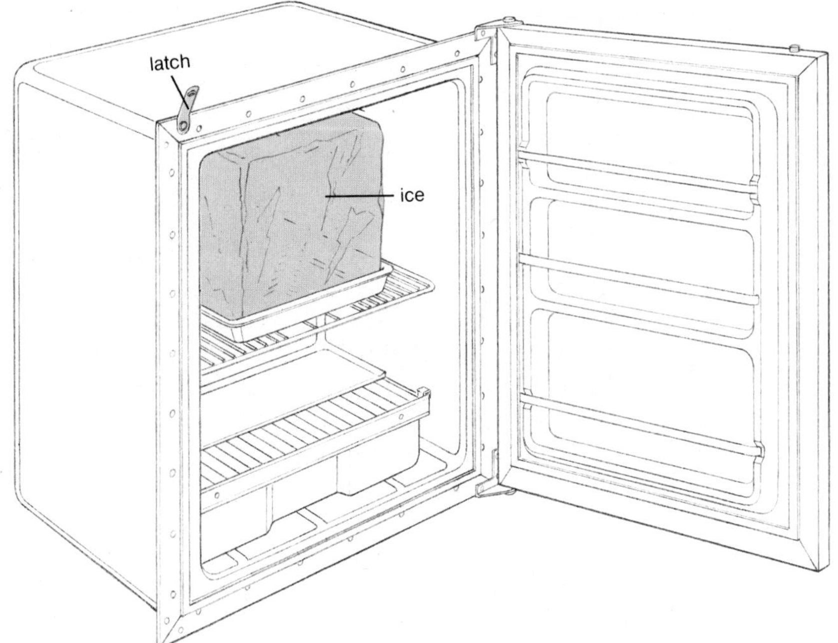

A front-opening box like the one at right consumes more ice than a top-opener—cold air spills out every time the door is opened —and requires a latch to keep the door from falling open when the boat rolls or heels. But it offers easier access to the food inside, has handy shelves for jars and bottles, and will fit snugly into a small space—beneath a galley counter, for instance—that lacks the overhead clearance a top-opener needs.

Seagoing Coolers

Devices for keeping food and drink cool aboard ship range from picnic-type styrofoam ice chests to large household-sized refrigerators. The kind of equipment used will depend in most cases on the size and type of the boat and the extent of the cruise. For a sailboat with no power source aboard, or with only an outboard or very small inboard engine, an ice chest is the only choice. In fact most modern cruising boats of medium and small size come already equipped with an ice chest like one of those at left. A 50-pound block of ice in a well-insulated ice chest will preserve perishables for several days.

But since ice melts and in some places is hard to come by, many cruising skippers use some form of mechanical refrigeration. Most marine refrigerators, like the devices shown at right and overleaf, work in the same manner as ordinary home models. A compressor circulates a non-flammable refrigerant, which then passes through the cooling coils of the condenser and on to another set of coils in the freezer compartment.

Some compressors get power directly from a belt connected to a pulley on the drive shaft of a boat's main engine, but most rely on their own electric motors. Some of these motors run on direct current and can be hooked into the boat's DC system. But some compressors come with AC motors. At sea they must get their power either through an inverter, which converts DC into AC, or from an AC generator. The latter is run by the boat's main engine or by a small supplementary engine.

While either kind of engine is running, it supplies the refrigerator with plenty of current. But few skippers want to run an engine constantly just to power the refrigerator. And with the engine off, the refrigerator can be run only at the risk of exhausting the battery. The installation of a second battery will provide spare power for the refrigerator, but a better answer to the problem of power drain is to run the refrigerator only intermittently, storing up cold to protect food until the next convenient time for running the engine. This can be achieved either by using a cold-hoarding device called a eutectic plate *(overleaf)* or by docking and running the refrigerator all night on pierside power.

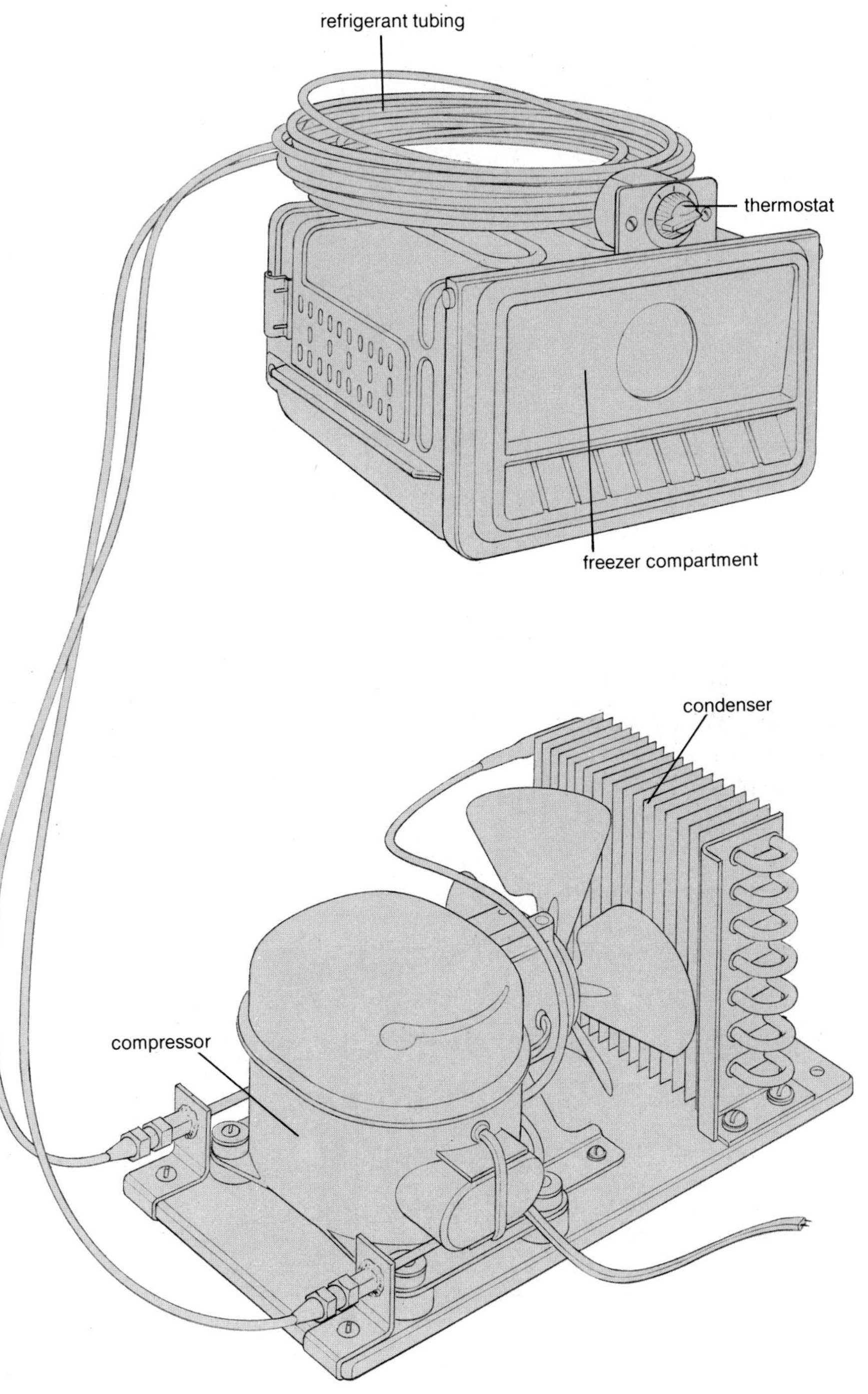

This simple machinery can be installed in a front-opening icebox to convert it into a refrigerator. Cut a hole in the box to admit the refrigerant tubing, and drill holes for mounting the freezer compartment. Pass the tubing carefully through its hole, mount the freezer in the space designed for a block of ice and seal all holes airtight with caulking compound. Bolt down the condensing unit in a well-ventilated area in the bilge, 10 or 12 feet from the box. Connect the tubing to the condensing unit, making sure that the tubing has no kinks or sharp bends.

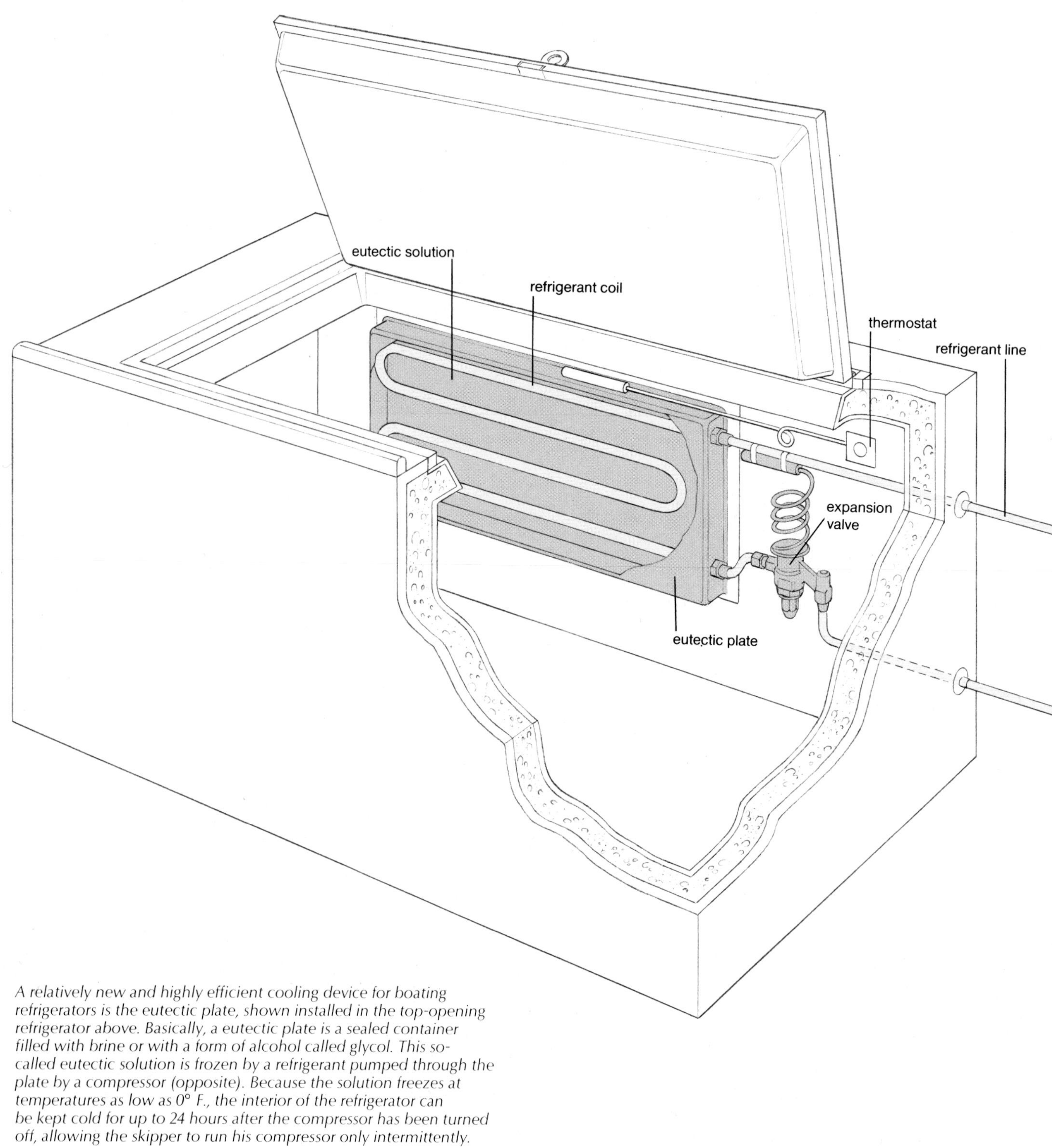

A relatively new and highly efficient cooling device for boating refrigerators is the eutectic plate, shown installed in the top-opening refrigerator above. Basically, a eutectic plate is a sealed container filled with brine or with a form of alcohol called glycol. This so-called eutectic solution is frozen by a refrigerant pumped through the plate by a compressor (opposite). Because the solution freezes at temperatures as low as 0° F., the interior of the refrigerator can be kept cold for up to 24 hours after the compressor has been turned off, allowing the skipper to run his compressor only intermittently.

Though the eutectic plate, a closed unit with no moving parts, is maintenance-free, its compressor system requires routine care. (The commonest—and simplest—repair to the compressor's electric motor is described below.) Tighten the belt between the motor and compressor if it can be depressed more than three quarters of an inch. A pink tinge in the sight glass between the receiver tank and the dehydrator indicates too much moisture in the refrigerant. Such moisture can freeze in the expansion valve, block the flow of refrigerant and cause the plate to defrost. If this happens, wrap a hot wet rag around the valve to melt the ice, and replace the dehydrator.

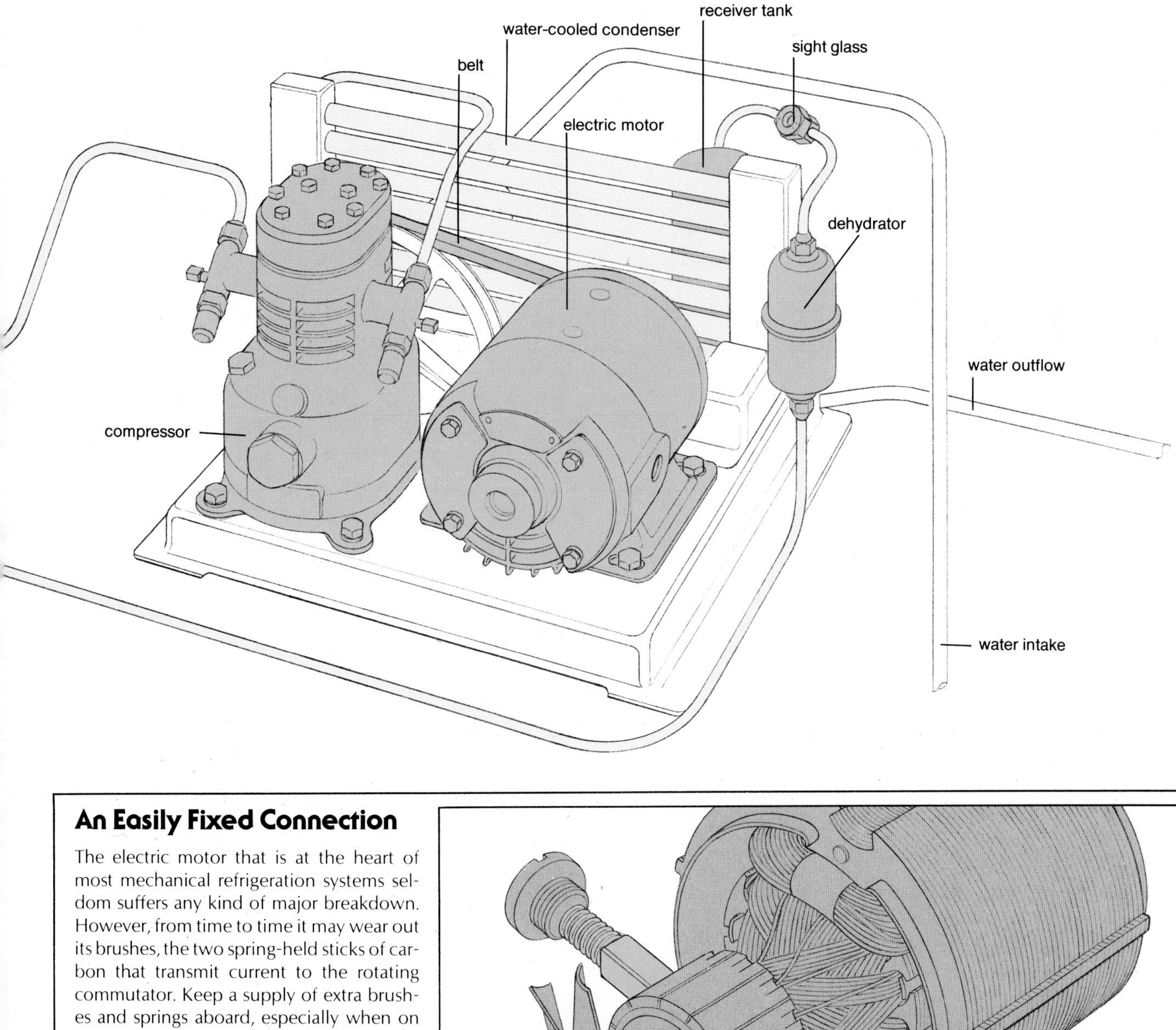

An Easily Fixed Connection

The electric motor that is at the heart of most mechanical refrigeration systems seldom suffers any kind of major breakdown. However, from time to time it may wear out its brushes, the two spring-held sticks of carbon that transmit current to the rotating commutator. Keep a supply of extra brushes and springs aboard, especially when on long cruises. If the motor should stop because of worn brushes, loosen the screws on each side of the motor casing. The brushes and the springs will pop out. Replace any brush that is less than half an inch long and any spring that seems too weak to keep its brush in contact with the commutator. After reinserting the brushes and springs, retighten the retaining screws. If the motor still refuses to operate, something more serious is wrong; remove the motor and take it to a serviceman for repairs.

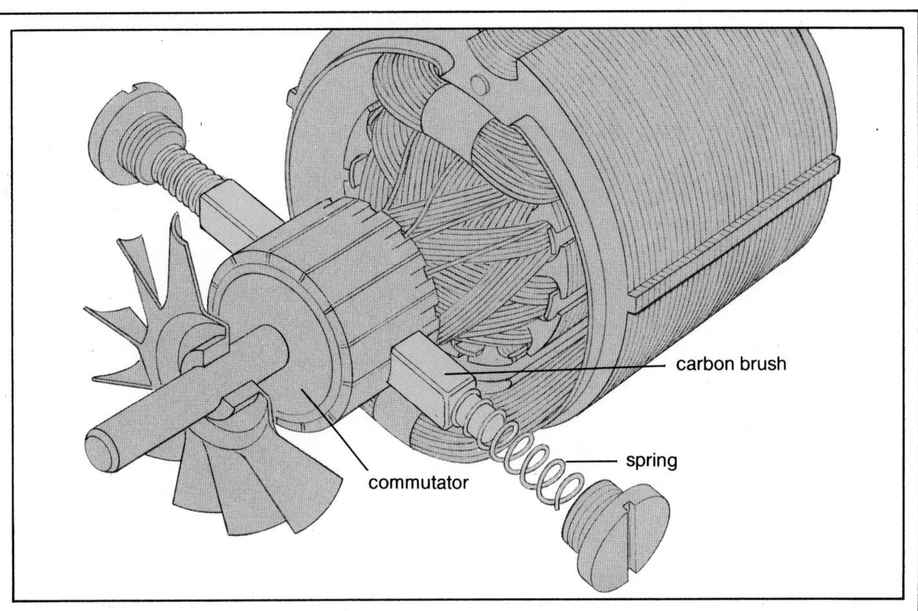

A typical installation of fresh- and raw-water systems for a galley sink is shown below. To prevent leaks that could drip down the cabinet and—on wooden-hulled boats—cause dry rot, the sink rim is firmly sealed in bedding compound. The pipes are made of a noncorrosive material like polyvinyl chloride. The seacocks on intake and outlet lines control the flow of water from outside the boat. The cabinet beneath has room for bulky items like dishes, and pots and pans.

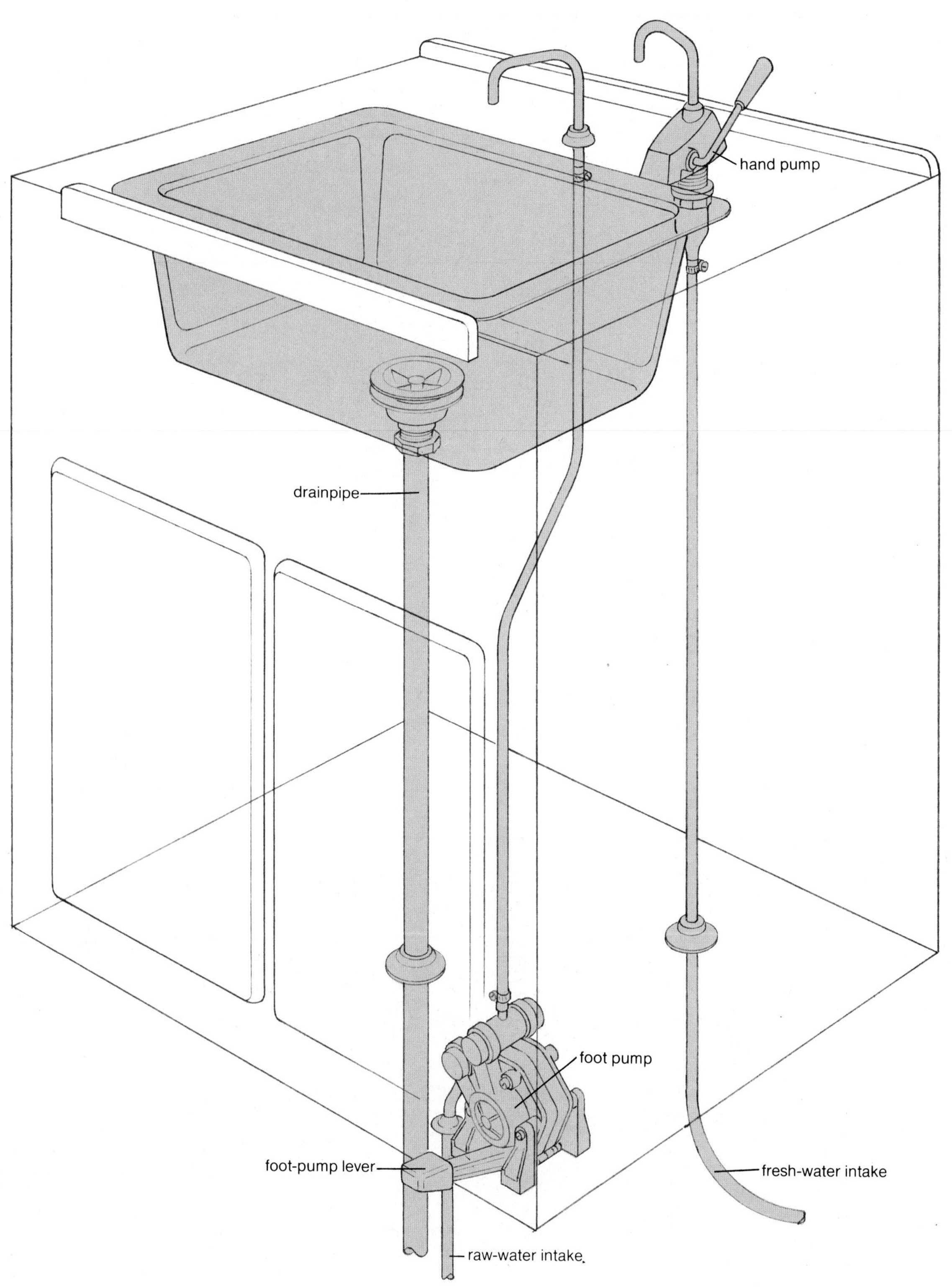

Sink Systems

Galley sinks are made in a variety of sizes and shapes to fit the available space aboard ship. On small powerboats and sailboats in the 25- to 30-foot range, the standard installation is an arrangement like the one at left, in which the deep, compact sink has a hand pump for fresh water—and sometimes a foot-operated pump for raw water. Larger, more luxurious craft can accommodate the electrically powered pressure system that is described on page 108.

With a dual system of the type shown here, fresh water can be conserved for drinking, since the raw water can be used to wash dishes or boil vegetables, pastas, etc. Both kinds of water exit down a common drain, which in turn is attached to a pipe connected to a through-hull fitting that carries the waste water overboard.

This galley sink is mounted in a countertop cutout. On boats whose space is more cramped, the sink may be bolted directly to a bulkhead. On a sailboat, the best mounting position is near as possible to the fore-and-aft centerline of the hull; this location allows the sink to drain when the boat heels, but is usually possible only on boats that have wide hulls and correspondingly broad cabin space. On smaller boats, the sink—and the galley—may be situated either on the port or starboard side, as a centerline arrangement would cramp already tight quarters.

While the location of a galley sink is important, so is the shape of the individual sink. A well-designed sink is both deep and narrow: deep to prevent spillage in rough weather, narrow to save space and to allow a minimum amount of water to fill the sink to a depth sufficient for easy dishwashing. A deep sink has another advantage: when empty, it can be used while the boat is underway as a secure temporary stowage compartment for such items as pots, coffee mugs and the fixings for luncheon sandwiches.

Repairing Leaky Pumps

In typical marine water pumps like those below, the parts that undergo the most wear and are thus likely to cause leaks are valves, diaphragms and washers—here marked in blue. To get at the bucket ring and cup washer of a leaky hand pump (upper drawing), remove the screws on the underside and pull off the bottom assembly. To remove the cork washer around the outlet pipe, first pull out the pipe, then push out the washer. To replace the washers around the pump lever, unscrew the lever knob and then unscrew and slide off the plastic nut at the base of the lever; the washers are inside the nut. To disassemble a foot pump (bottom), remove the bolts that hold the pump housing together; this will expose the diaphragms, valves and washers. Take care in removing the last bolt; otherwise, the operating spring will expand suddenly, forcing the pump apart and spraying parts far and wide.

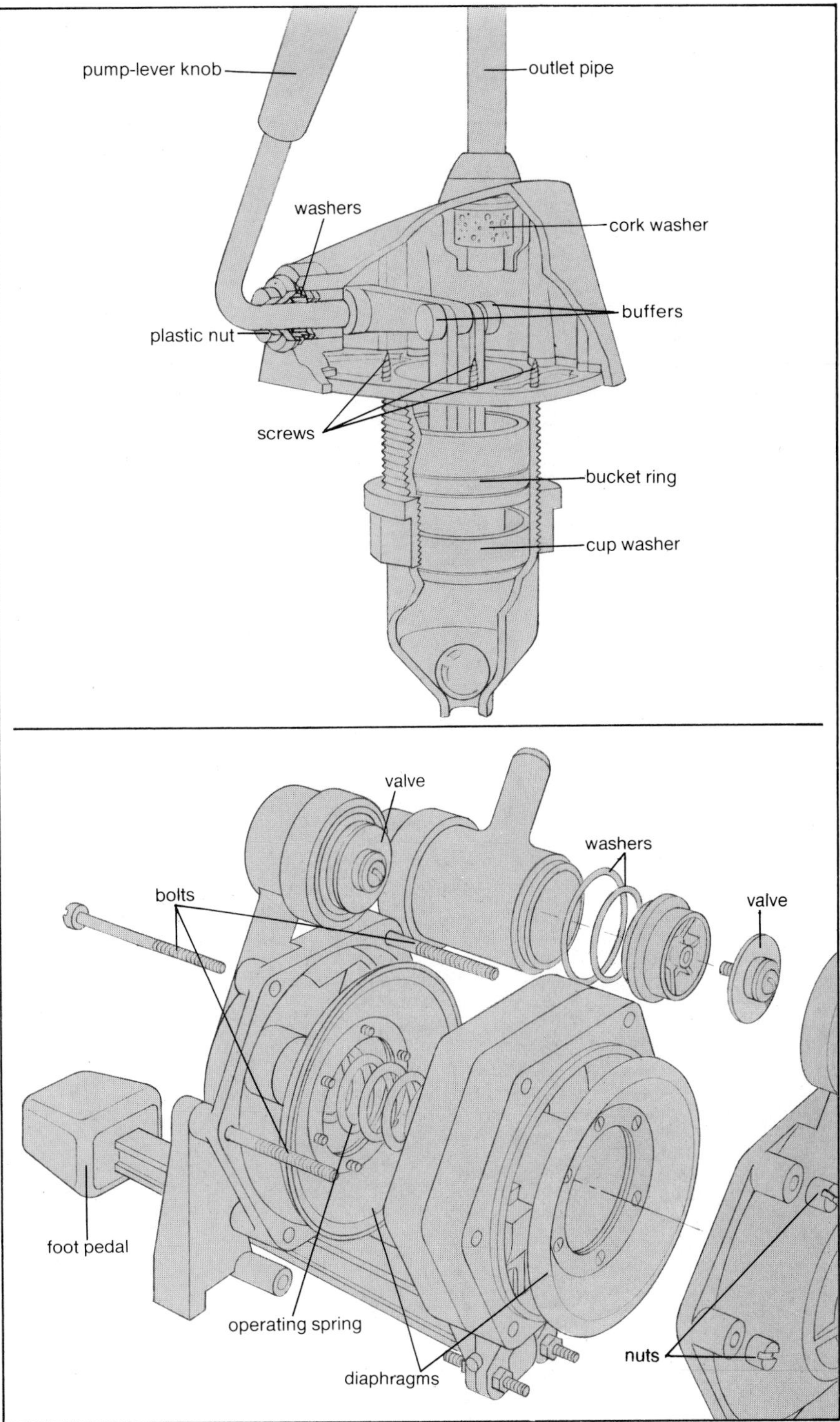

Expanding the Galley

A few ingeniously simple additions to a galley can greatly boost its utility at no extra cost in space. In fact some of the additions actually give the cook more working room. Round-cornered drop-leaf extensions of counters, and removable tops that fit over stoves and sinks—and stow away handily when not in use—can double or triple the available counter area. Sliding doors on the lockers beneath stoves not only save leg space but are more likely than the hinged variety to stay closed when a boat heels.

A two-piece folding stool that is securely fastened in a central location allows the cook to work sitting down—a boon particularly in small-boat galleys where headroom is limited.

In the modified galley layout pictured here, the icebox has two compartments, each with a lid for easy access; one section is for perishable foodstuffs, the other for cold drinks. The double sink facilitates cleaning up; dishes can be washed in one sink and rinsed in the other.

Such twin facilities as these are best installed by a professional. But most of the other conveniences can be added afterward by the boatman himself, using plywood veneered with plastic for the countertops and plain three-quarter-inch plywood for the folding stool. He can also install, where needed, additional handholds; fiddles—the rails around countertops that keep dishes from sliding off; fastenings for attaching the galley strap that holds the cook upright in heavy weather; and brackets and a turn button to hold a cutting board.

The removable countertop immediately below rests on supports on either side of the stove, and stows behind the stove when the burners are lighted. At far right, below, is a drop-leaf extension hinged to the side of the sink cabinet and supported by folding braces. The cutting board beneath it covers either of the two sinks. Both the board and the stool hinged to the side of the icebox are held in place by turn buttons, small wooden or metal retainers pivoted on screws. Eye straps are used to provide secure anchorage for the galley strap.

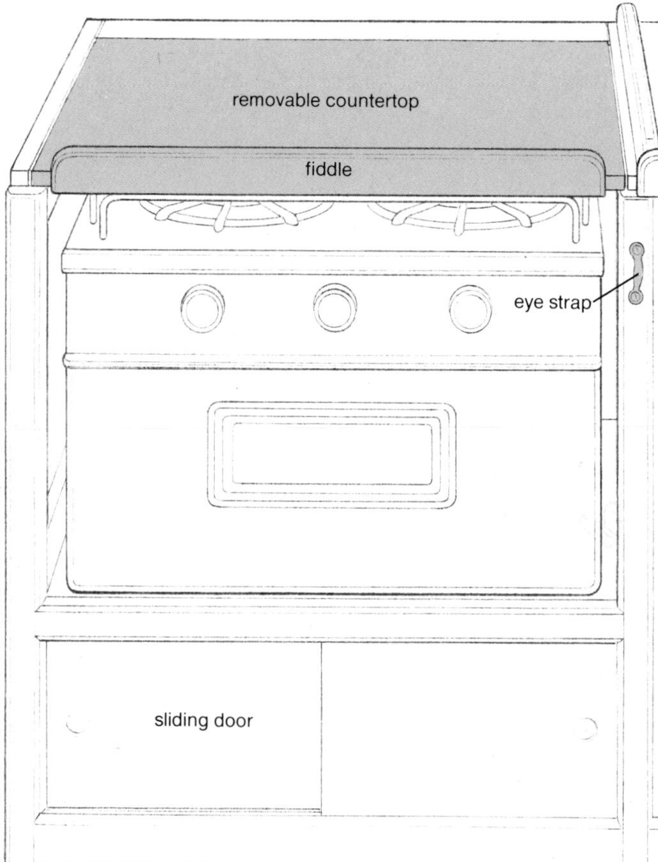

Stoves for Special Uses

Some galleys include auxiliary equipment for cooking in especially bad—or good—weather. The ministove at right can be hooked into its wall bracket whenever stormy seas prohibit cooking on the regular stove. Gimbals keep it on an even keel even when the boat is pitching severely. A can of Sterno held in the lower ring provides heat; the upper ring snugly encircles a pot. Next to the swing stove is a marine charcoal broiler for use in calm anchorages. A metal arm on the broiler goes into the boat's flagstaff bracket—or, as here, into a special bracket permanently screwed to the boat's stern. Either attachment holds the broiler outboard so that spilled coals cannot burn the cockpit. Since a vessel faces into the wind while at anchor, the smoke drifts astern, away from the boat.

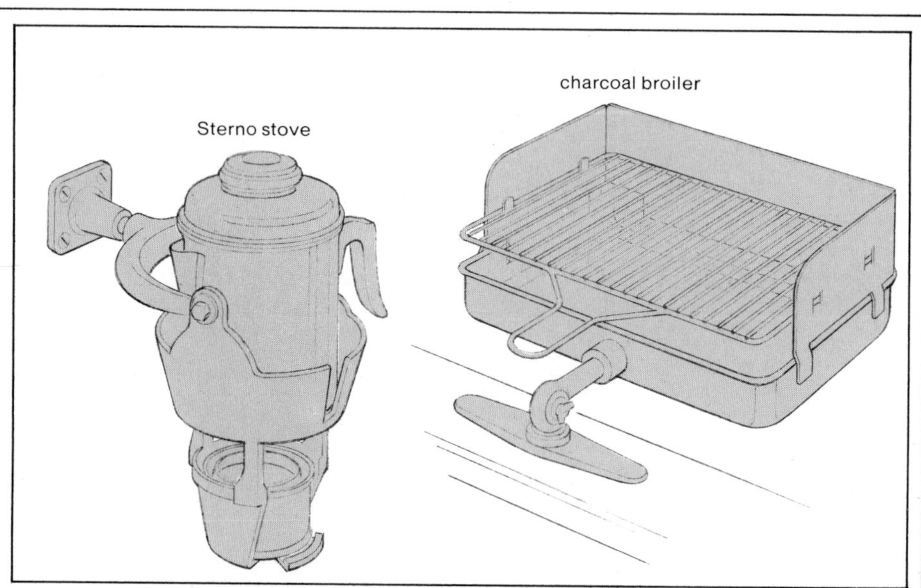

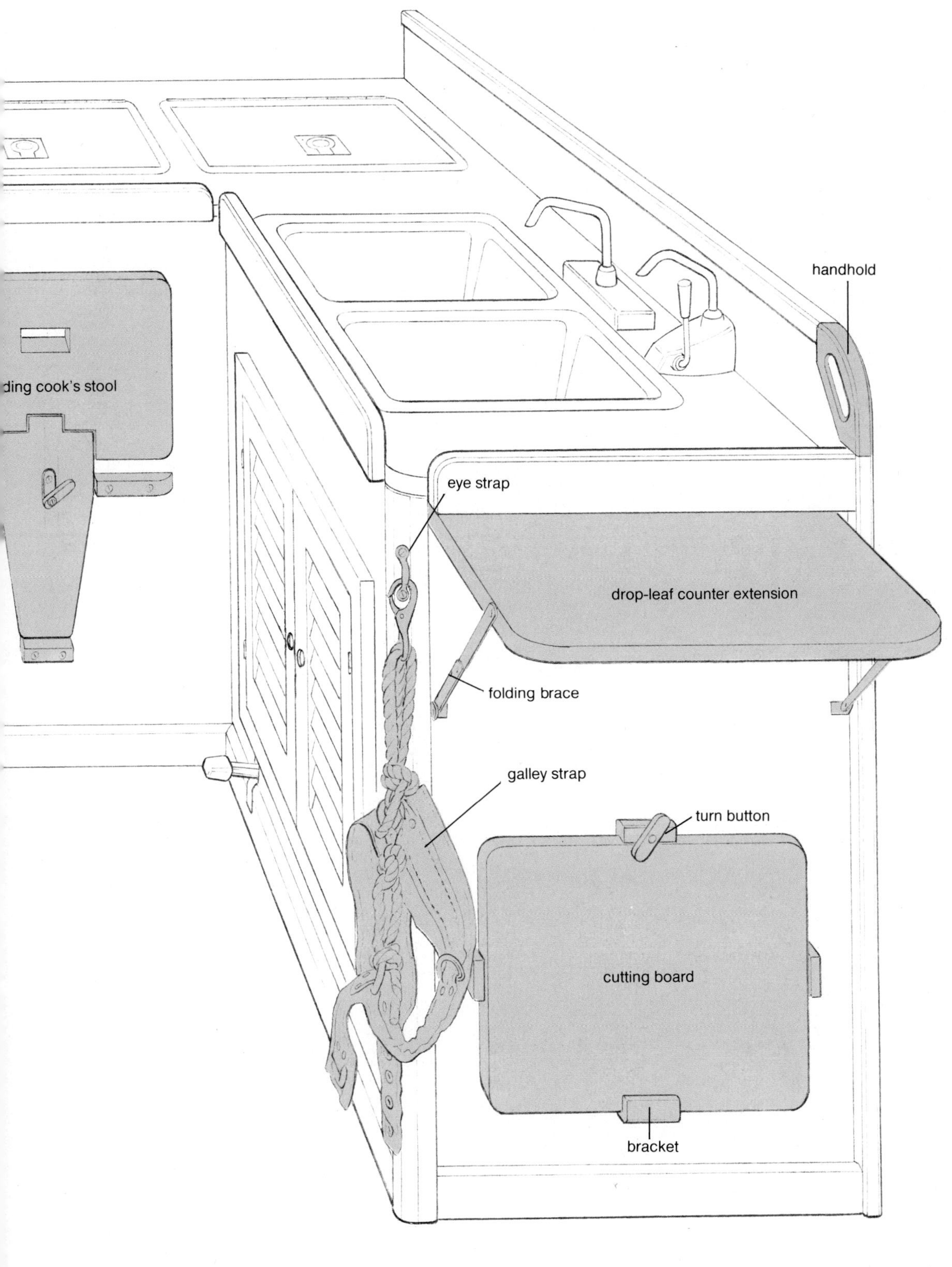
handhold
ding cook's stool
eye strap
drop-leaf counter extension
folding brace
galley strap
turn button
cutting board
bracket

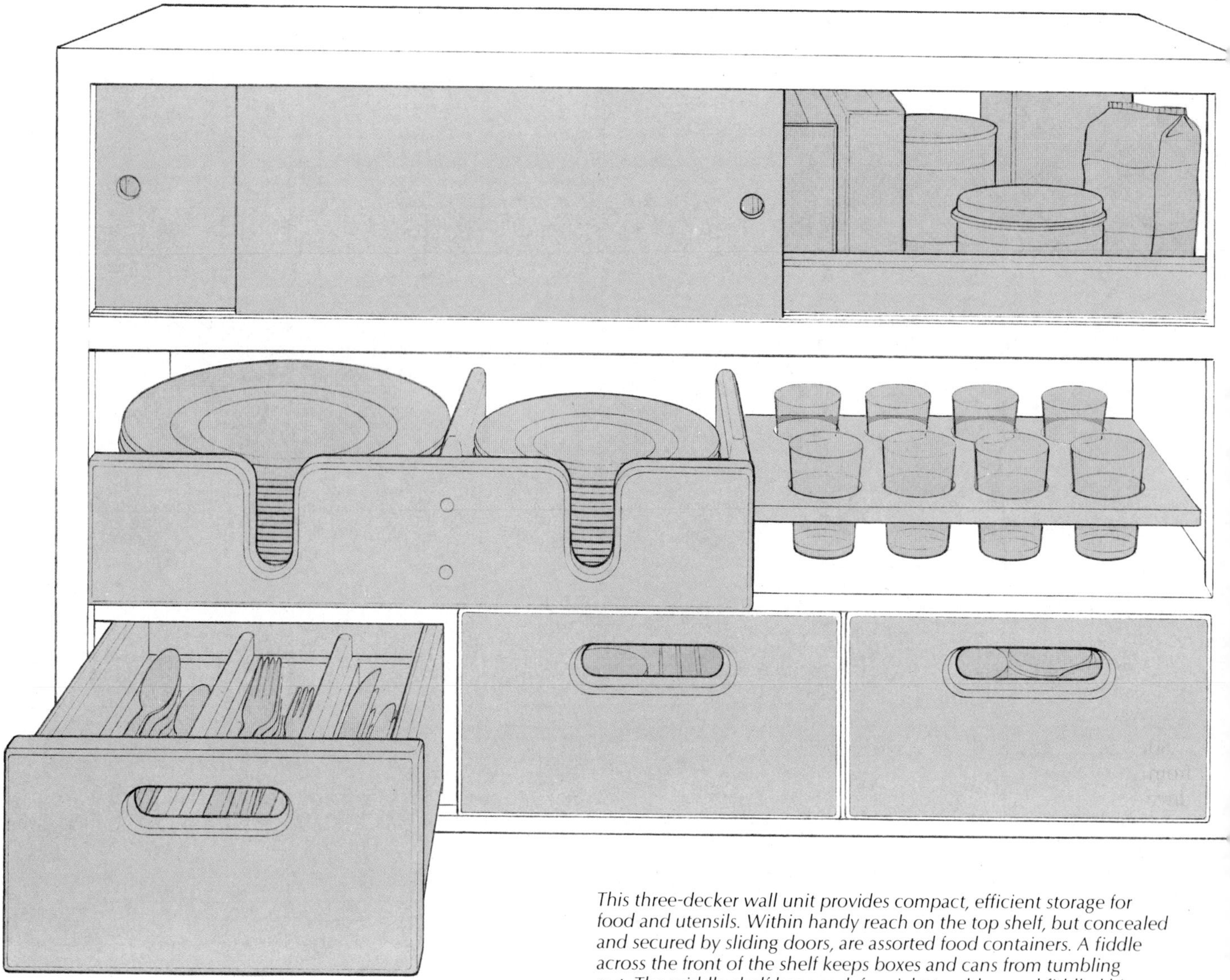

This three-decker wall unit provides compact, efficient storage for food and utensils. Within handy reach on the top shelf, but concealed and secured by sliding doors, are assorted food containers. A fiddle across the front of the shelf keeps boxes and cans from tumbling out. The middle shelf has a rack for eight tumblers and fiddled bins for two sizes of plates. The drawers at the bottom of the unit can be partitioned, like the one at left, for various kinds of utensils.

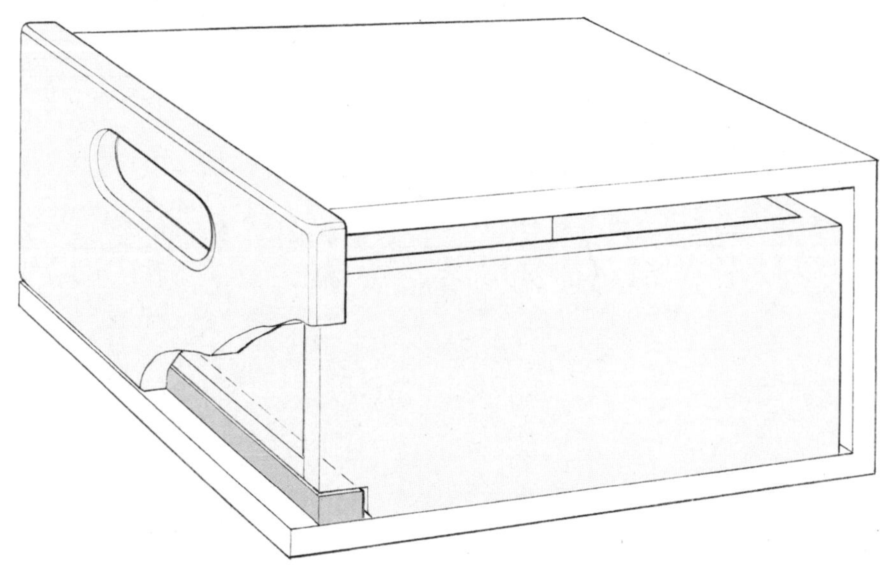

The simple device shown at right will keep a drawer firmly shut no matter how much the boat heels. Notches about a quarter of an inch square cut in the front of each of the wooden drawer runners fit over a wooden cross brace of the same size. To open the drawer, simply lift it up a quarter of an inch to clear the brace and then pull it out.

Order in the Galley

For convenience—and to avoid pandemonium in rough weather—pots, pans, dishes, cups and cutlery urgently demand proper galley storage. Otherwise, these generally benign tools of the cook's trade can damage not only each other but also the person and morale of anyone who tries to work among them.

The three keys to proper galley stowage are compactness, security and accessibility. Stowage should be planned according to the size and weight of the articles to be stowed. Put heavy items, such as Dutch ovens, low down and as close to the center of the boat as possible; smaller, lighter items can go higher up. Frequently used devices such as bottle openers and mugs should be mounted with hooks or snaps on a bulkhead, both for instant access and to save drawer space. The illustrations on these pages suggest a number of ways to make a galley both safe and handy to work in. Many boats come already equipped with some of these storage devices. In others they must be installed; fortunately, they are for the most part both simple and inexpensive for a boatman of normal ingenuity to make.

Once he has provided proper stowage, the wise boatman also picks his utensils with care. Plastic dishes, for example, are far more convenient and durable than glass. And thermal mugs, though less elegant than crockery, will keep cold drinks colder and coffee hotter.

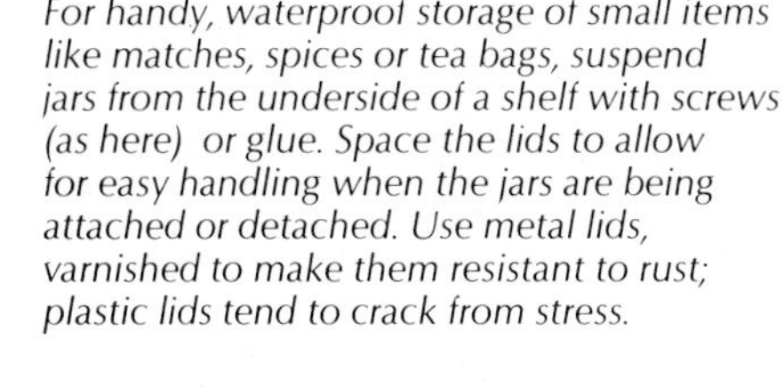

For handy, waterproof storage of small items like matches, spices or tea bags, suspend jars from the underside of a shelf with screws (as here) or glue. Space the lids to allow for easy handling when the jars are being attached or detached. Use metal lids, varnished to make them resistant to rust; plastic lids tend to crack from stress.

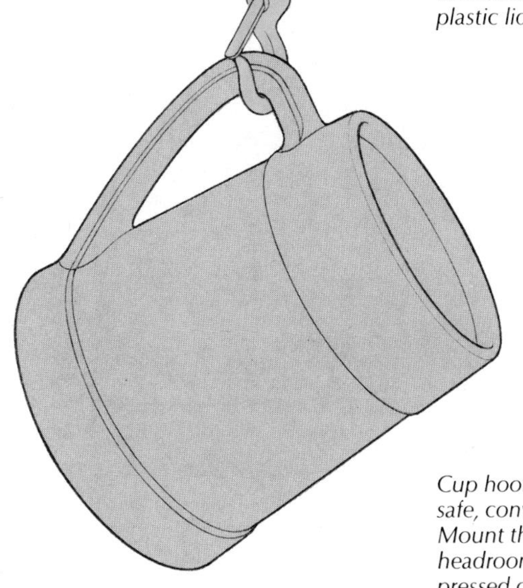

Cup hooks with safety closures will provide safe, convenient moorings for bulky mugs. Mount them where they do not infringe on headroom, but are handy when a hard-pressed crewman needs a quick refresher.

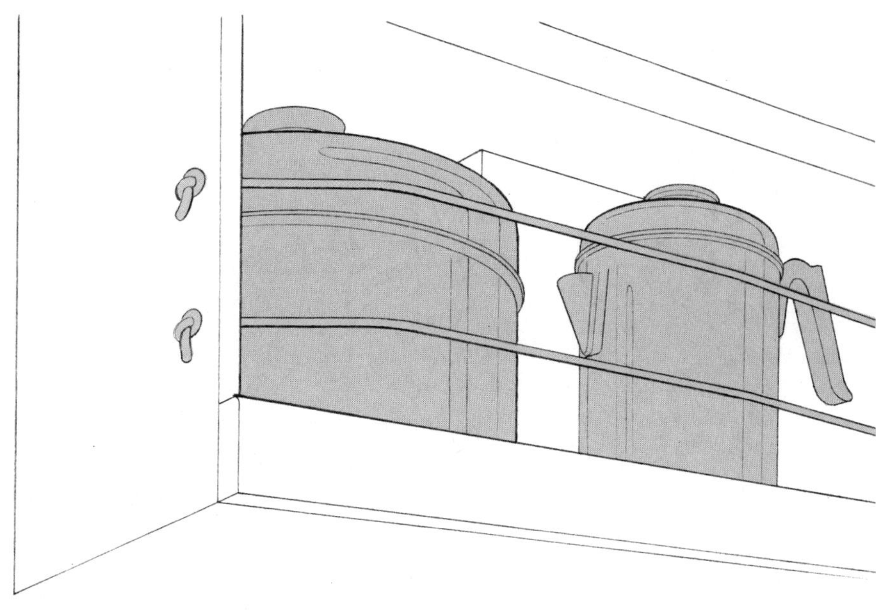

Utensils too tall to stow behind low fiddles can be held in place by shock cord drawn across the front of an exposed shelf. Here the elastic cord was led through small holes at the ends of an open cabinet, and knotted with sufficient tension on the line to keep the knots secure and to restrain the pots yet permit their easy removal by the cook.

Four pots and pans, ranging in sizes up to 10 inches in diameter, are cleverly designed to nest into the single, neatly latching unit shown in the drawing at top right. The total package, which occupies less than a cubic foot of space, includes three detachable handles, two standard lids and a skillet that can serve as lid for the largest pot—or vice versa. Other versions, scarcely much larger, may incorporate dishes and cups.

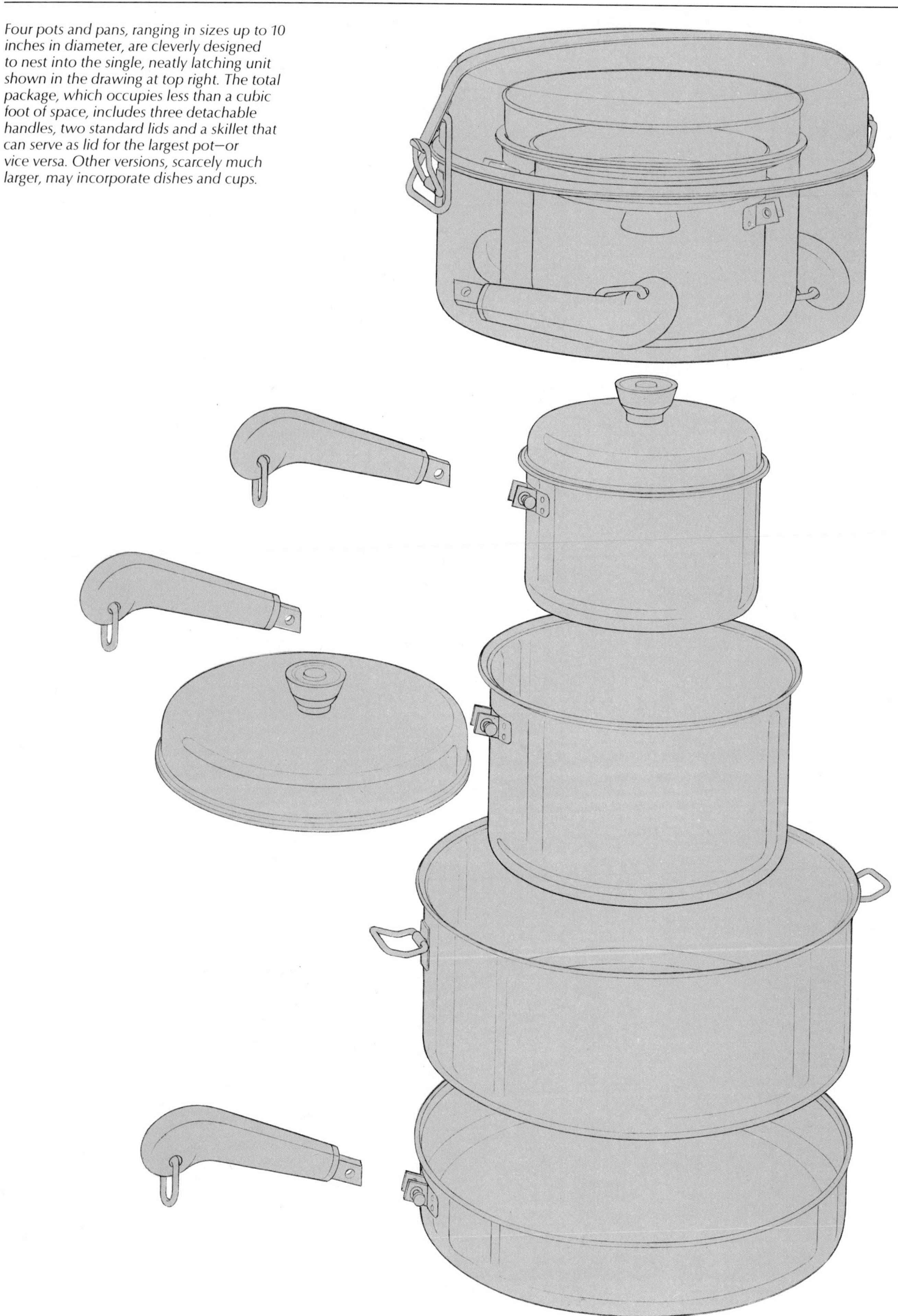

Compact Cookware

A good shipboard cook keeps the crew fat and happy while using only a half-dozen or so well-chosen pots and pans. In selecting these kitchen utensils, the cook should look first for versatility, and then for ways to save cooking fuel and to expand the cooking capability of shipboard stoves—which are typically small in size and heat-generating capacity.

For example, a large, heavy skillet with a lid added doubles as a casserole. A four-quart pot that holds a hot one-dish meal for the entire crew later serves as a dishpan. A pair of two-quart stewpots can also be used to heat soup and vegetables. A big (12-cup) coffeepot does extra duty as a general-purpose kettle. A double boiler allows vegetables, eggs, soup or coffee water to be boiled in the lower half while the upper half is heating, and each half can function at other times as a separate pot. A Dutch oven adds baking capability to the smallest stove. And a pressure cooker saves precious water—as well as the cook's precious time—and can be used as a simple saucepan as well.

Finally, in selecting kitchenware, the smart cook considers compactness and durability. Nested pots like those shown at left take up the least stowage room—and allow more room aboard for food. Shape is important, too. A straight-sided pot is much less likely to slop over than an outward-flared pot, and presents proportionally more bottom surface to its burner. Two tall, straight pots can stand so close together on the stove that they touch without encroaching on each other's burner space.

Pots and pans made of heavy-duty stainless steel or aluminum resist denting and require little maintenance to keep them gleaming. Many ship's cooks, however, insist on taking aboard at least one cast-iron frying pan. Cast iron, though heavy, is durable, easy to clean and more efficient than most lighter metals used for cooking. With regular wipe-downs of cooking oil, a cast-iron skillet will probably outlast the boat. Moreover the iron skillet's weight keeps it firmly on the stove burners when the boat rocks. Enamelware should be avoided; it chips easily and so is unsuitable for a knockabout life at sea.

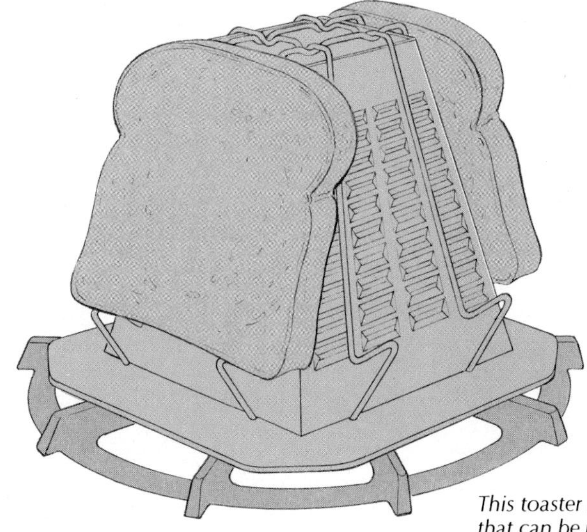

This toaster is one of a number of devices that can be used to add to the usefulness of a galley stove. With perforated sides for distributing the heat, it sits directly over the stove burner, holds four pieces of bread at a time and turns out toast almost as quickly as a conventional electric model.

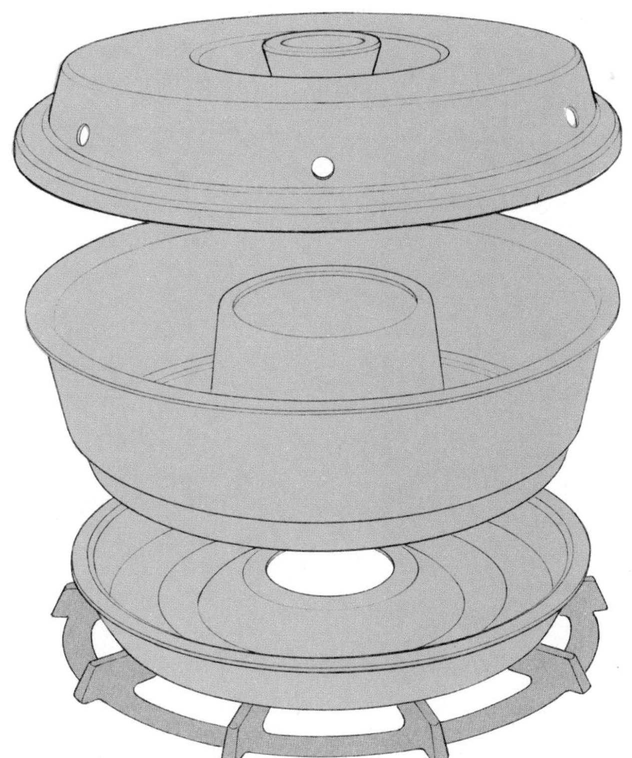

This portable stove-top oven, a sophisticated variation on the old Dutch oven, consists of a base rack that spreads part of the burner's heat over the bottom while directing the rest up a center flue, a middle baking dish that receives evenly distributed heat from the bottom and the flue, and a lid with side vents that bleed off excess water and pressure.

THE RECIPE FOR GOOD COOKING

There is no reason why a cruising yacht's bill of fare need consist of a dreary succession of canned stew and peanut butter sandwiches. With a little more galley time, a touch of imagination and some advance preparation ashore, seagoing meals can be made almost as varied and inviting as restaurant food, as has been demonstrated by avid nautical chef William O'Donovan, seen at right.

Few boatmen are as handy with a skillet as O'Donovan, a lawyer turned restaurateur, but his method of planning the meals on his 35-foot sloop might profitably be applied to almost any cruise. He first draws up a menu for every meal of the trip, taking into consideration the number of mouths to feed, the boat's storage and refrigerating capacities, and the length of the cruise. The fare includes many dishes cooked and then chilled or frozen before being put on board.

Prior preparation offers many advantages. Cooking at home is almost always easier and more efficient than cooking at sea. The cook can vary the shipboard meals with dishes that would take too much time, trouble, fuel and dishwashing to prepare underway. Also, precooked items, packed in their plastic containers, take up little space, and serving them is, if anything, simpler than opening a can.

Inevitably, the greater part of a cruising menu must be prepared aboard, and much of it will consist of canned goods. Even here a cook's ingenuity can bring variety and elegance to otherwise drab ingredients. A sprinkling of sherry will perform wonders with canned shrimp, for example, and canned peaches take on new zest when laced with rum or kirsch. By supplementing the canned dishes with fresh vegetables and fruit, picked up during stops for gas or ice, a well-organized sea cook can turn out three tempting meals a day without repeating a single dish or straining the capacities of a standard two-burner alcohol stove.

Preparing at home for a cruise, sea cook William O'Donovan spoons boeuf bourguignon, a French beef stew, into a plastic container for freezing. It will be the main course of the third night's dinner afloat. The artichokes at left will be chilled—but not frozen—for the same meal. The peppers and other vegetables are for a ratatouille, or Mediterranean vegetable stew, to be frozen and used later in the trip.

Arranging Provisions

After a skilled sea cook such as William O'Donovan *(right)* has accumulated the food that he needs for a cruise, he packs it aboard systematically and efficiently. Stowing foodstuffs and drinks on a boat involves problems seldom encountered in kitchens ashore. Supplies must be tucked into the bilge and assorted lockers, bins and drawers. Boxes, bottles and cans are firmly wedged into place to prevent rattling, spilling or breakage. And the experienced hand will work up a list showing where every item is kept—thus reducing the time spent rummaging through the various hideaways.

On most boats, conserving the ice in iceboxes and refrigerators is an important consideration. Since some amount of cold air escapes every time the door is opened—even on a top-opening box—the wise cruising person digs into the icebox as seldom and as briefly as possible. O'Donovan, for example, minimizes icebox raiding by installing a supplementary ice chest that holds cold drinks for the crew. And by arranging food in the main icebox in the order of intended use and marking all containers plainly, he makes doubly sure of quickly finding what he needs for each meal.

Canned drinks are packed tightly into a portable ice chest secured on deck or in the cockpit, where thirsty crew members can get at them. The drinks have been chilled in advance to help prolong the life of the ice block, and the chest has been precooled by filling it with extra ice on the night before loading. As the drink supply is used up, it will be replenished by other cans that have been kept cool in the bilge.

To protect fragile bottles stored in a galley locker, O'Donovan surrounds them with shock-absorbing boxes and packets. A sliding door helps to keep the contents of the locker in place when the boat is underway.

An exception to the first-in, last-out rule for loading the icebox is made for frozen foods. Here O'Donovan places plastic containers of precooked frozen food at the bottom of the galley chest. He will then put the ice block on top of them for maximum chilling. A tray of vegetables and other perishables can be laid on top of the ice.

Planned Economy

A good cook like William O'Donovan, whose techniques and suggestions are set forth on these pages, plans his seagoing menus with due regard for the perishability of his stores. Fresh and frozen foods dominate the bill of fare at the outset of the cruise; thus the cook's perishable stores diminish at about the same rate that his ice melts. As they dwindle, they are cunningly supplemented with canned or other long-lived stores. By the end of the cruise, he will have virtually emptied his larder without having let anything rot, molder or turn sour.

A cruising chef's most perishable commodity of all is time; it is best conserved by detailed advance planning. If, as on most cruises, the cook must tailor his menus to the limited capabilities of a slow-heating two-burner alcohol stove, he plans meals that use no more than two cooking utensils, a saving of time in both preparation and dishwashing. Similar results are accomplished by making utensils do double duty—for example, by using the pot in which macaroni was cooked to heat the accompanying sauce. Alternatively, each meal might include at least one dish that requires no heating—and hence no pot. O'Donovan's frozen ratatouille, for instance, needs only to be thawed and served at room temperature.

Heating canned foods right in the can further economizes on utensils and burner space. By putting three different cans —peas, potatoes and Vienna sausages, say—into a single pot of boiling water, a cook can produce three hot dishes simultaneously. (Before heating, open any can to keep it from exploding.)

A Guide to Preserving Perishables

A general idea of how long foodstuffs can be expected to remain palatable and safe to eat is vital to the planning of cruise menus. Fresh fruits, vegetables, meats and dairy products obviously spoil sooner than frozen, dried or canned foods; but some fresh foods keep better than others. The clever cook not only uses his most perishable items first but also tries to provide the best possible storage arrangements for all his supplies to minimize the deleterious effects of moisture, heat and motion. The food-preserving suggestions listed below are based on the average keeping times of foods likely to be carried on cruises during normal weather in temperate climates. A cook must make allowances for different cruising conditions. For example, fresh foods will spoil more quickly in tropical heat, and turbulent waters may cause fruit to bruise.

- *Fresh milk not only requires constant refrigeration but is easily churned into curds and whey by the motion of the boat. To avoid this hazard, freeze milk in plastic bottles at home, leaving space for expansion. Frozen milk kept on ice will last for several days; when thawed and vigorously shaken it is quite palatable.*

- *Iced butter keeps for a week, and margarine for up to 10 days. Liquid margarine lasts for a week unrefrigerated.*

- *Iceberg lettuce, the most durable of salad greens, lasts for 10 days or so if wrapped in plastic and kept on ice. Like other fresh fruits and vegetables carried aboard, it should not be washed until just before serving; moisture hastens rot.*

- *Limes and lemons wrapped in foil stay good for a month. Other citrus fruits keep for several weeks if hung in string bags where air can circulate around them. Inspect them often; a moldy orange or grapefruit will contaminate its neighbors.*

- *Bananas should be bought in several stages of ripeness so they can be eaten as they mature; green ones take about a week to ripen. If possible, bananas should be stored by hanging them in a cool, dry spot.*

- *Green tomatoes wrapped in tissue paper and stored in a cool, dark place last up to six weeks. Ripen them as needed by unwrapping them and exposing them to any light but direct sunlight, which tends to rot rather than redden them.*

- *Potatoes hung in string bags last for a month; wrapped in plastic, they may rot.*

- *Hard, sound onions sprout in damp air but last a month in a cool, dry place.*

- *Fresh eggs, unrefrigerated, will keep for several weeks in a cool place. Store them in rigid boxes, and turn the boxes frequently to prevent the yolks from settling. Eggs will keep even longer if dipped in boiling water for 30 seconds to harden the layer next to the shell, or if coated with petroleum jelly, which seals off air. Cracked eggs may harbor bacteria and should be discarded.*

- *Commercial bread, made with preservatives, lasts up to three weeks in double plastic bags. Unsliced, homemade-style bread will keep for several weeks if it is sprayed with vinegar to retard mold and then double-wrapped in plastic.*

- *Most canned goods will keep safely on a boat for a year, but those stored in the bilge require special precautions. Remove all paper labels; otherwise, they would inevitably soak off and might clog the bilge pump. Using indelible ink, label the contents of each can. Varnish any cans that may be stored in the bilge for a month or more; this will inhibit rust, which could cause the cans' seams to leak.*

- *All dried and dehydrated foods should be kept in airtight plastic or metal containers. Rice, the longest-lasting of staples, will remain weevil-free for two years; macaroni and flour, for a year. Tea bags last for six months; instant coffee, after being opened, will last about the same time.*

After little more than half an hour in the galley, O'Donovan serves up a sumptuous dinner for four. The main course, cooked in a single pot, is chicken fricassee and dumplings. He first thawed the meat, which he had parboiled and frozen at home, then browned it in butter and added canned mushrooms, broth, chicken soup and herbs. The dumplings were made from a packaged mix and popped into the simmering stew. While the stew cooked, he concocted a salad of thinly sliced oranges and Spanish onions. Canned plums, enlivened with a dash of kirsch, and coffee will complete the repast.

Tidying Up

After-dinner cleanup chores are no one's idea of fun, but they are inevitable facts of cruising life. Fortunately, contemporary cleaning materials such as paper towels and detergents take most of the drudgery out of dishwashing, and plastic garbage bags make refuse stowage a relatively simple task.

In the interests of neatness and hygiene, it is wise to wash up directly after a meal. Most cooks heat the dishwater while serving the dessert course. Master galley hand William O'Donovan uses the largest cooking pot, wiped clean with paper towels, for the purpose. To extend the boat's fresh-water supply, yachtsmen often soap the plates in salt water and rinse them in fresh; the rinse must be thorough, however, because the slightest hint of detergent left on a plate can cause stomach problems. To avoid the risk of food poisoning, hot water is safest for both soaping and rinsing.

Garbage disposal is governed by law. A federal act, in effect since 1899 and reinforced with new environmental regulations in 1974, prohibits the dumping of any refuse overboard. The law applies not only to beer cans, but to such biodegradables as bread and orange peels. Thus, all garbage should be bagged tidily—preferably in a double thickness of plastic—until it can be disposed of ashore. If there is more garbage than can fit in its locker, it can be towed in the dinghy.

To give dirty dishes a prewash rinse, O'Donovan lowers them overboard in a string bag. They will be trailed astern while the boat is underway. Knives and forks remain in the galley; they could pierce the netting or work out through the holes and be lost. A bowline holds the bag, and a fisherman's bend secures the line to a stanchion.

With a sparing splash of fresh water, O'Donovan gives a lathered plate a quick second rinse to remove the last traces of detergent. Before washing, all cutlery and dishes are wiped off with paper towels.

The day's refuse from the galley, bound inside a doubled pair of plastic bags, goes into a pair of larger garbage bags for stowage in the lazarette. Doubling the bags is a wise precaution, because a single bag could split if knocked about when the boat is underway.

4

The bedrock of happy cruising is a comfortable boat. In the plush, pioneering days of pleasure boating, cruising yachts owned by industrial barons *(pages 28-37)* featured ballroom-sized cabins trimmed in teak and mahogany, hand-carved furniture, ornate draperies and rugs, heavy brass fittings, and a hired crew to polish them up—and sumptuous expenditures to keep the ensemble afloat. For all its glamour, however, such high-style cruising is no longer fashionable or practical. Today the typical cruising boat is a compact, reasonably inexpensive craft that packs a surprising amount of seagoing comfort into a relatively small package. In fact, a modern yacht of

LIVING COMFORTABLY AFLOAT

the 24- to 30-foot class, a length considered barely suitable for a two-person weekender as late as the 1950s, now carries a family of four or five with comparative ease for 10 days or more.

This jump in interior capacity is due to two revolutionary developments —one in hull design, the other in material. In both sailboats and power craft, a continuing search for speed has produced hulls that tend to be shallow but fairly beamy, enabling builders to cram more creature comforts than ever before into the wider space belowdecks. Moreover, the majority of these hulls are built of fiberglass, which is molded as a unit. This eliminates space-gobbling frames, stringers and deck beams, and supports and bracing for counters, seats and lockers—which are cast in the original mold. Wooden elements that survive are strips of trim for bulkheads, tabletops, shelves and, occasionally, interior planking, as in the cabin at left.

The single most important component of belowdecks comfort is the bunk space, where the crew spends a third of its time. Therefore, every possible bit of footage in the tight world of a boat's interior is pre-empted by sleeping accommodations—V-berths in the forward cabin, and various ingenious arrangements of transom berths, settee berths and quarter berths in the main saloon. Within the space available, bunks for adults are designed to measure at least 6 feet 3 inches long. But, with the exception of the double berths found in some modern craft, bunks are generally no wider than 27 inches; otherwise, a recumbent crew member will roll about uncomfortably when the boat is underway. Removable sides, called bunk boards, can be installed to keep the sleeper from sliding out when the boat heels.

Another basic facility in a vessel's cabin is the dinette table. In many contemporary boats, as at left, it stands on removable or recessed pedestals, allowing it to be dropped to the level of an adjacent settee, thus creating a queen-sized bunk for use at anchor or dockside. In a cabin with sufficient space, the table may be swung on gimbals atop a pair of legs bolted to the cabin sole, enabling the crew to eat off a level surface when the boat rolls. A third type of table is hinged to fold up against a bulkhead.

Other amenities aboard a modern cruising boat include galley and head facilities, various kinds of electric lighting, stowage lockers and efficient ventilation and water systems. Skippers can augment any of these standard facilities by adding hot-water showers, wood or charcoal heating units, stereo systems, and even air conditioners, as illustrated in the following pages. To help keep order belowdecks, they can modify the craft's existing locker facilities; for example, stowage space can be doubled by fitting lockers with shelves. Small hammocks serve as compact stowage compartments for personal gear, as do shoe bags, which can be hung on hooks from a bulkhead or locker door. And to ensure that all hands know where to find—and to replace —each article of gear, a well-organized skipper posts an updated list of the contents of every locker and stowage bin.

Laid out for comfort and utility, the mahogany-trimmed cabin of this 32-foot ketch includes a dinette that doubles as a berth, a stereo tape deck, and a pair of kerosene lamps.

The after port section of this cabin shows the astonishing variety of stowage and living facilities that can be fitted into a small space by careful planning. Behind the companionway is a ventilated hanging locker, accessible through an oblong opening, for foul-weather gear. Next to the locker is a quarter berth with stowage beneath, a bookshelf above; a spacious, well-lighted navigator's table (whose hinged top covers a storage bin) sits atop the drawered cabinet. Open-faced and closed shelves fit above the settee's back—which swings down to give access to additional locker space.

Two different types of bunks line the starboard side of this 35-footer's main cabin. The upper bunk, called a pilot berth, is set out of the way of cabin traffic. The transom berth below serves as a narrow settee in daytime, and at night it can be pulled out partway into the cabin passageway, trundle-bed fashion—the position shown here. Small cupboards between berths provide space for personal gear. Additional cupboards and drawers, as well as a commodious hanging locker, are tucked forward of the berths, along the passageway to the forward cabin.

Compact Quarters

In the cabin of a well-planned boat, berths and lockers are fitted in so snugly and by such artful design that it is often impossible to tell where one leaves off and the other begins. In the cabin section at left, the plaid settee doubles as a bunk whose headboard is one side of a locker with two drawers and a cabinet; underneath the mattress there is a pair of stowage bins for items such as canned goods, tools or spare engine parts.

No matter how craftily bunks and lockers are dovetailed, however, some storage space occasionally must be sacrificed to leave adequate sleeping room for the crew. A quarter berth, for example, generally encroaches into area that would otherwise be occupied by a sail locker. But even the berths themselves can double as temporary stowage bins when not in use—for folded bedding during the day, say, or for extra pillows or cushions. And even in small boats, both berthing and storage facilities can be extended by some of the ingenious devices shown here and overleaf. The root berth below, for example, provides an extra bunk at no permanent cost in space. The following pages offer suggestions for creating convenient stowage in unused cabin areas.

An important aspect of planning stowage space is to be certain that lockers are not only sizable but also easy to get at. And in order to make sure that all hands know the proper place for everything on board, a skipper who takes aboard a rotation of guests would be well advised to label each locker with a list of its contents. Otherwise, dirty clothing, or even last night's damp anchor rode, is likely to pile up atop clean bedding—or worse yet, on the cabin sole.

The forward cabin of a 27-foot cruising sloop incorporates a pair of V-berths with generous stowage bins beneath. The cutout openings across each bin provide quick access to gear stored inside, while keeping it from sliding onto the cabin sole. To add roominess to the sleeping space, a wooden inset, covered by padding, can be fitted across the open area between the two berths.

A Canvas Hideaway Bed

The root berth, originated by the yachtsman son of statesman Elihu Root, provides comfortable sleeping space for an extra crewman at night and rolls up for compact stowage during the day. Basically, it is a canvas stretcher that is supported between cabin bulkheads. The canvas is held to the outboard bulkhead by a strip of molding screwed down every five or six inches. Its inboard edge is stitched around an aluminum pipe that fits between two athwartships bulkheads. Pairs of U-shaped wood pads hold the pipe, both when the berth is extended in use and when it is rolled up and stowed away. Additional pads can be screwed to the bulkheads to raise or lower the bunk's inboard edge when the boat is underway, keeping the sleeper level on either tack.

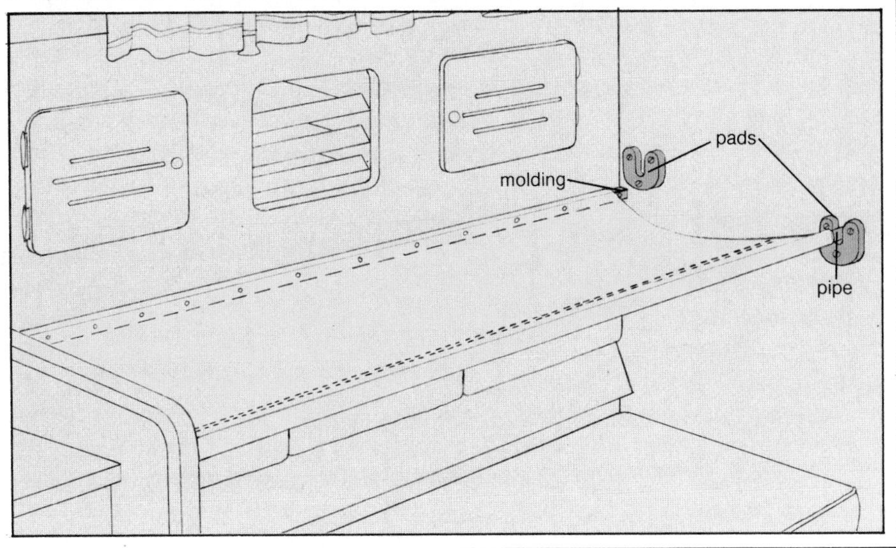

Tips for Stowage

The open-faced locker below, divided into half a dozen cubbyholes, provides individual niches for small items like crew members' toiletry kits. Constructed from three-eighth-inch plywood, the locker is nailed and glued together, then screwed to a bulkhead. The key facet of its design is the plywood facing. It has been cut out to leave a lip around each bin; shock cord is then knotted through holes in the facing to keep stowed articles in the bins during rough weather.

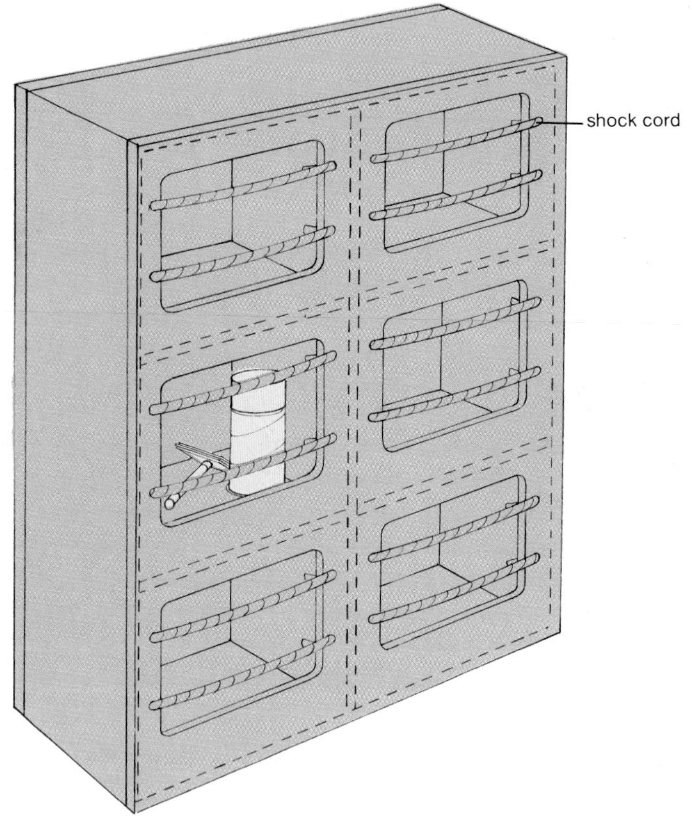

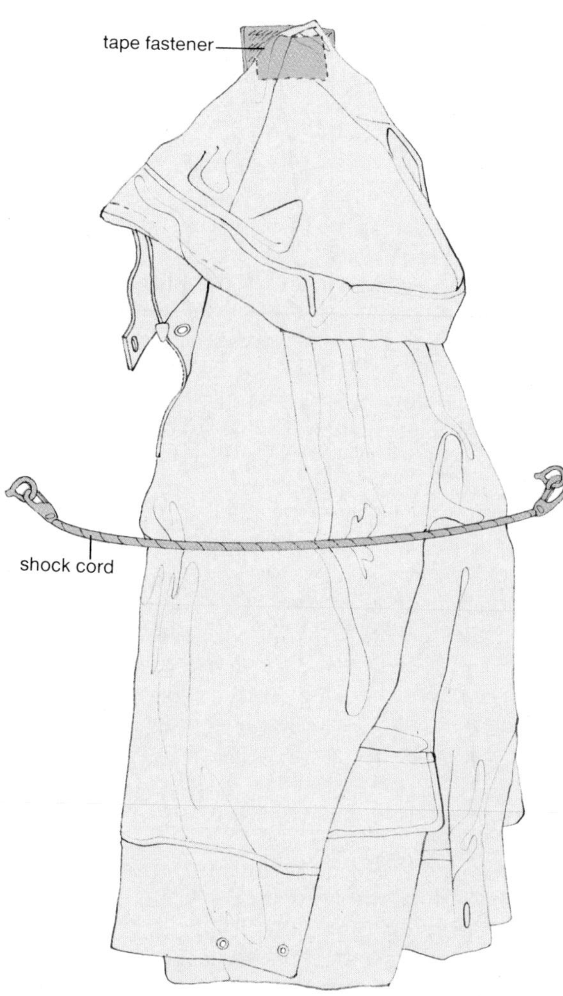

On a boat too small to have full-sized hanging lockers, damp foul-weather gear can be hung on a bulkhead by the method shown here. This foul-weather jacket is supported from the neck by companion strips of the adherent tape fastener called Velcro. One segment of the fastening strip is sewed to the jacket; the other is epoxied to the bulkhead. Shock cord, hooked through eyes screwed into the bulkhead, secures the oilskin.

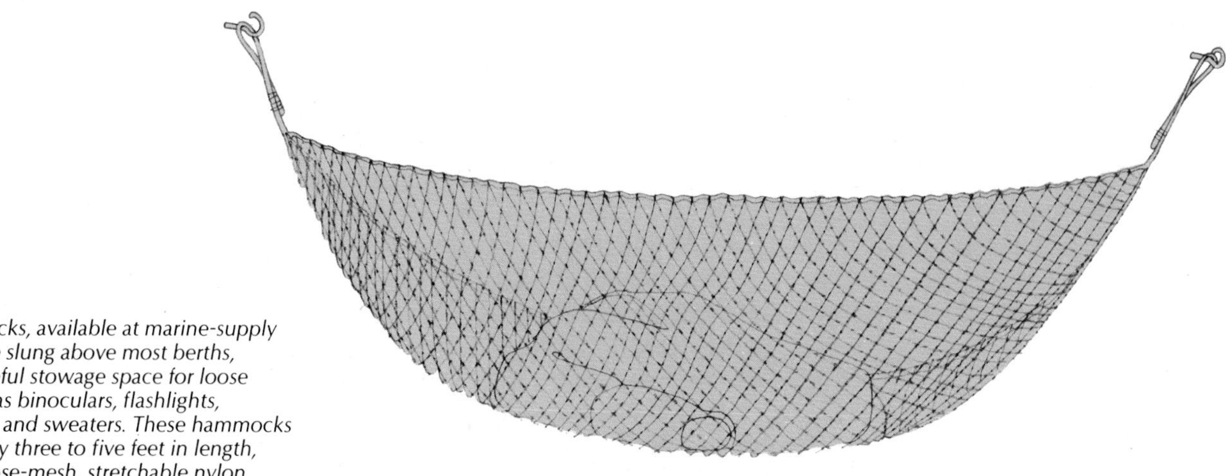

Gear hammocks, available at marine-supply stores, can be slung above most berths, providing useful stowage space for loose articles such as binoculars, flashlights, tissues, boots and sweaters. These hammocks are commonly three to five feet in length, and are of close-mesh, stretchable nylon.

Sheets and blankets can be stuffed into zippered pillow covers like this one during the day, thus conserving valuable drawer and cupboard space—and at the same time creating comfortable settee cushions.

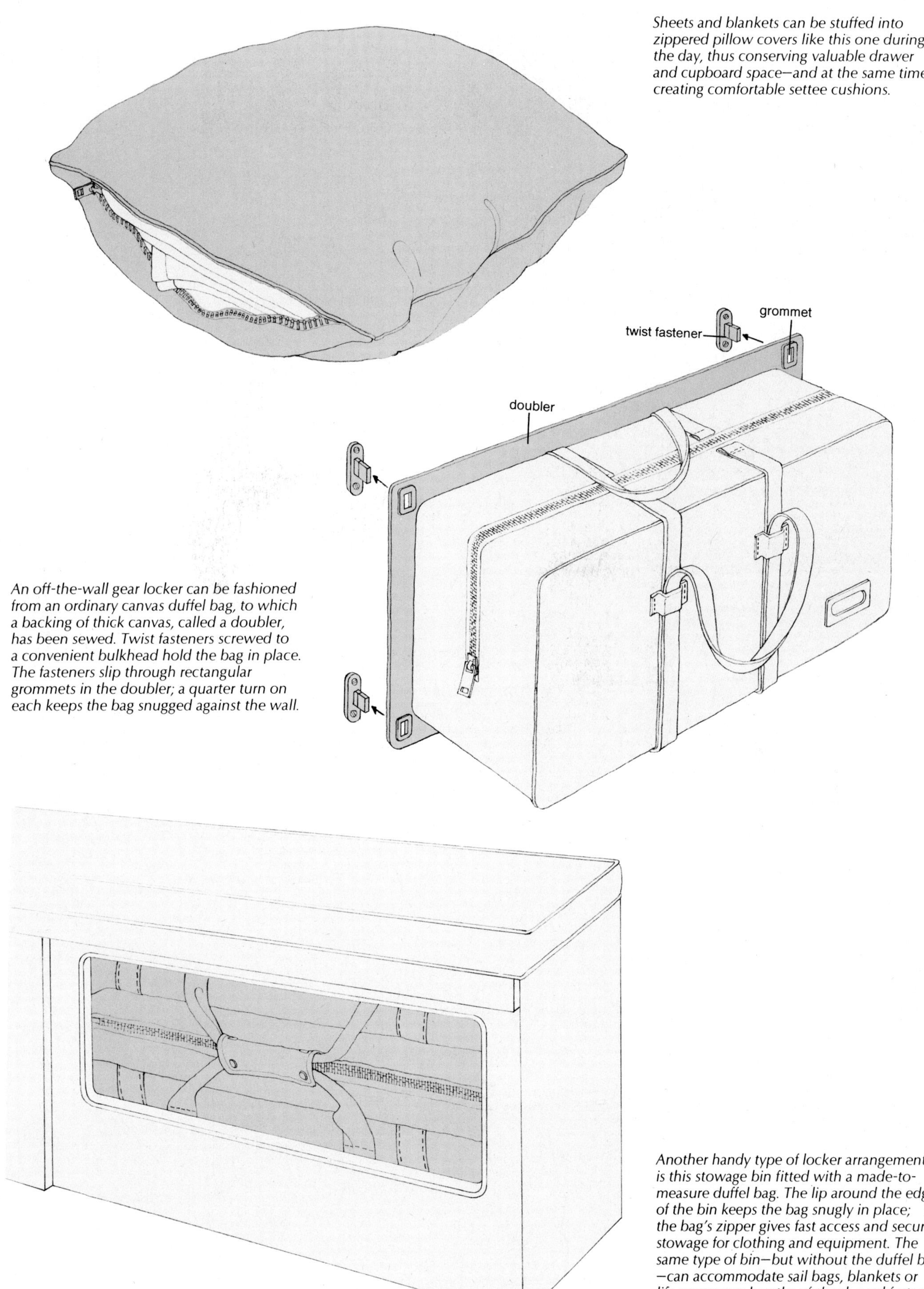

An off-the-wall gear locker can be fashioned from an ordinary canvas duffel bag, to which a backing of thick canvas, called a doubler, has been sewed. Twist fasteners screwed to a convenient bulkhead hold the bag in place. The fasteners slip through rectangular grommets in the doubler; a quarter turn on each keeps the bag snugged against the wall.

Another handy type of locker arrangement is this stowage bin fitted with a made-to-measure duffel bag. The lip around the edge of the bin keeps the bag snugly in place; the bag's zipper gives fast access and secure stowage for clothing and equipment. The same type of bin—but without the duffel bag—can accommodate sail bags, blankets or life preservers; lengths of shock cord fastened across the openings provide added security.

The Head

The head on a cruising boat may be no more than a tiny alcove closed off by a curtain. Or it may be a relatively luxurious facility that includes hot and cold running water, storage cabinets, a counter with built-in sink, a shower, and even an electrically operated toilet that flushes at the push of a button.

Every head, no matter what its size, must be well ventilated and spotlessly clean to keep the cabin atmosphere fresh. Nothing should find its way into a marine toilet except bathroom paper and the waste elements it was designed for. Anything else—cigarette butts or human hair, for example—can block the valves, causing a stoppage that will necessitate dismantling the toilet. In addition, clogging can occur from improper flushing. On a typical marine toilet like the one at right, flushing is a four-step operation: open the valve next to the pump handle; pump to flush the bowl; close the valve; pump at least half a dozen more strokes to be sure the plumbing is cleared. Never leave the valve open after using the toilet, or sea water will flood the cabin.

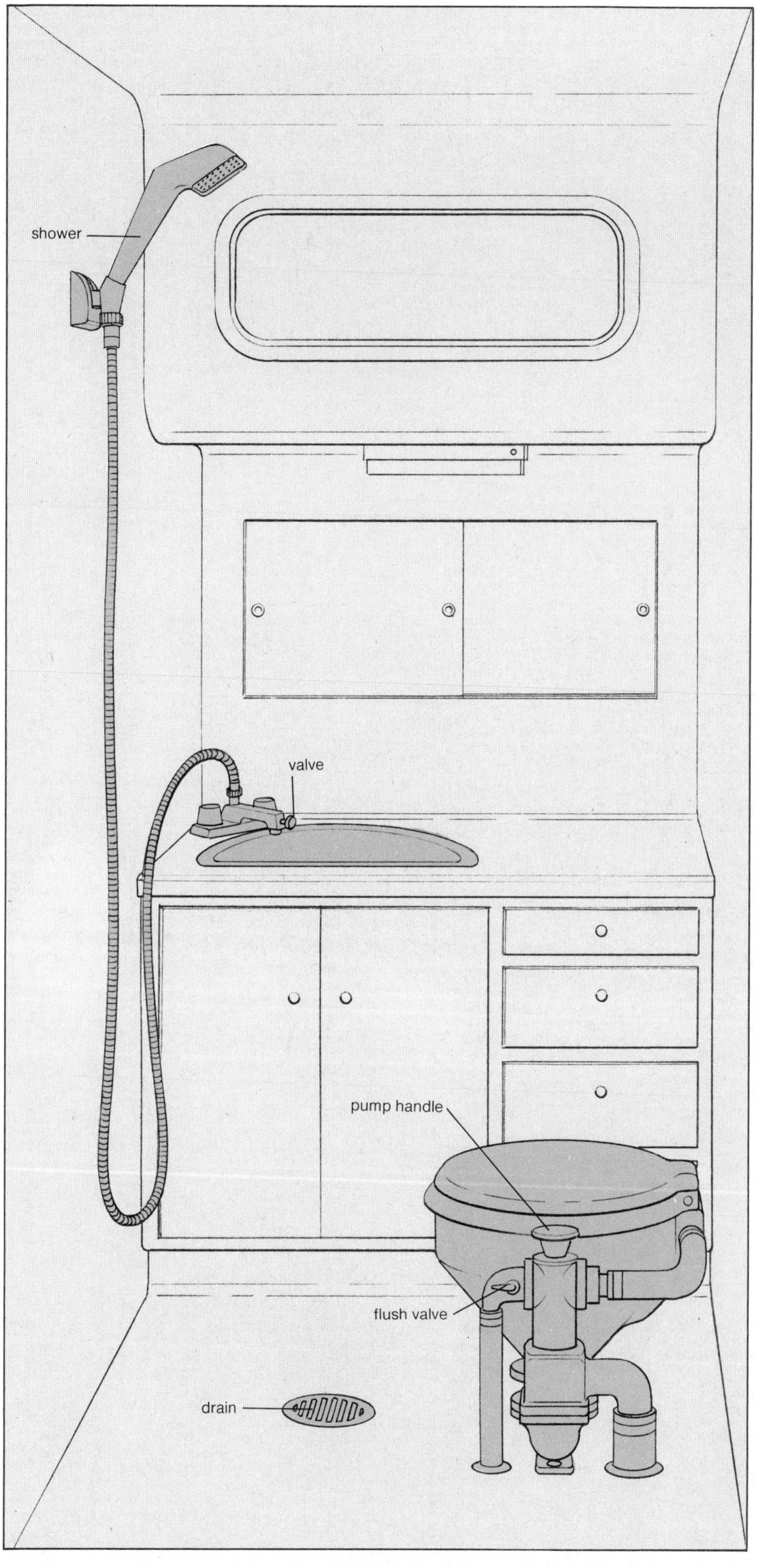

This compact head aboard a fiberglass cruising boat includes a complete bathroom in the space of a small closet. Cupboards and drawers for toilet articles and linens are tucked around the washstand. Opposite the toilet is a shower supplied with water by a pump and water heater (pages 108-109). The shower water, routed from the lavatory faucet by a diverter valve, sprays out the nozzle and runs through a drain in the floor. If the drain is below the waterline, the shower runoff must be pumped overboard by a small electric pump, usually located in the bilge.

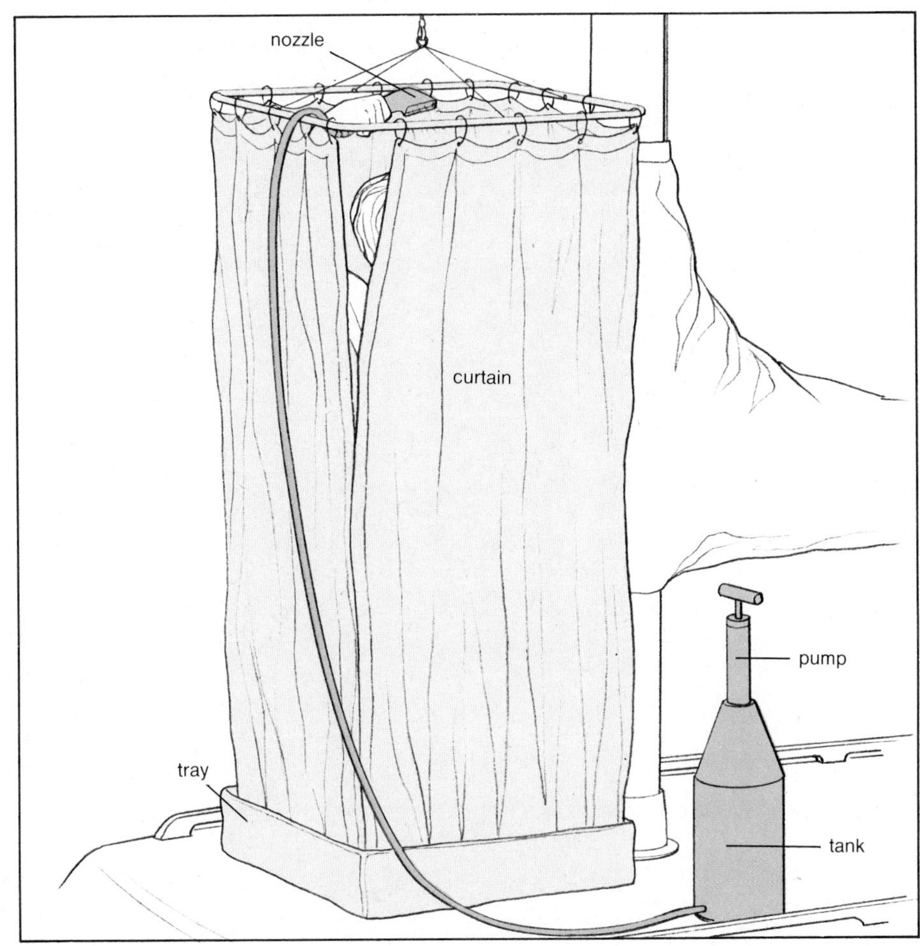

An on-deck shower stall that can be assembled when needed and then stowed away below provides a fresh-water rinse on boats with no pressurized water supply. The shower tank is filled with water and pressurized by means of the pump. When a valve on the shower nozzle is depressed, the pressure forces the water out of the tank and through the nozzle. A shower curtain held by a halyard hangs with its lower edge inside a plastic tray that catches runoff.

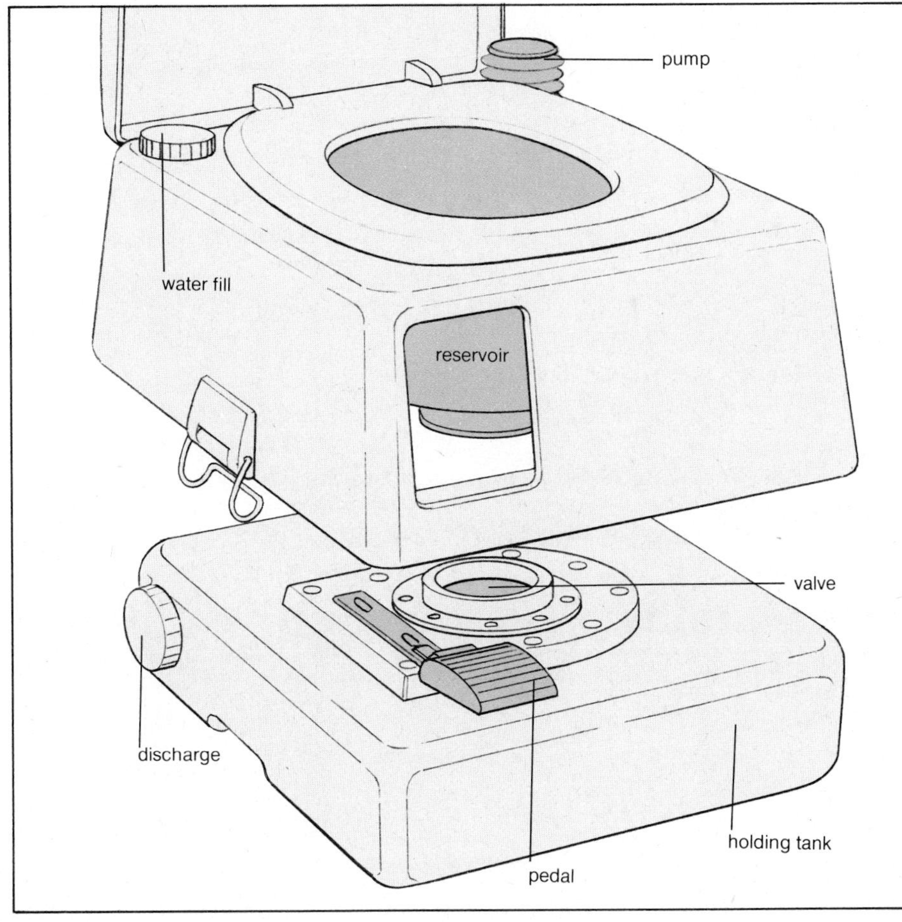

Portable toilets, increasingly popular on small cruising boats, are made up of two major sections that latch tightly together. The lower section is a holding tank; the upper section houses the bowl, which is surrounded by a two-gallon water reservoir. When the toilet is flushed, water pumped from the reservoir sluices waste from the bowl through a pedal-operated valve into the holding tank, which contains a waste-treatment solution. After approximately 50 flushes, when the supply of flush water is exhausted, the holding tank is detached and then is emptied through a discharge opening into a toilet ashore.

A Hot-Water System

Nearly every cruising boat is equipped by the builder with a water tank, and with pump-type faucets or a small electric pump to deliver the water to the sink. But the supreme cruising luxury is a plentiful supply of hot water for showers, shaves and after-dinner dishwashing. In order to provide it, the fresh-water tanks must be fitted with a pressurized water system like the one at right, which includes a one-twelfth-horsepower electric pump and a small electric water heater.

The pump, preferably a self-priming type, runs off the boat's 12-volt batteries, and keeps up a constant pressure of about 25 pounds per square inch. The heater, usually a 6-to-12 gallon glass-lined metal tank containing an electric coil, requires dockside power or an auxiliary generator; the coil draws so much current (most units run at 1,000 watts) that it would discharge an ordinary storage battery in less than an hour. But the tank's one and a half inches of fiberglass insulation will keep water hot up to four hours after unplugging from the dock. The tank's heating capacity can be boosted by fitting on a heat exchanger, which borrows heat from the engine's cooling system to generate piping-hot water while the boat is underway.

A boat's fresh-water tank is simply a sealed container constructed of corrosion-resistant metal, fiberglass, plastic or reinforced flexible rubber. In addition to openings for filling and emptying, the tank is equipped with a vent that allows air to enter or escape, thus equalizing air pressure inside and outside as the water level changes. Rigid tanks like the metal one below contain one or more baffles to moderate the surge of water when the boat rolls or pitches.

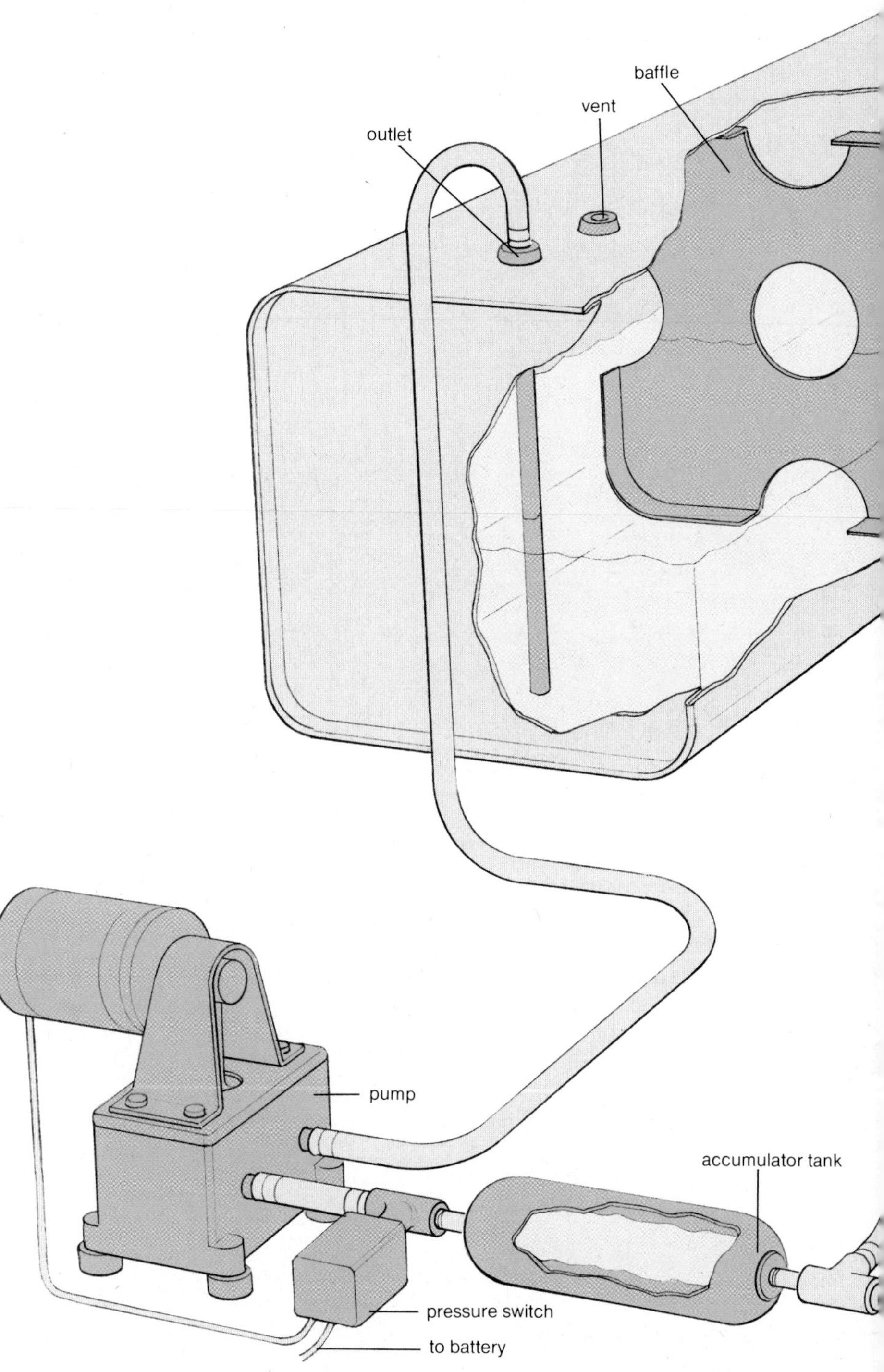

The 12-volt electric pump that provides force for a boat's running water is activated automatically by means of a pressure switch, shown here connected to a small, one-quart accumulator tank. If any of the boat's fresh-water faucets are turned on, pressure in the accumulator tank drops; when it falls below a prescribed minimum—usually 20 pounds per square inch—the switch trips on, operating the pump until pressure is restored. Since the tank allows up to 16 ounces of water to be drawn before triggering the switch, the system saves wear on the pump —and conserves the boat's batteries.

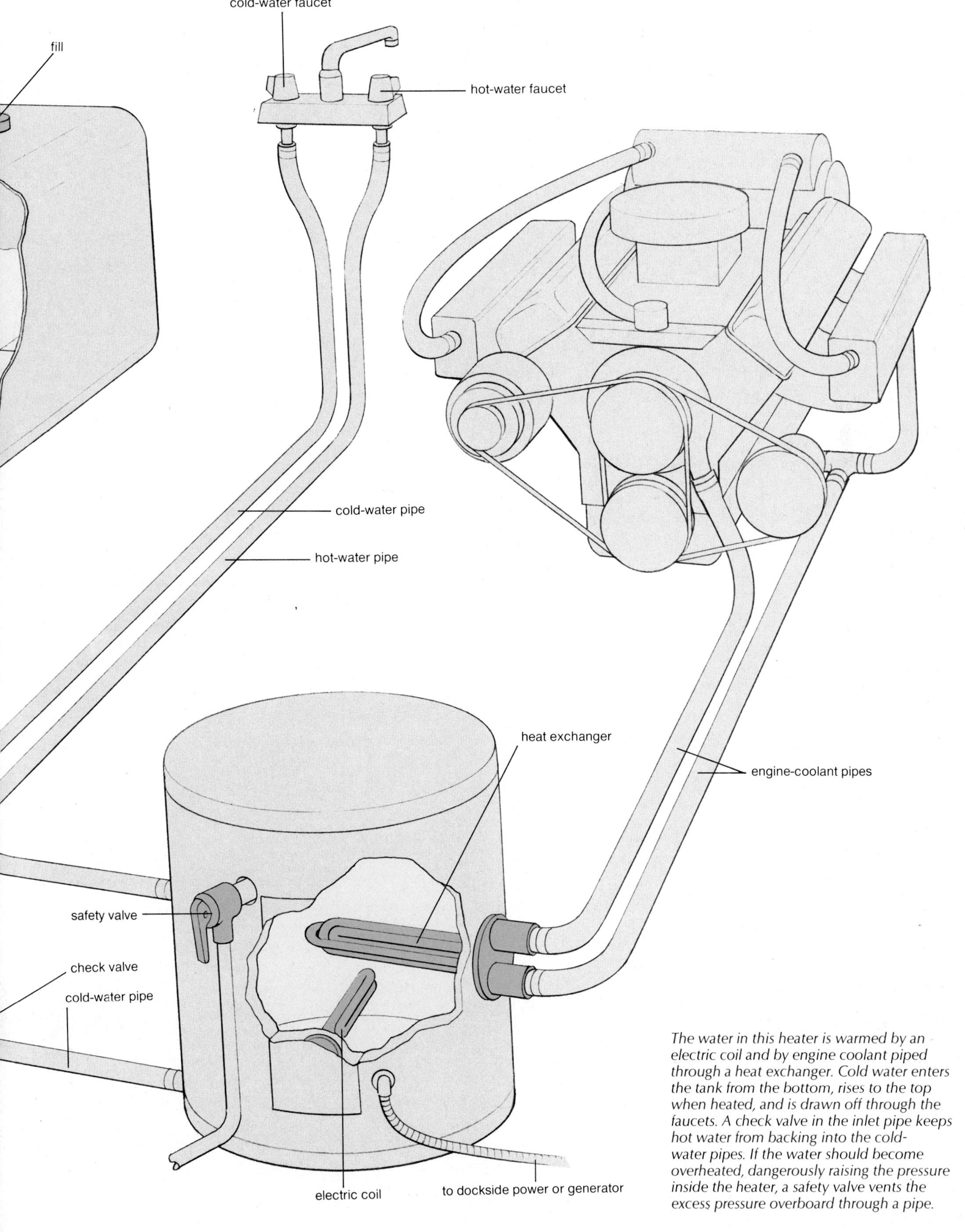

The water in this heater is warmed by an electric coil and by engine coolant piped through a heat exchanger. Cold water enters the tank from the bottom, rises to the top when heated, and is drawn off through the faucets. A check valve in the inlet pipe keeps hot water from backing into the cold-water pipes. If the water should become overheated, dangerously raising the pressure inside the heater, a safety valve vents the excess pressure overboard through a pipe.

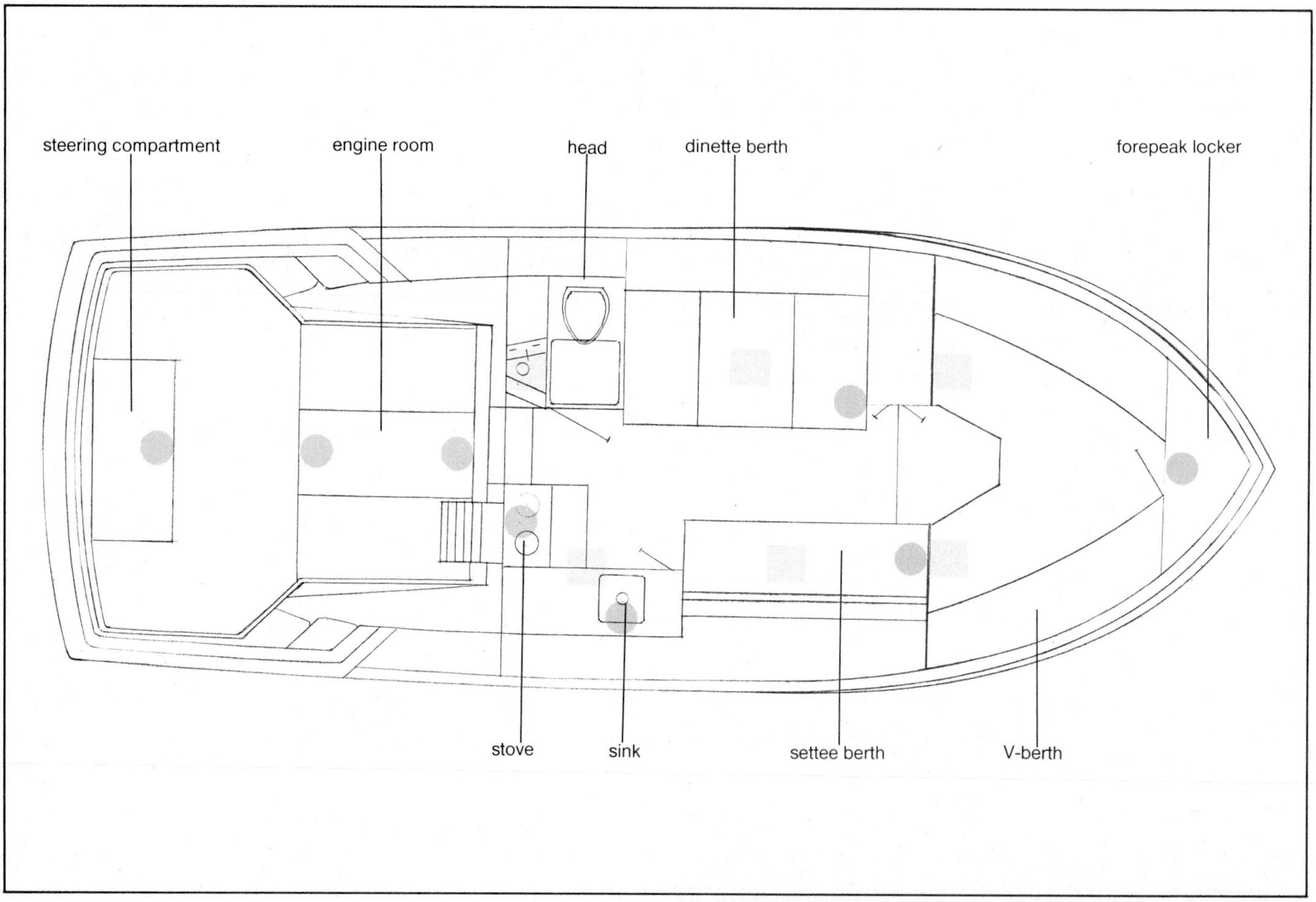

steering compartment
engine room
head
dinette berth
forepeak locker
stove
sink
settee berth
V-berth

The circles in this diagram show where extra lights might be placed on a medium-sized powerboat to augment the original fixtures, indicated by squares. Work lights added to the steering compartment and engine room facilitate emergency repairs at night. A single light suffices for the head, but extra lamps above the stove and sink are a welcome addition to the galley's overhead fixture. Directional reading lamps are added above main-cabin berths—like those already installed over the V-berths. Finally, a light fixture tucked into the forepeak locker makes it easy to untangle a fouled anchor line.

A gooseneck lamp screwed to a bulkhead in the navigator's nook illuminates the chart table with a sharply defined circle of light without disturbing crew members sleeping nearby. The flexible stalk allows the light to be directed toward the chronometers and the depth finder mounted on the bulkhead.

Light Below

The lighting units that come with some of the production-model cruisers may consist of no more than a single overhead fixture in the center of each cabin. But by installing supplementary lights like the ones shown on these and the following pages, the boatman can greatly improve belowdecks illumination for cooking and reading, navigating and making repairs.

Since every additional electric light increases the drain on batteries, a boatowner must take care to balance the demands of his lighting system against the vessel's electric-power supply. He can increase the available power by adding extra storage batteries or an auxiliary generator. He may also want to install a battery charger—an ingenious device that can tap dockside current to recharge the batteries while running the lights at the same time.

Even with an augmented supply, he should conserve electricity whenever possible. One simple but effective method is to scrupulously turn off all lights not in use. Another is to install fixtures for fluorescent tubes or the high-intensity bulbs used in automobile taillights, both of which produce more candle power per watt than ordinary incandescent bulbs.

There is one method for avoiding the need for lights below during a cloudy day. The deck light shown on this page channels daylight through a prism in the deck. It can brighten lockers, lazarettes, quarter berths and engine compartments. However, it is difficult to install, and should be put in by a professional. Many boatmen also carry kerosene lamps *(overleaf)*—for emergency lighting in case of a power failure, for warmth and for the cozy, cheerful glow they impart to a cabin.

The brilliant stripe of light in the ceiling of this head marks the location of a prism deck light. This power-saving light source floods the compartment with a soft, natural glow, even in stormy or overcast weather.

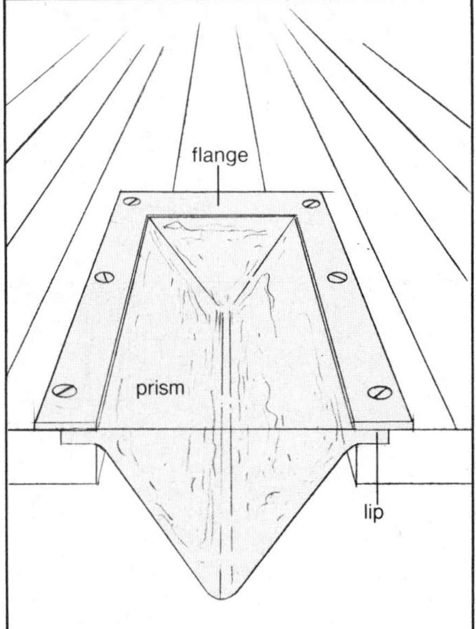

A prism deck light consists of an inverted solid-glass pyramid whose slanted lower surfaces are rippled with a series of random corrugations to diffuse the light. The unit fits into a slot cut through the deck, and is held in place by a molded lip and a bronze flange.

The lantern at right, which burns vaporized kerosene, produces as much candle power as a 200-watt electric bulb. The key element in this highly efficient light source is its mantle —a loosely woven bag composed of rayon. When first exposed to flame after installation, the mantle is transformed into a fragile network of ash; thereafter, heat causes it to incandesce like a light bulb's filament. Although the carbonized rayon will crumble if touched, it will last indefinitely if left undisturbed. A frosted-glass chimney softens the lamp's glare and keeps off drafts that could dim the light by cooling the mantle.

To light a typical kerosene-vapor lantern, first pressurize the fuel tank with the built-in air pump. Insert a lighted match through the hole below the chimney, while slowly opening the valve that admits kerosene into the preheater, which will ignite. Continue pumping while the preheater warms the vapor tube—it takes about 50 seconds; then open the burner valve. Pressure forces the kerosene through the tube—where heat vaporizes it—and into the mantle, where it is ignited by the preheater's flame. Turn off the preheater and pump in more air to restore pressure lost during the preheating stage.

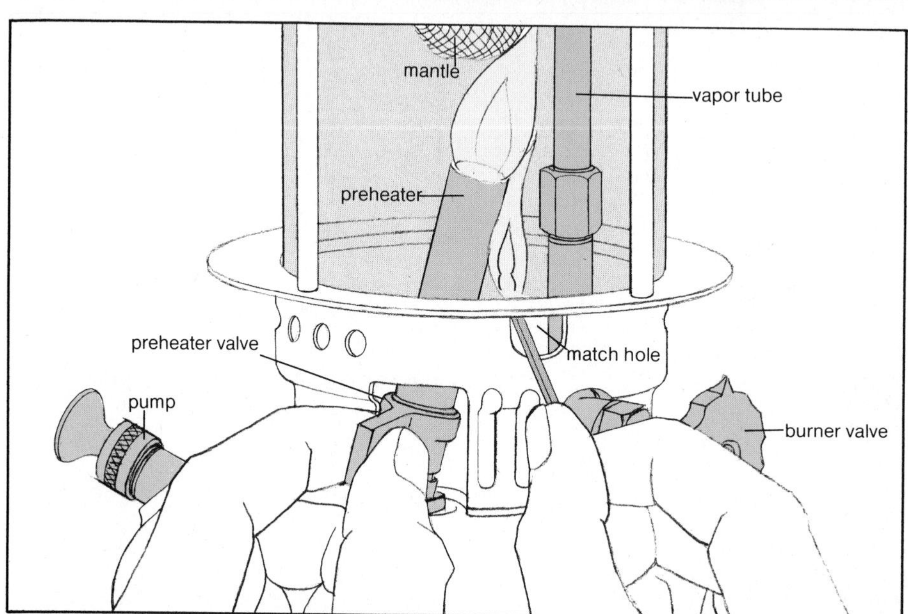

Firm Foundation for a Lantern

A kerosene lantern can be firmly secured to a tabletop or other flat surface by the method shown at right—which will also allow the lamp to be readily detached. Using epoxy glue, attach three brass nuts to the bottom of the lantern; after the epoxy has dried, insert into the nuts three brass machine screws about three eighths of an inch long. With a drill or a routing tool, gouge three hollow spaces in the tabletop to receive the screwheads. Cover the hollows with flat brass keyhole escutcheons, which are available at hardware stores; secure the escutcheons to the tabletop with small finishing nails. When the lamp is set in place, the screwheads should fit through the round ends of the keyholes and into the hollows below. By giving the lamp a slight twist, the screwheads will lock into position. A twist in the opposite direction frees them.

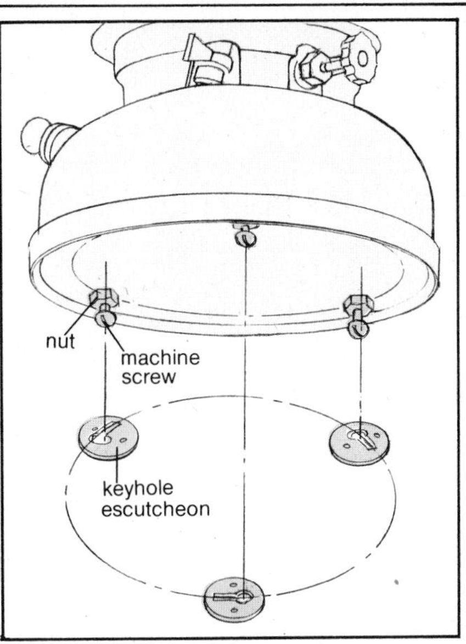

Old-fashioned kerosene reading lamps bathe this 42-foot schooner's cabin in a gentle glow. Though the boat was built in 1967, the owner excluded electric lights, thus enhancing the vessel's traditional character. The lamps are a simple wick-type; they burn liquid kerosene drawn by the wick from a reservoir located in the lamp's base. Each lamp is attached to a bulkhead by means of gimbals, which keep it vertical so that kerosene does not spill when the boat rolls or pitches. A metal shield, or smoke bell—which is visible above the lamp in the background—will keep lampblack from smudging the overhead.

When anchored head to wind, the principal airflow pattern belowdecks is usually from the rear of the cabin forward—a paradox explained by the fact that wind passing over the deckhouse loses speed, spills into the cockpit and eddies back into the cabin through the open companionway. The air empties through the forward hatch (hinged from the forward edge to keep out spray or rain), where suction from the wind above helps pull it out. The stern vent faces forward, to air out the aft section of the boat, and the bow vent is also angled forward, creating a small direct airflow through the forepeak.

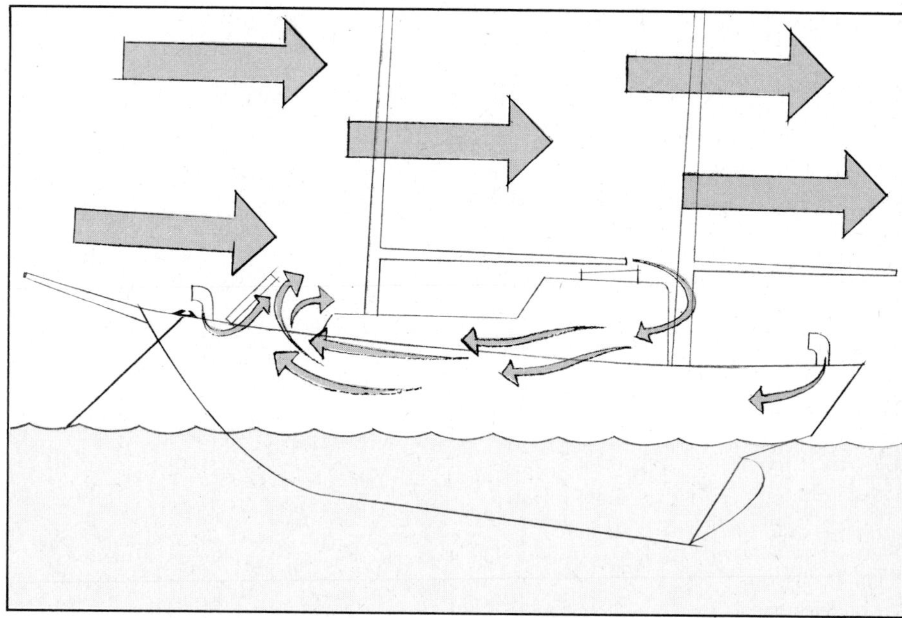

On calm, dry evenings, anchoring stern-to may help channel stray breezes belowdecks, particularly on boats that have high deckhouses and large companionways. The airflow is direct, from stern to bow, so the foredeck hatch should be hinged by its after edge to act as an exhaust. When anchoring by the stern, the tiller should be lashed to keep the rudder from swinging, and the boat should never be left unattended—in a squall, it might fishtail from side to side and collide with a neighboring vessel.

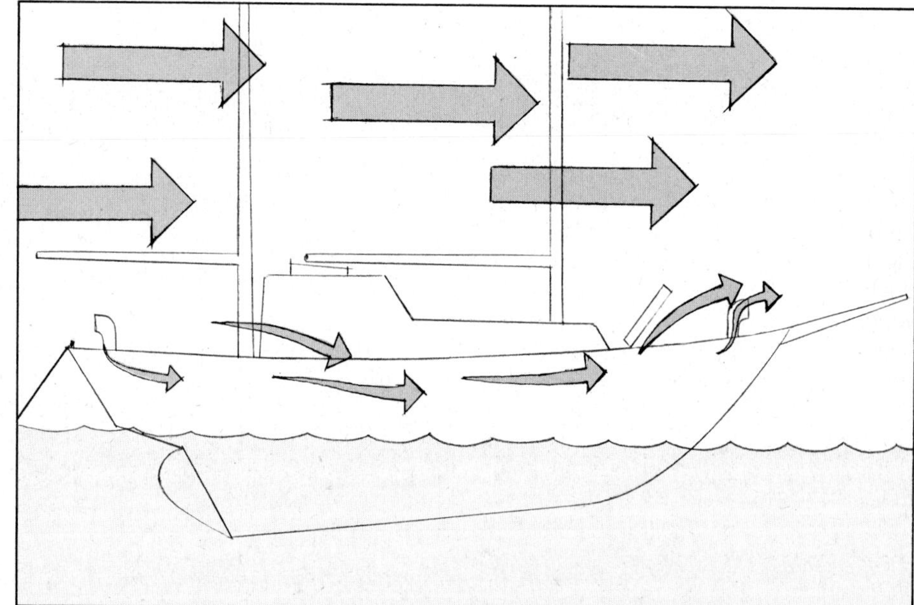

Bug Barriers

Nylon mesh secured by self-gripping Velcro tape makes a tight, lightweight, long-lasting screen for a hatch, a porthole or a companionway. Such screens can be installed or removed in seconds, will roll up for compact stowage when not in use, never rust, and can be popped into a washing machine when they get dirty. Using one of the kits available at marine-supply stores, a boatman can quickly and easily make a screen to fit any size or shape of hatch on his vessel. To make a screen like the one at right, glue strips of Velcro tape around the inside rim of the hatch and around the edges of a piece of nylon screening cut square to fit the rim. To install the screen, press the Velcro strip on the screen against the matching strip on the hatch. To remove, take hold of one corner and pull the screen away.

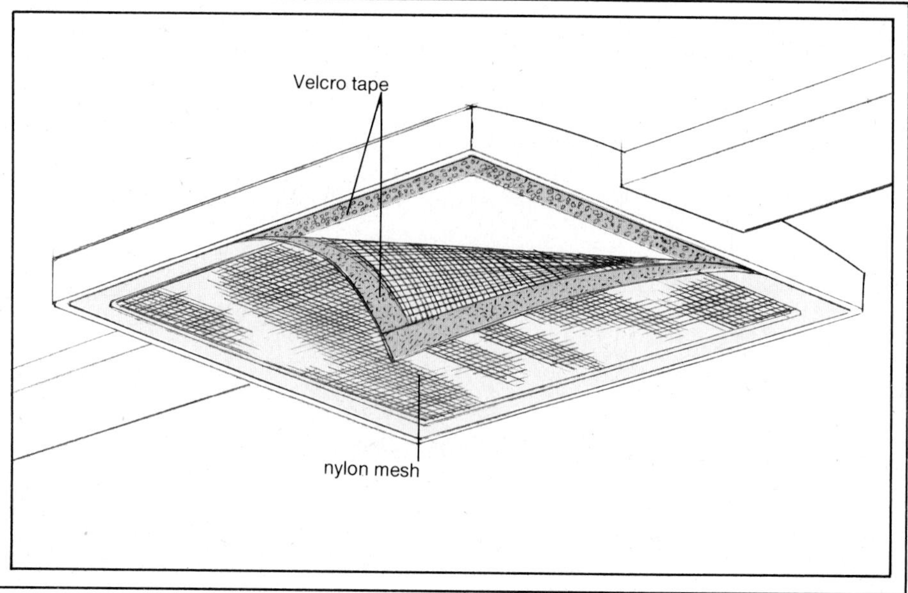

Ventilating the Cabin

A steady flow of fresh air through a boat's cabin is essential for comfortable cruising. Without it, a cabin becomes intolerably stuffy—and full of mildew, a musty-smelling fungus that discolors fabrics and mars the finish of woodwork. Most cruising boats are ventilated primarily by the wind, usually abundant when the vessel is underway on open water, but often sparse at anchor. To exploit the slightest zephyr, the skipper should take advantage of the basic, through-boat airflow principles illustrated at left; in addition, he may want to hoist a wind scoop like the one in the picture at right.

The key to adequate ventilation, however, is the presence aboard the vessel of a fair complement of well-placed vents. Knowledgeable cruising skippers recommend equipping a boat with at least one ventilator in the bow and often another in the stern. An additional vent in the head is advisable, and in multiple-cabin boats, added comfort can be provided by a vent for each compartment.

Hatches also serve as ventilators; many are hinged both fore and aft so they can be opened in either direction by removing the pins from one pair of hinges. With the hatch cover's after edge lifted and the wind on the bow, the hatch acts as an exhaust vent, while blocking wind-driven spray. Opened the other way, and complemented by a wind scoop, it channels air directly into the cabin.

Belowdecks circulation of air can be further improved by minimizing the resistance to airflow presented by such obstacles as doors and lockers. The boatman can install louvers in doors between fore-and-aft compartments, or saw off the doors four inches or so above the cabin sole. In tropical cruising grounds, he can replace the doors with curtains. Experienced cruising hands will also cut three-by-six-inch air holes into the sides of lockers to allow the breeze to circulate inside, thus keeping the contents fresh and relatively dry.

A wind scoop funnels a breeze directly through the forward hatch into the cabin, reversing the airflow shown at the top of the opposite page. This model is made from lightweight cotton with top edges sewed to form a pocket. The bottom of the scoop is hooked to the rim of the hatch; the top is supported by the jib halyard. Three guys hold the scoop upright against the wind. One guy stretches from the forestay to the top of the scoop; the other two run from the life lines to a thin wooden rod that is slipped through loops sewed to the scoop to help it hold its shape. A bow vent, cabin vent and cabin hatch, all facing forward, reinforce the effect of the scoop.

A critical element on any marine stove is the smokehead that crowns the flue above the deck and allows fumes to escape, while keeping out the rain and eliminating most downdrafts. The key fixture in the smokehead is a dome that is slightly larger in diameter than the flue itself; the dome acts as an umbrella, spilling rain beyond the flue's edges and out the bottom of the smokehead.

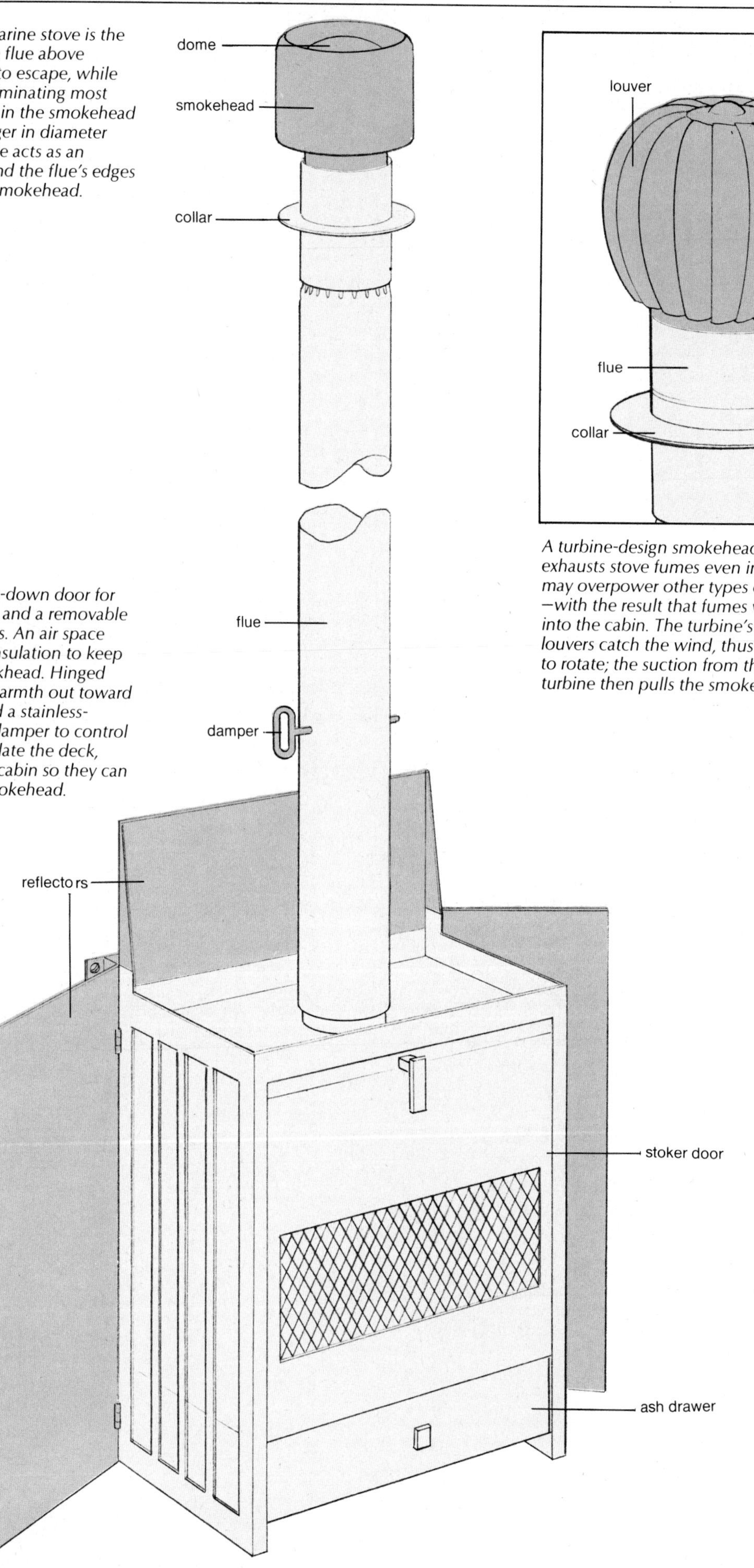

A turbine-design smokehead effectively exhausts stove fumes even in high winds that may overpower other types of smokeheads —with the result that fumes will back down into the cabin. The turbine's overlapping louvers catch the wind, thus causing the unit to rotate; the suction from the spinning turbine then pulls the smoke out of the flue.

The stove at right has a drop-down door for lighting and stoking the fire, and a removable drawer for disposing of ashes. An air space behind the stove serves as insulation to keep heat from scorching the bulkhead. Hinged steel reflectors help direct warmth out toward the middle of the cabin. And a stainless-steel flue, equipped with a damper to control the draft and a collar to insulate the deck, carries the fumes out of the cabin so they can be dispelled through the smokehead.

The Temperate Cabin

Any skipper who cruises off-season in northern waters such as those of Maine or Canada needs heat in his cabin. In small boats, the morning chill of September or early June can be banished from the cabin by lighting the galley stove and kerosene lanterns. But larger boats often rely on a wood- or coal-burning stove like the one at left. The stove must be insulated from the woodwork around it. It must also have a flue to lead smoke and poisonous carbon-monoxide fumes out of the cabin, and plenty of fresh air to replenish oxygen consumed by the flames.

Cruising boats that venture to sultry climes as well as chilly ones can maintain cabin comfort with a marine air conditioner that will either cool the cabin or warm it. The key to both of these operations is a substance called refrigerant, which flows through a network of sealed piping. During its circulation, according to need, the refrigerant abruptly changes from a liquid to a gas or condenses from a gas to a liquid—absorbing or giving off large amounts of heat in the process.

The source of the refrigerant's heat, or the means of carrying off heat that it has absorbed in cooling the cabin, is sea water, piped aboard and placed in close proximity to the refrigerant at an engine-room component called a condenser. A cabin switch controls the direction of the refrigerant's flow, and it is the flow direction, rather than the temperature of the sea water, that determines whether the air conditioner will heat or cool the boat's interior. Thus, the air conditioner can keep the cabin at a balmy 70° by wringing calories out of sea water whose temperature is 20° lower; or cool off a cabin when surrounding sea water is as warm as 78°.

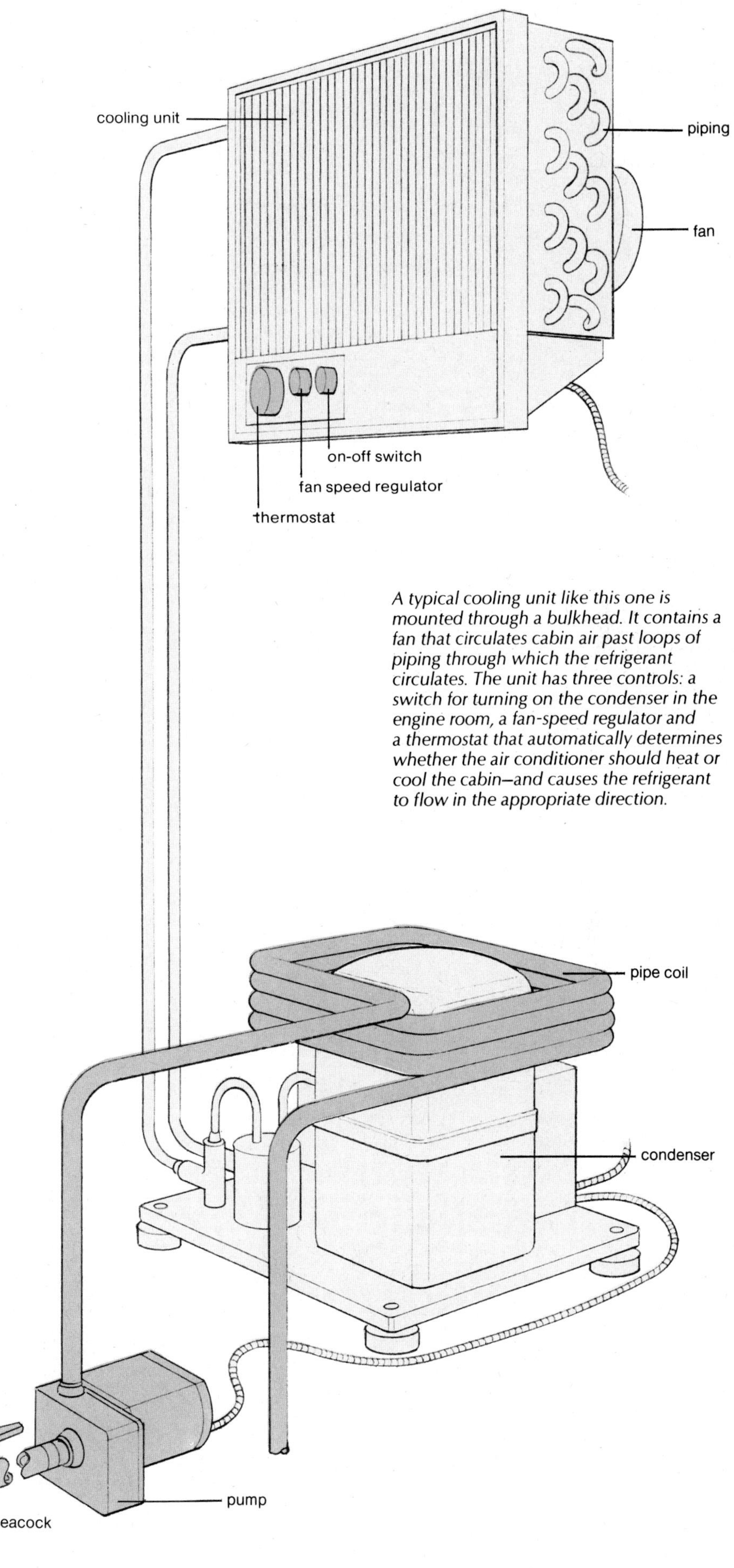

A typical cooling unit like this one is mounted through a bulkhead. It contains a fan that circulates cabin air past loops of piping through which the refrigerant circulates. The unit has three controls: a switch for turning on the condenser in the engine room, a fan-speed regulator and a thermostat that automatically determines whether the air conditioner should heat or cool the cabin—and causes the refrigerant to flow in the appropriate direction.

An air conditioner's engine-room machinery includes an electric pump that supplies sea water used to alter the temperature of the refrigerant. The pump draws water through a seacock, circulates it around the condenser by means of a coil of pipe, then discharges the water overboard. The sea water either carries off heat absorbed from the cabin by the refrigerant or replaces the heat lost by the refrigerant in warming the cabin.

This sailboat's dodger is supported by a two-piece folding frame of steel tubing, and secured to the cabin top by metal snaps. Tensioning lines in the dodger's after corners pull the canopy taut against the snaps. In fine weather, the dodger can be struck by undoing the tensioning lines and snaps, pushing the frame members together and laying them on the cabin top forward of the companionway. Covers in matching fabric protect the wheel, binnacle and cockpit winches.

A Panoply of Canopies

So many waking hours of a cruise are spent topside that a boat's deck and cockpit become important living spaces. To make the abovedecks areas as comfortable as possible, many boatmen equip their vessels with canopies and awnings that fend off sun, spray and rain.

The dodger on a sailboat *(left)* and a powerboat's Bimini top *(right)* are both semipermanent canopies of heavy-duty, sun-resistant fabric such as acrylic or vinyl, supported by folding metal frames. Both types of canopies must be custom ordered to fit any particular vessel, and once mounted on a boat they are generally left on for the duration of the cruising season.

The dodger shields a sailboat's companionway from spray and driving rain when the boat is underway, while allowing the hatch to remain open for cabin ventilation. Plastic windows set into the fabric permit visibility forward. The Bimini top (namesake of the sun-drenched Bimini islands off the Florida coast) is usually mounted on a powerboat's flying bridge. Not only does it provide shade for the helmsman, but with the addition of side curtains *(bottom right)* it will keep him warm and dry in case of rain.

Some powerboats also carry permanent awnings installed over the cockpit on tall metal stanchions. Sailboat awnings are commonly fashioned with a minimum of supporting framework *(pages 120-121)*, and since they are set above the boom, they must be rolled up and stowed below when the boat is underway.

A Bimini top is suspended above the bridge of this powerboat by a hinged three-piece tubular frame through-bolted to the bridge coaming. Guys running from each corner of the canvas to the coaming help hold the top in position. As with a dodger, these lines can be untied and the canopy lowered by folding the frame together, then tipping it forward to rest on the cabin top.

An All-Weather Bridge

Transparent curtains snapped to the Bimini top on this vessel offer a snug topside command post in the cold or rain. A rolled-up flap in the rear curtain permits access to the bridge. When the boat is underway, this opening is an escape route for wind that blows into a flap in the front curtain; the airflow between them reduces the shelter's wind resistance.

A typical sailboat awning shades the cockpit and deck areas from mast to backstay. The awning is supported by the boom, by an athwartships pipe or wooden batten at its after end, and by a variety of tielines. Besides warding off sunrays coming from directly overhead, this awning is rigged so that its port and starboard edges become vertical side flaps to block the afternoon sun. Such an awning also gives rain protection at anchor and while motoring on calm days.

Roof for Roughing It

A day sailer can be converted into a vest-pocket cruiser by means of a boom tent, as shown here. The tent consists of a rectangular canvas draped over the boom and hooked to the shrouds and gunwales. This makes an effective shelter for someone spending the night aboard in a sleeping bag—and also serves as a rain cover for a permanently moored boat.

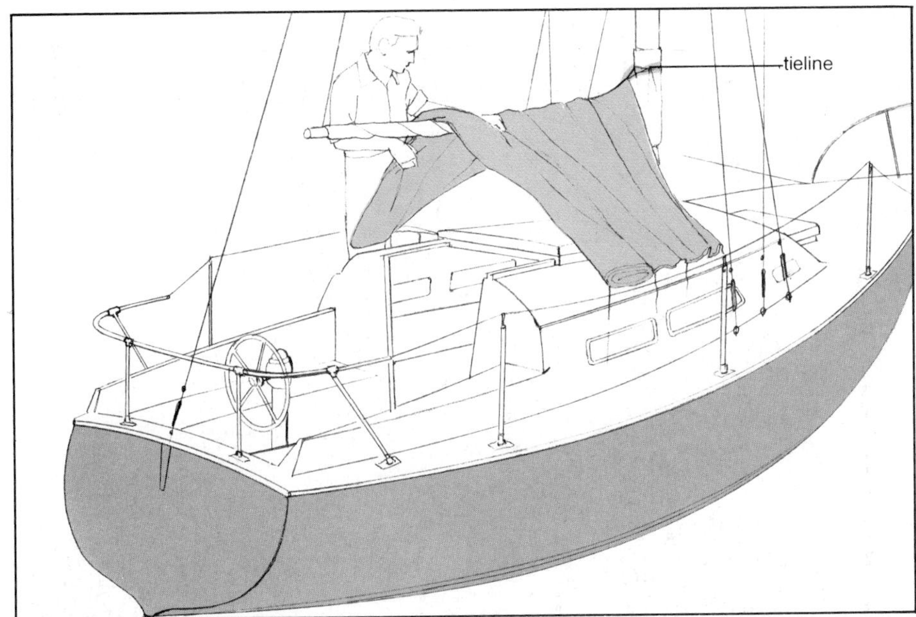

To put up a sailboat awning like the one on the opposite page, center the rolled-up canvas on the boom, and secure its forward end to the mast with a tieline. Then, working aft, unroll the awning along the boom.

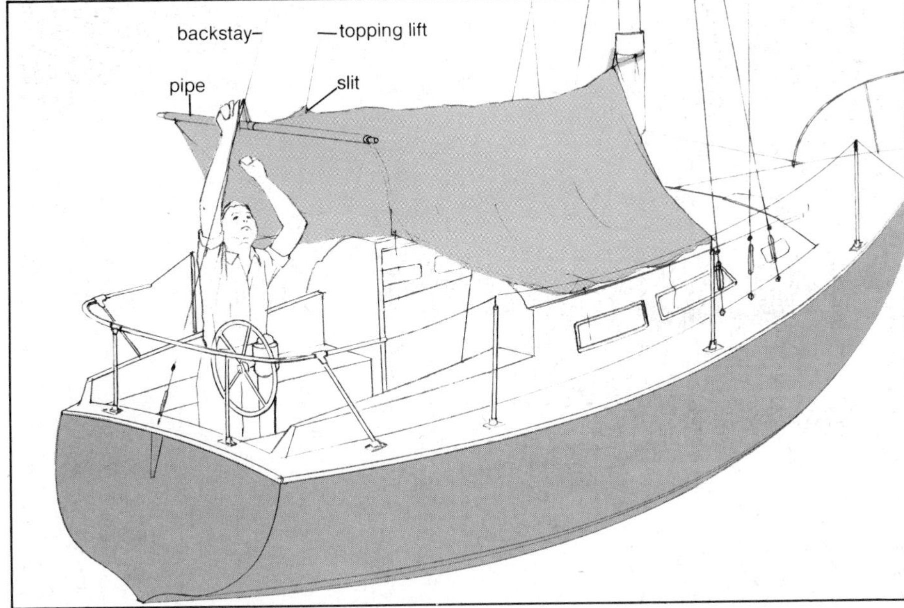

A slit in the awning's after section allows it to extend past the topping lift and over the rear of the cockpit. Once the awning has been completely unrolled, a supportive pipe or wooden batten is slid through the hem at the after edge and lashed to the backstay.

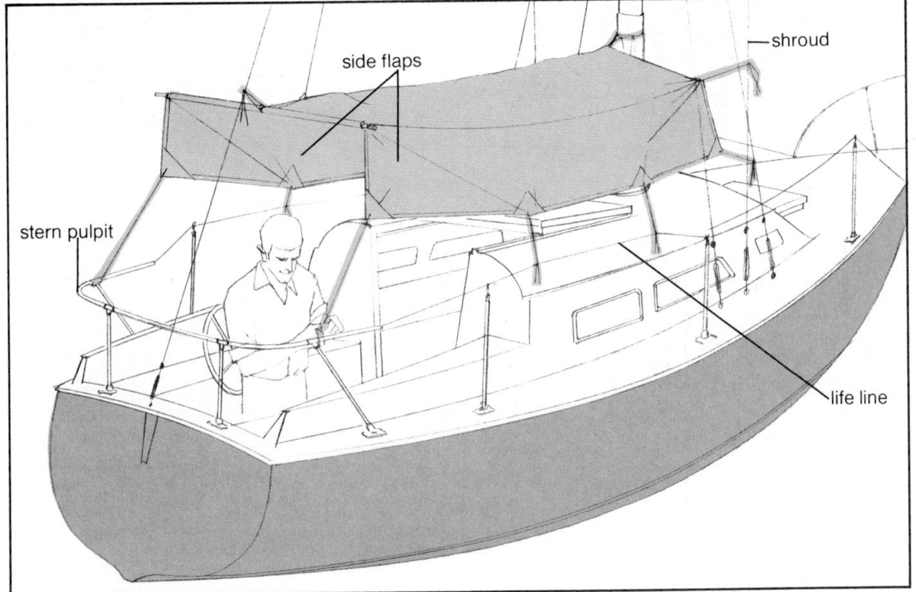

To give the awning its final shape, secure the remaining lines: one pair, to the shrouds, holds up the forward edge; the canopy's long side flaps are kept taut with other tielines, some fastened lower down on the shrouds and some to the life lines and stern pulpit.

PLENTY OF ROOM ON A PINT-SIZED SLOOP

Take a family of five on a three-week cruise in a sloop that measures only 24 feet overall? For most skippers the prospect would be unthinkable. Yet that is the way Peter and Mary Gray and their three daughters spend their vacations. Every spring they load their sloop, *Presto,* onto a trailer and drive from their front yard in upstate New York to Florida—there to embark for the Dry Tortugas or the Bahamas. And on a long summer weekend, they may trailer to the St. Lawrence River to spend a few leisurely days poking about the Thousand Islands.

Before attempting to fit his family into *Presto's* 24 feet, Gray, a research physicist with a flair for carpentry, made some radical belowdecks alterations. He converted a portside bunk into cabinets, with space for a portable stove and an icebox. The result: a full galley. To make up for the lost bunk, he turned a gear locker under the cockpit into a quarter berth.

With his wife's aid, Gray also made meticulous plans for the efficient use of the rest of *Presto's* limited space, as shown in the belowdecks layout on pages 124-125. (As one example, bulky, commercially packaged groceries are repacked in space-saving plastic bags.)

Before beginning any trip, the family spends long hours rereading the logs of past voyages, in which ideas for improvements are regularly jotted down. After one voyage in the Bahamas, on which a log entry had noted that Dacron-filled sleeping bags are bulky and overly warm in the tropics, Mary Gray made new ones from oversized Turkish towels.

Once underway, cooperation among the family members is essential. Sleeping bags must be rolled up every morning, all personal gear stowed and chores evenly shared. But as the years of happy cruising—and the pictures on the following pages—prove, the forehanded planning of the Grays contains lessons from which any other cruising boatman may benefit.

The Gray family—Peter, Elizabeth, wife Mary, Margaret and Jennifer—stand between their tiny sloop, Presto, and a small mountain of gear at the start of a four-day cruise through the Thousand Islands. Ingenious planning ensures that with everything aboard—food, fuel and water, and duffel—all hands will still have plenty of room.

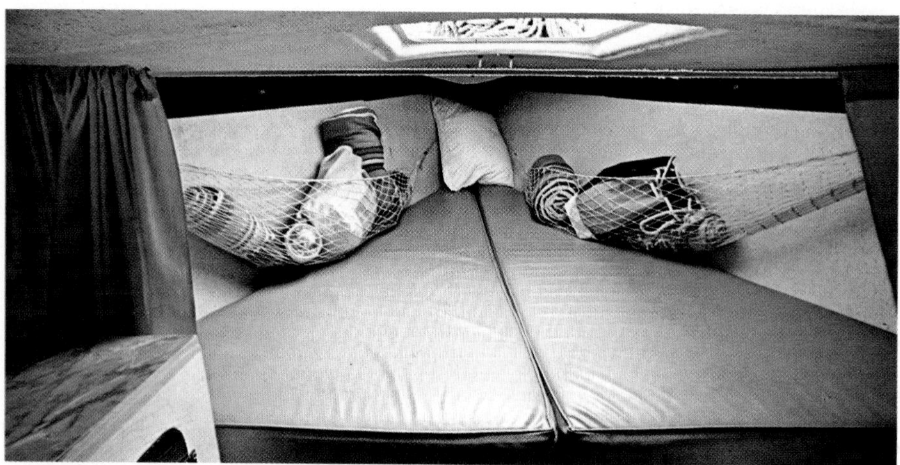

A double V-berth in the forward cabin serves as sleeping quarters for the two younger Gray girls. String hammocks hold small duffel bags, tightly rolled towels and light, easy-to-stow terry-cloth sleeping bags. The starboard-side hammock also contains a flashlight; additional flashlights are stowed in the galley, head and after sleeping quarters. During the day, both pillows are stowed together in one zippered case. A large area beneath the bunks is used for stowing the wooden flooring for Presto's inflatable dinghy.

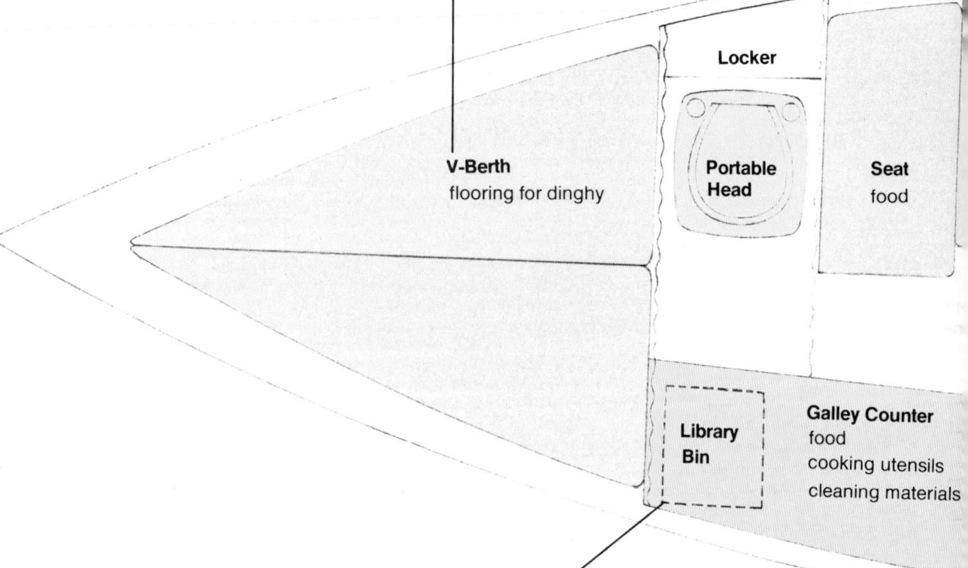

A plastic bin on the galley countertop holds the family library and navigation instruments. Besides light reading, the books include a ship's log, nautical almanacs, a first-aid manual and a cookbook. In rough weather, the library is moved off the countertop and stowed on the cabin sole. Underneath the counter, food lockers hold enough provisions for the first week of a voyage; additional food supplies are stashed away under the forward dinette seat and the quarter berth.

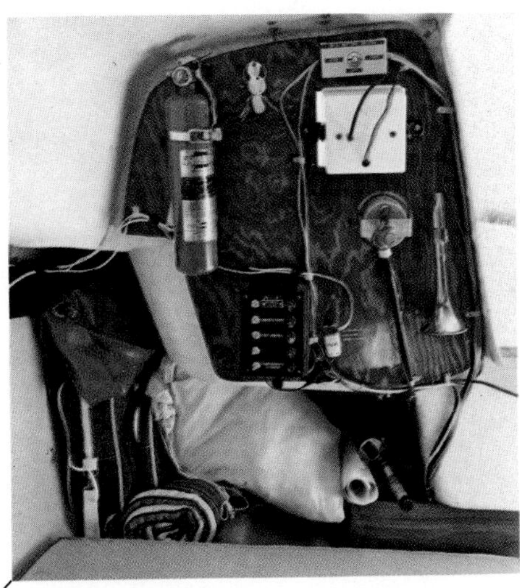

Critical items such as keys, fire extinguisher and ship's horn hang conveniently on the boat's central control panel. Beneath, a space leading under the cockpit holds charts, a fishing rod and the parents' sleeping bag.

After filling his on-deck gas tank, Gray stows the empty can in the lazarette—which also gives access to the gear locker under the starboard cockpit seat. This combined storage area contains, among other items, the boat's fresh-water supply, in five-gallon plastic jugs.

Seat
spare 6-volt battery
mosquito netting
spare bulbs
awning
spare flashlight batteries
companionway covers

Gear Locker
life preservers
water jugs
foul-weather clothing
inflatable dinghy

Lazarette
spare anchor
outboard spares
swimming ladder
scuba gear
gas cans
toolboxes

nvertible
nette

Quarter Berth
food

Stove

Icebox

Sink

A quarter berth tucked into the 14-inch-high space beneath the port cockpit seat provides sleeping quarters for Jennifer Gray, the eldest daughter. During the day, it holds Jennifer's rolled sleeping bag, pillow and duffel. The projecting forward end of the mattress serves as a cabin seat. A locker under the mattress provides supplemental storage space for Presto's food supply; the food supply could include up to 1,000 cans of assorted edibles when the vessel is fully provisioned.

Preparing to shift out of the playsuit she has been wearing, Elizabeth Gray reaches into her carefully prepacked wardrobe and selects shirt and shorts for the cool afternoon aboard. Before the cruise begins, each girl's changes of clothing are selected and then packed as units in individual zip-lock plastic bags that can be broken out as needed. Besides providing compact convenience, the bags keep the clothing free of dirt and mildew. Empty, they hold such beach-front souvenirs as seashells and colorful rocks.

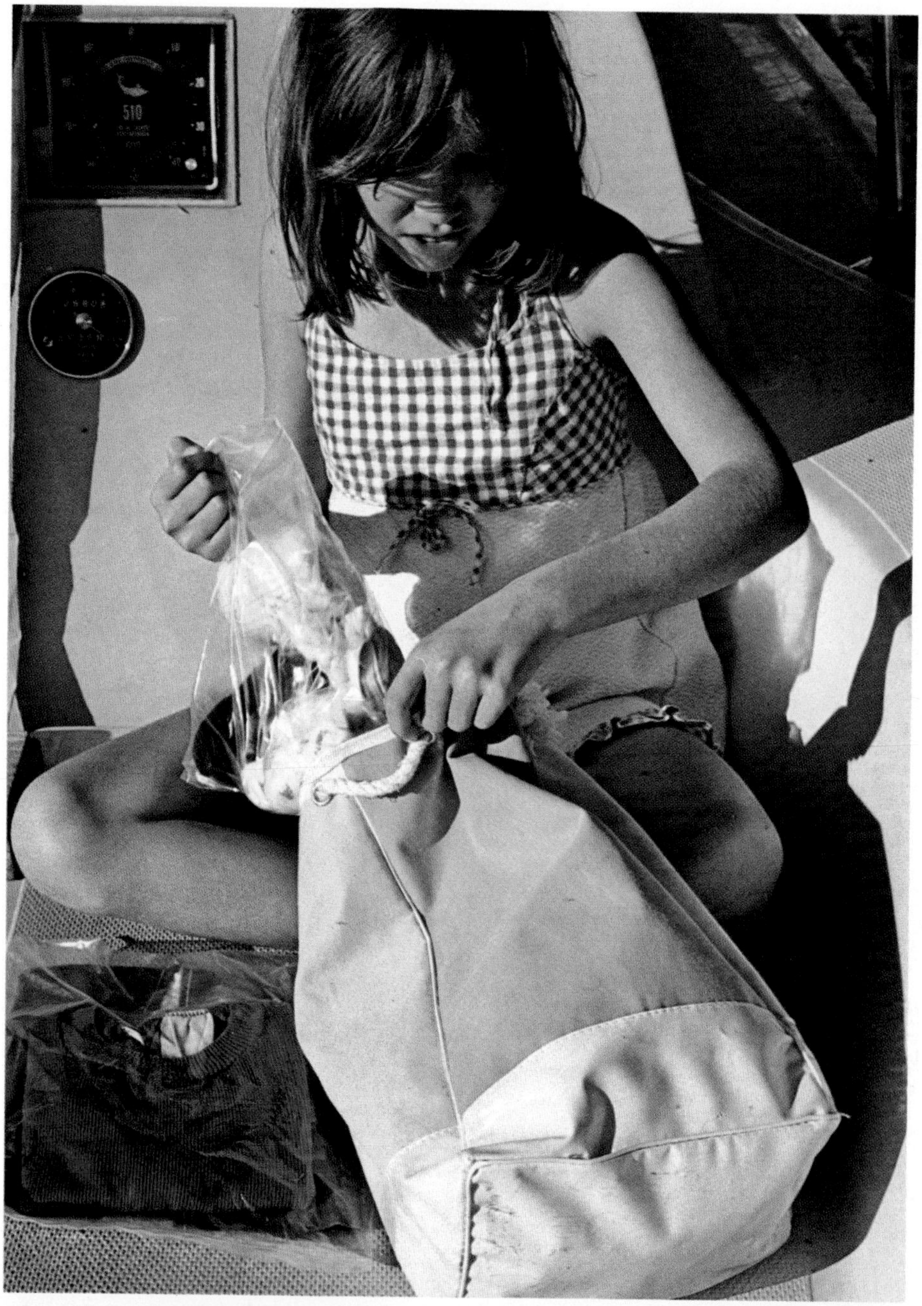

Completing the job of food stowage, Mary Gray pours noodles from their rigid paper carton into an airtight, zippered plastic bag, which occupies minimum space alongside other provisions in a plastic galley bin. The bags keep food dry; the bin affords the cook quick and visible access to whatever may be needed for a meal—avoiding the trouble of rummaging through cramped shelves.

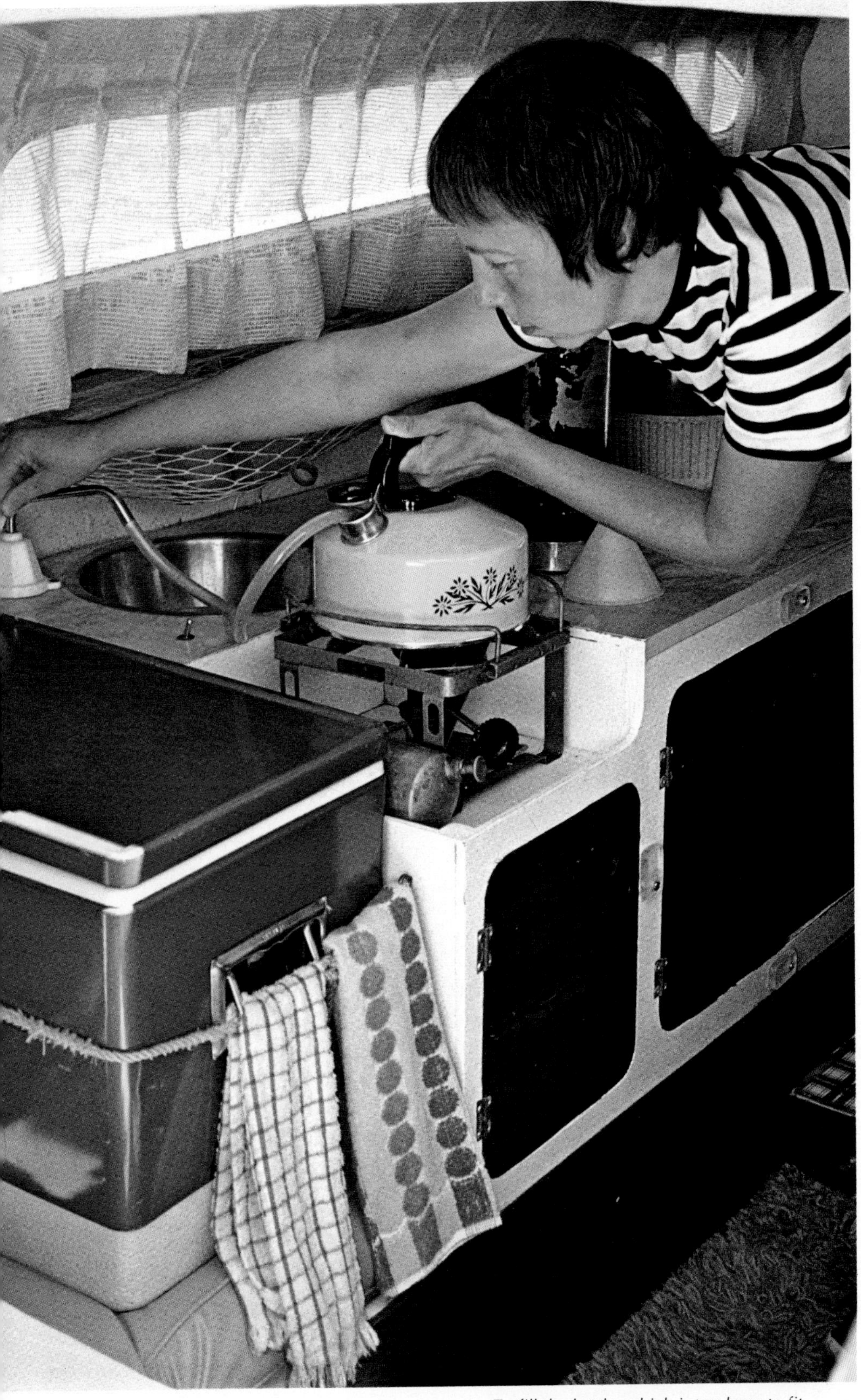

To fill the kettle, which is too large to fit under the sink faucet, Mary pumps water through a piece of plastic tubing. The same tubing also aids in rinsing pots and pans. Contrary to most galley arrangements, the stove is positioned in front of the sink; otherwise, flames from the burner would char the overhead. A line secures the portable ice chest and doubles as a towel rack.

A mosquito net for the companionway—here attached by Mary Gray, who designed it—is held by two loops of shock cord fastened to the jib-sheet cleats. The net's forward end leads over the hatch cover and is secured near the mast. Peter Gray, inside the cabin, adjusts the heavy canvas edging whose weight holds down the net's vertical flap.

When rain threatens, the netting comes off, the hatch cover is closed and a Dacron rain cover is fitted over the companionway. Loops of shock cord sewn to the cover's upper corners fasten to the jib-sheet cleats. The air space between the Dacron and the closed hatch—and around the loose bottom and sides—is sufficient for ventilation.

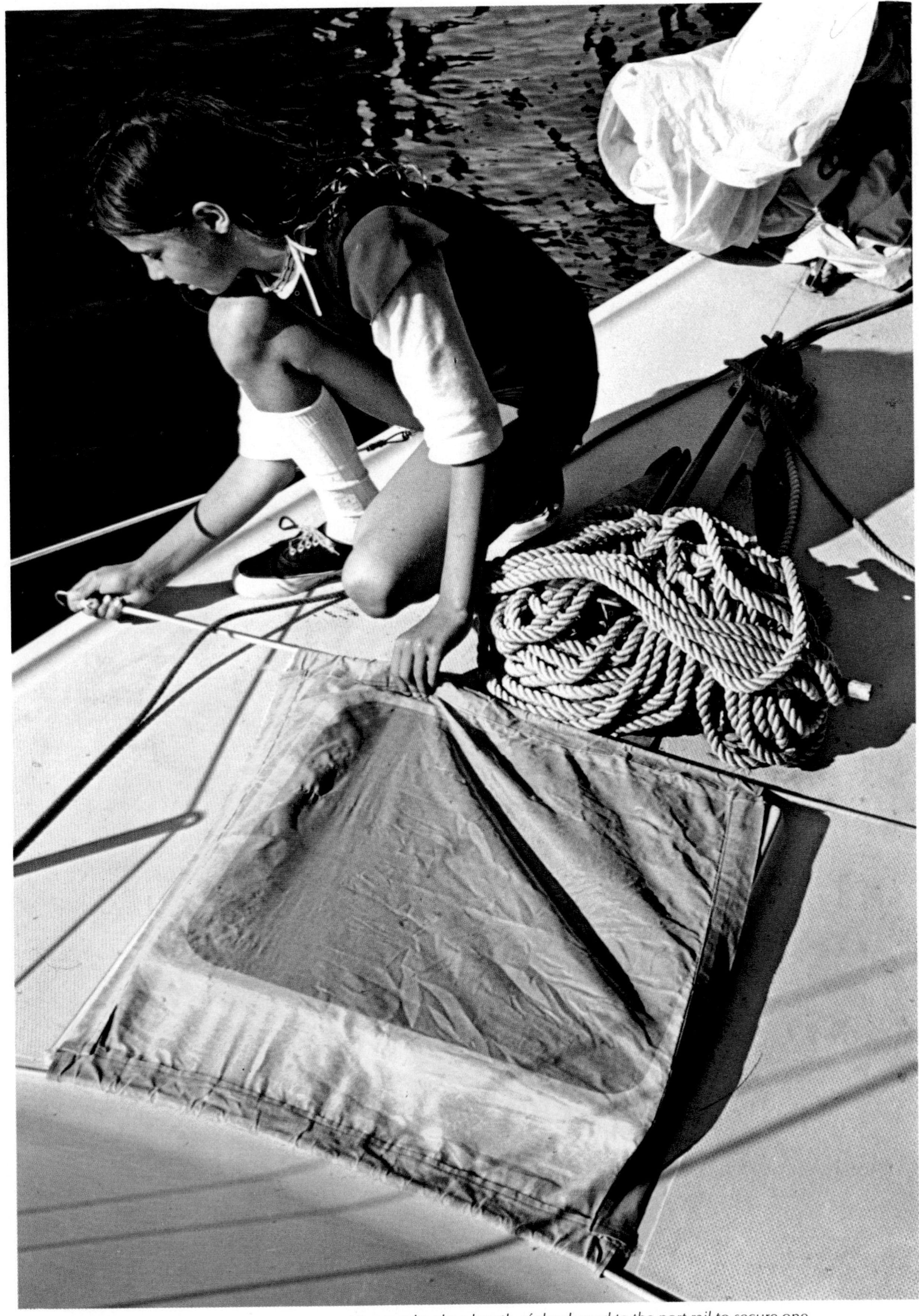

Margaret hooks a length of shock cord to the port rail to secure one end of a mosquito net covering the forward hatch. Two cords running athwartships through the hems hold the net to the deck; the hatch stays open to provide air and light for the forepeak sleeping quarters. When not in use, the net stows with Margaret's gear in the forepeak.

Mosquito netting with canvas edging, made by Mary Gray, keeps insects from invading the cockpit when the family and friends relax after a day's cruise. The thwartship poles at the forward and after edges of the netting, tied to the boom, hold the shelter aloft. Canvas strips give shape to the corners and also provide sufficient weight to make the sides hang vertically within the cockpit. Based on an idea formulated during a Bahamian cruise, this bug-free porch took two days to make and required only $12 worth of materials.

Moored before banks of lush foliage in the Thousand Islands, the Grays take a daytime break under the shade of a homemade Dacron awning. On most boats, such an awning is suspended from a pole placed above the boom. Gray, however, frequently rigs his pole under the boom, as here, securing it by lines attached to the boom itself, to the shrouds, and to various cleats and stanchions. Although this arrangement may sacrifice a little headroom in the boat's cockpit, it gives occupants better protection in case of a sudden rainstorm.

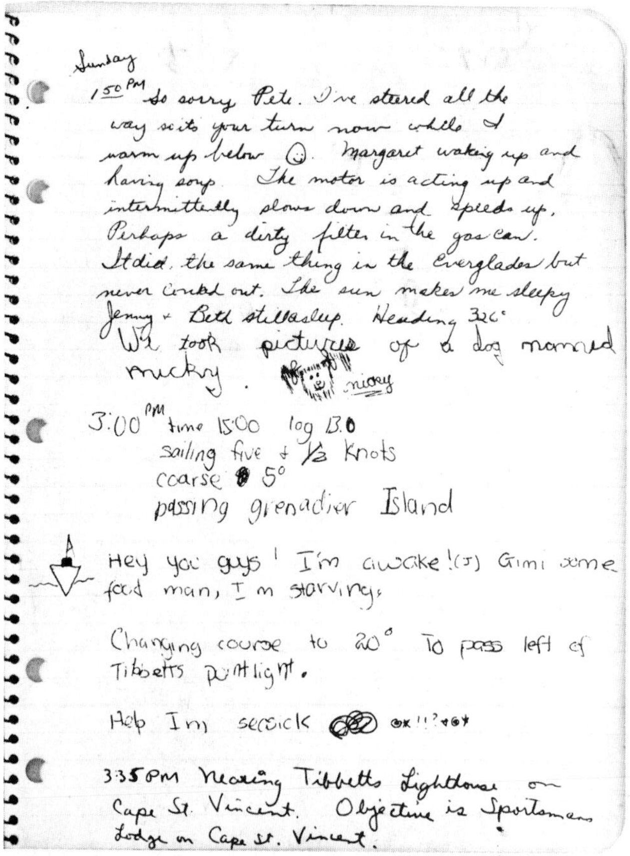

Sunday
1:50 PM So sorry Pete. I've steered all the way so it's your turn now while I warm up below ☺. Margaret waking up and having soup. The motor is acting up and intermittently slows down and speeds up. Perhaps a dirty filter in the gas can. It did, the same thing in the Everglades but never conked out. The sun makes me sleepy. Jenny + Beth still asleep. Heading 320°
We took pictures of a dog named micky. micky

3:00 PM time 15:00 log 13.0
sailing five + 1/2 knots
coarse 5°
passing grenadier Island

Hey you guys! I'm awake! (J) Gimi some food man, I m starving.

Changing course to 20° To pass left of Tibbetts point light.

Help I'm seasick !!?

3:35 PM Nearing Tibbetts Lighthouse on Cape St. Vincent. Objective is Sportsmans Lodge on Cape St. Vincent.

Taking advantage of a quiet moment at anchor, Margaret Gray makes an entry in the ship's spiral log. As the sample page at top indicates, everyone on board is a contributor. Entries are both serious and frivolous—relating to navigation, memorable sights seen, demands for food from a mutinous crew and despair of seasickness.

At day's end, the Grays moor close inshore and debark for a cookout. Part of the meal has been prepared aboard, but the rest will be charcoal-broiled on a portable grill. Whenever circumstances make it possible, the Grays camp ashore to eat or sleep, giving all hands a chance to stretch before returning to the close order of the little vessel.

10

5

No matter how adept a boatman may become at day sailing, his seamanship is rarely put to any real test until he goes cruising. Then he may routinely find himself maneuvering into a slip in a crowded unfamiliar marina, riding out a blow at anchor in an unprotected bay, or sailing at night to a distant landfall. Each of these situations calls for skills and quick decisions that are not demanded of a skipper in his home harbor. Perhaps even more challenging, he may have to cope with weather conditions that are rare at home—or that no sensible day sailor ventures out in. For example, the dense fog that rolls in through the island thoroughfares of the Maine coast may be an entirely new

SEAMANSHIP FOR CRUISERS

experience for a yachtsman visiting from balmy Louisiana, but if he and his crew are due in port by a specific date, he will have to voyage through it. Like the skipper of the socked-in schooner at left, he must remember to post lookouts, to sound his horn at the intervals prescribed by the maritime Rules of the Road, and to proceed slowly and as quietly as possible to catch the sound of foghorns, bells or breaking surf that will tell him where to head—and where to stay clear. Additionally, he can pick up some fogwise seaman's tricks from local mariners: in some cases, because of the warming effect of land areas, fog may be less thick on the leeward side of islands and headlands, and a knowledgeable skipper will plot his course accordingly. And whenever possible he will head slightly downwind of the bells and horns he expects to encounter, since sound travels farther in that direction.

Night sailing demands other knowledge and techniques to ensure a safe and comfortable cruise. The skipper must be certain that he can interpret the light signals displayed by other vessels, and he should make sure his own running lights are in prime working order. In plotting the course, he should plan to sail from lighted buoy to lighted buoy, and he should scrupulously avoid taking shortcuts through unmarked channels. All extraneous on-board lighting ought to be doused to allow the helmsman's eyes to adapt to the darkness. And if the skipper intends to sail on through most of the night or until the dawn, he should set alternate watches so that all of the crew members get a chance to bunk down below.

The trickiest part of a cruise may turn out to be the short leg between any harbor entrance and dock, both on the way in and on the way out. Many entrances are narrow, with swift currents, fast-shoaling water and rocks on either side. Inside the harbor, the mooring and docking areas are often jampacked with other boats. The difficulty of maneuvering in such cramped quarters is compounded by the design of many cruising vessels—which typically are heavy craft with long keels or high, wind-catching topsides and cabins. While these cruisers are comfortable and stable at sea, they may be clumsy and uncooperative at dockside—being not only hard to stop but also slow to answer their helms.

In addition, mooring arrangements vary endlessly from harbor to harbor. In a single port, the skipper may find an attractive, modern marina that—if it is not already filled—will offer him a tight dockside slip with preinstalled fenders and lines, and right next to it may be a concrete commercial wharf with barnacle-encrusted pilings where he will have to carefully lay out his own lines and fenders. Each of these mooring arrangements presents special problems in seamanship. And even if a skipper negotiates his landing with seamanlike adroitness, he may find himself wind- or tide-bound when he wants to leave port. At this point he will find essential a knowledge of how to coax his vessel away from the pier with a judicious combination of docking lines, rudder and engine, as described on the following pages.

Ghosting through fog, this schooner has a lookout forward—and jib down to reduce speed. At one-minute intervals the skipper sounds two horn blasts to show he is on the port tack.

Moored alongside a finger pier when the wind is light and not much tide is running, the skipper of this powerful twin-screw cabin cruiser will have little difficulty getting underway. After taking in his lines and fenders, he will simply put his engines in reverse and move gently away from the pier, keeping his helm amidships until his bow clears. He can then swing around to go down the channel. But if the wind had piped up astern strongly before his departure and slued his stern around, the skipper would have had to use one of the undocking techniques shown opposite and on the following pages.

When no one is on the dock to let go the final line securing a boat—or when the distance between boat and dock is too great for a crew member on the dock to cast off and jump back aboard safely, the solution is to double the line. Secure one end to a cleat on the boat; run the other end around a dockside cleat or bollard, then back aboard. As the boat draws clear, pay out the end slowly. When clear of the dock, drop the end and quickly haul in the line to avoid fouling it around the propeller or rudder.

Leaving a Strange Port

When spending the night in a strange port, the cruising skipper can often ride at anchor or on a mooring close by a marina or a yacht club. But just as frequently, he will find that he has to tie up alongside a dock or in a slip, crowded in among other boats. And if he is not used to bringing his boat alongside a dock, he should know the techniques for doing so *(pages 156-157)* —and also the tricks of casting off and getting underway that are shown here.

Getting away from a dock may be no problem if conditions are right. With wind and tide at a minimum, and on a boat with good power and maneuverability, the skipper starts his engine in neutral and casts off, beginning with the slack mooring lines. If there is no bystander at dockside to help him let go the last line, he can free it with a technique called doubling *(opposite, bottom)*. Then, putting the engine in gear, he motors smoothly away.

But in a fresh breeze or a swift tide, the skipper must often make skillful use of his mooring lines to pivot his boat away from his berth safely—particularly when his craft is a heavy cruising auxiliary with minimum engine power for the weight of the vessel.

These pivoting techniques are known collectively as warping; and in warping his boat the skipper generally employs a spring line, his engine and some skillful play with the rudder. In the examples on this page, the vessel's engine, working against the spring, forces one end of the boat against the pier; the contact point becomes a fulcrum, turning the boat's other end into the wind or current until the vessel is properly aimed to leave its berth without hitting any obstructions. The same principles can also be employed to perform other useful dockside maneuvers *(overleaf)*.

To warp away from a dock with wind or current astern (blue arrow), cast off all lines except one—a spring line led from a bow cleat to the dock (1). Power slowly forward with the rudder turned toward the dock, using a fender to protect the bow; the boat will pivot against the dock as the stern swings clear. Now cast off the spring line (2) and back slowly with rudder amidships until the bow is clear. Shift into forward and put the helm over to turn into the channel.

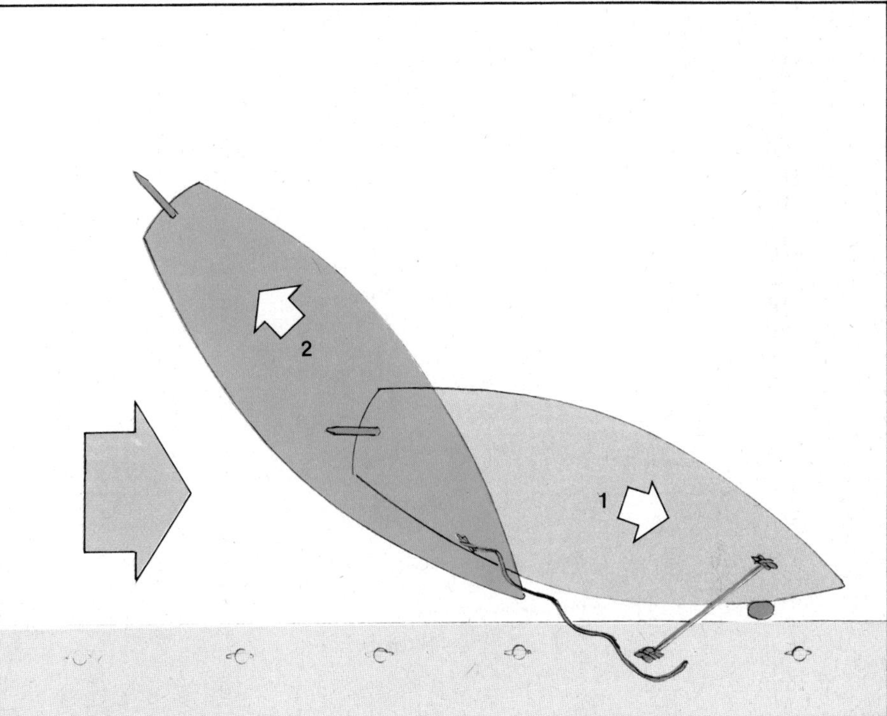

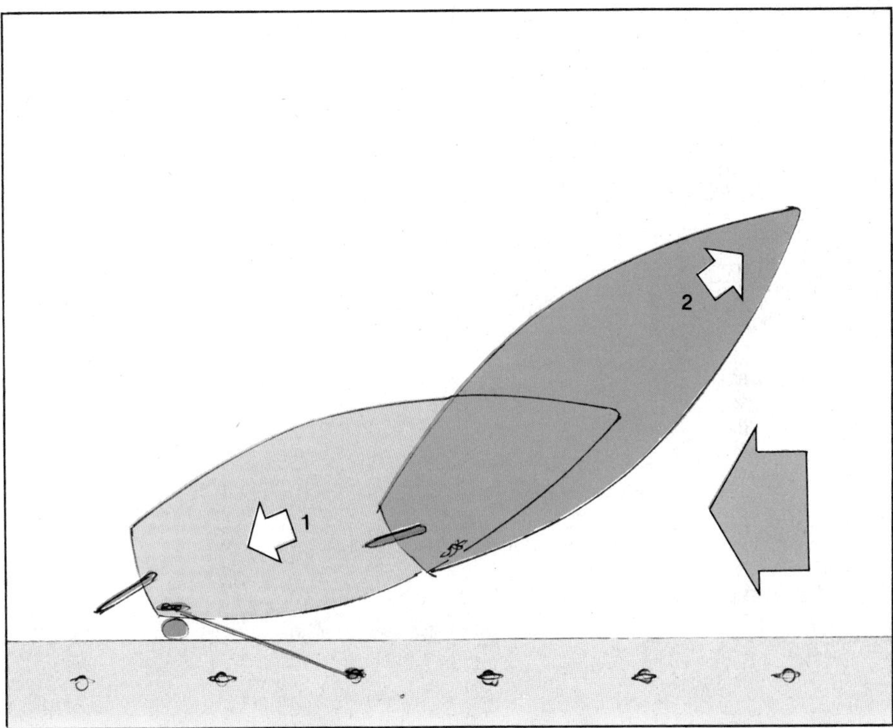

To get away from a dock with wind or current on the bow, begin by casting off all lines except a spring line led from a stern cleat to the dock (1). Place a fender on the quarter to prevent the boat from chafing on the pier. Then turn the rudder toward the dock, and back down slowly. This will force the stern into the dock against the fender, thus turning the bow away from the pier. When the boat is pointed out toward the channel (2), cast off the spring line. Put the engine ahead and the rudder over. Motor slowly into the channel.

To get away from a dock when pinned against it by wind or current (1), use a spring line leading from the stern. Place a fender at the stern to protect the topsides. With the rudder hard over toward the dock (2), back the boat against the spring; this pivots the stern against the fender and swings the bow outward. When headed away from the dock (3), cast off the spring; use a doubled line (page 136) if no one is on the dock. Put the helm amidships and move ahead slowly, watching the quarter as it swings toward the dock. With stern well clear, put the rudder over away from the dock and power ahead.

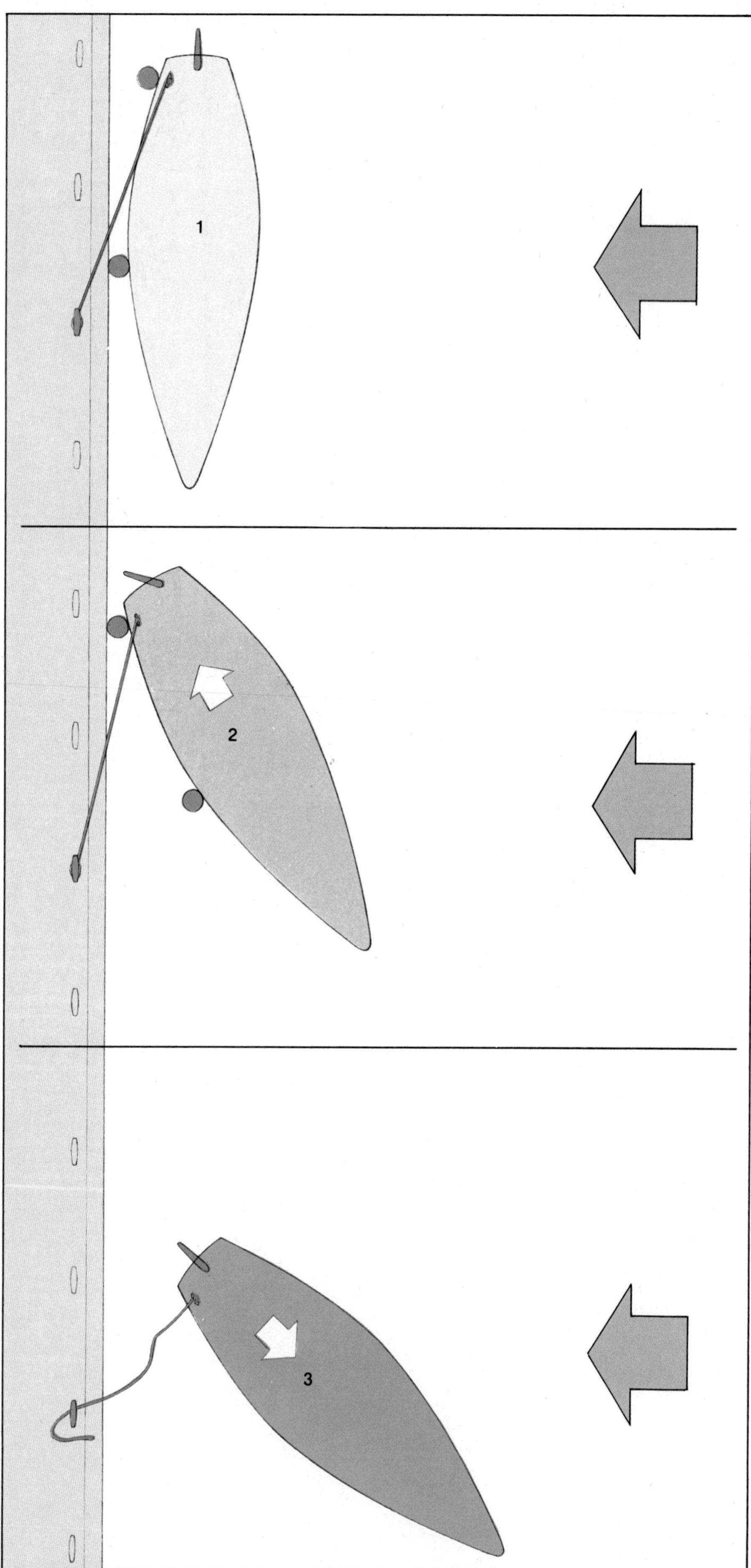

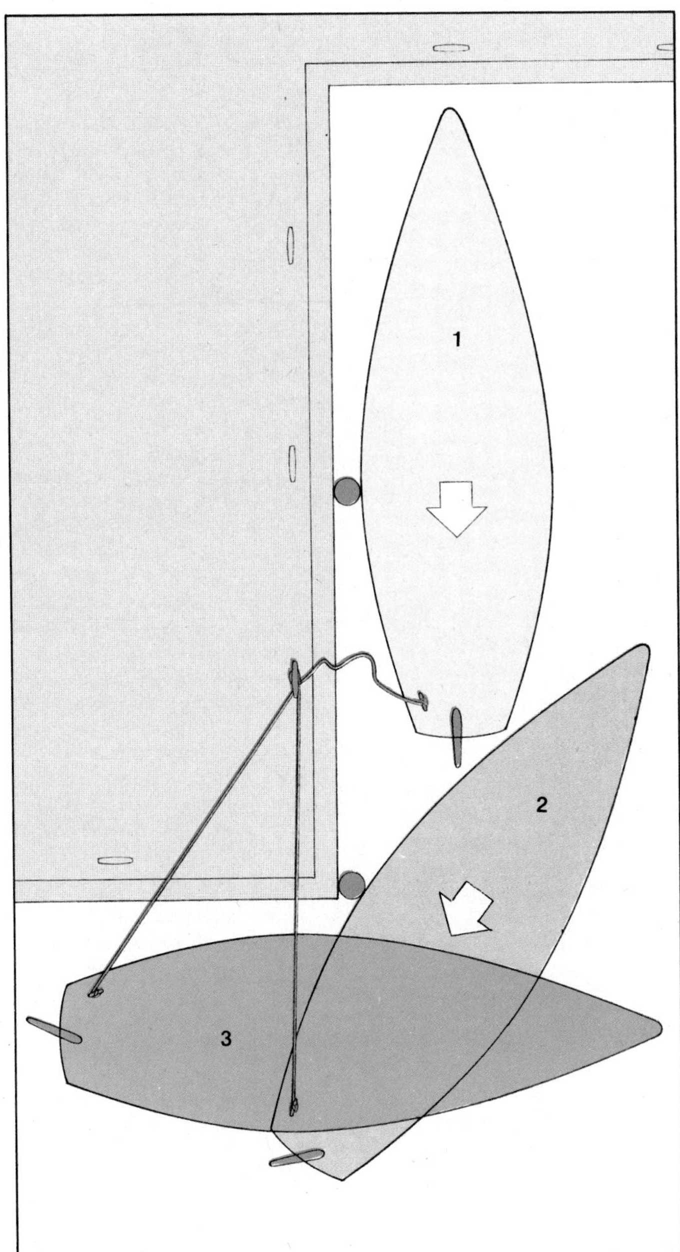

To back a boat around the corner of a dock (1), use a spring led from the dock to the stern. Place a fender at the corner of the dock for the boat to pivot on. With rudder amidships, back the boat slowly, paying out on the spring, which should be kept slack during the early part of the maneuver. When the corner of the dock is abeam of the boat (2), have a dockhand or a crew member take a strain on the spring. This prevents the boat from backing farther, at the same time swinging the stern around. A slight turn in the same direction helps to bring the boat parallel (3) to the end of the dock.

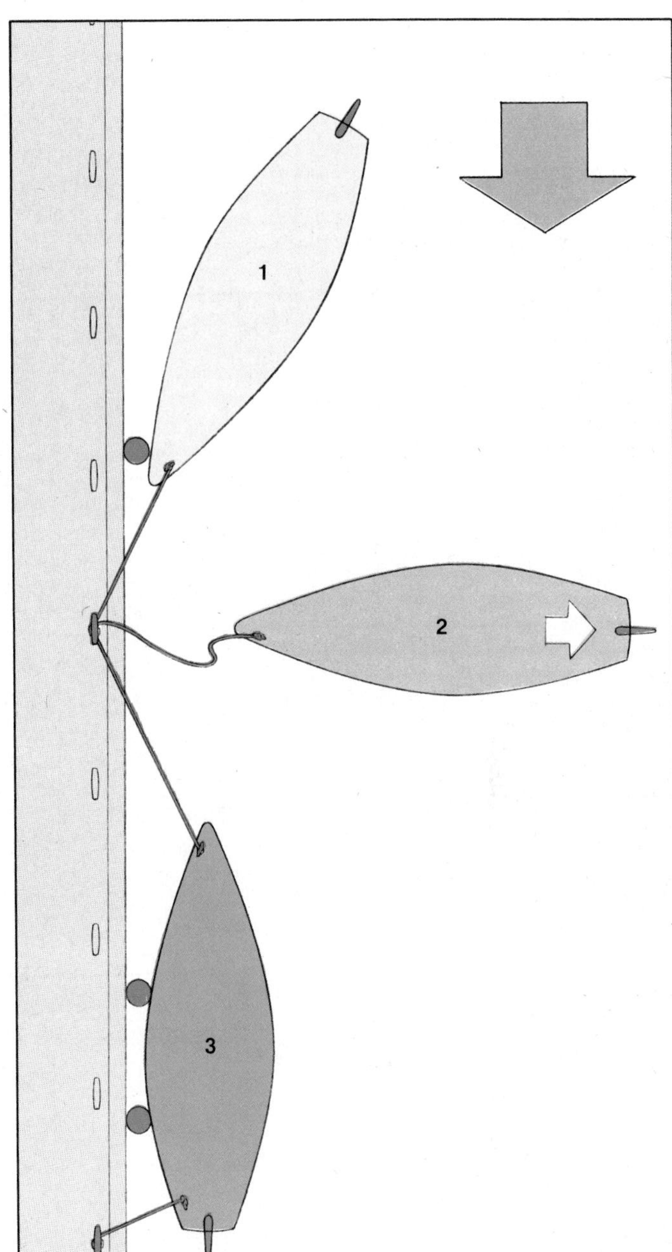

When a boat is moored with its stern facing into the current, it can be brought head-to—the preferred position—by the simple turning maneuver shown above. First, place a fender at the bow to protect it, and cast off all lines except a bow spring (1); the force of current will tend to swing the stern out to port. As the boat turns perpendicular to the dock (2), the helmsman may have to back off slowly with the engine to keep the bow clear. While the stern is continuing to make its swing (3), set fenders on the port rail, and heave a stern line to a dockhand in order to bring the boat snugly alongside.

Getting away from a dock (previous pages) can seem like a simple process compared to maneuvering away from the slips provided by some marinas and yacht clubs. The arrangement shown above is typical of many: bow lines are attached to rubber tires that float up and down on pilings with the rise and fall of the tide; stern lines are cleated to a floating dock. The procedure for this and similar tie-ups—detailed in the pictures on the opposite page—should be followed carefully to avoid hitting the pilings.

A Well-timed Flick of the Wrist

Instead of doubling the final line to cast it off a bollard or post (page 136), some skippers employ the method shown below. To use it, the bollard must be smooth surfaced and the line secured by means of a loop, such as a bowline or an eye splice. As the boat departs, the deckhand gives a quick flick on his end of the line; the other end will flip up, lifting the eye over the top of the bollard and freeing it.

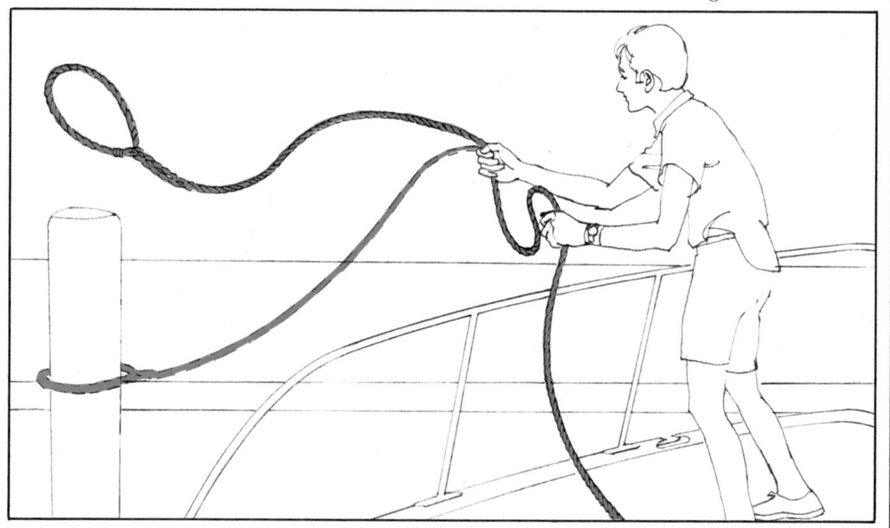

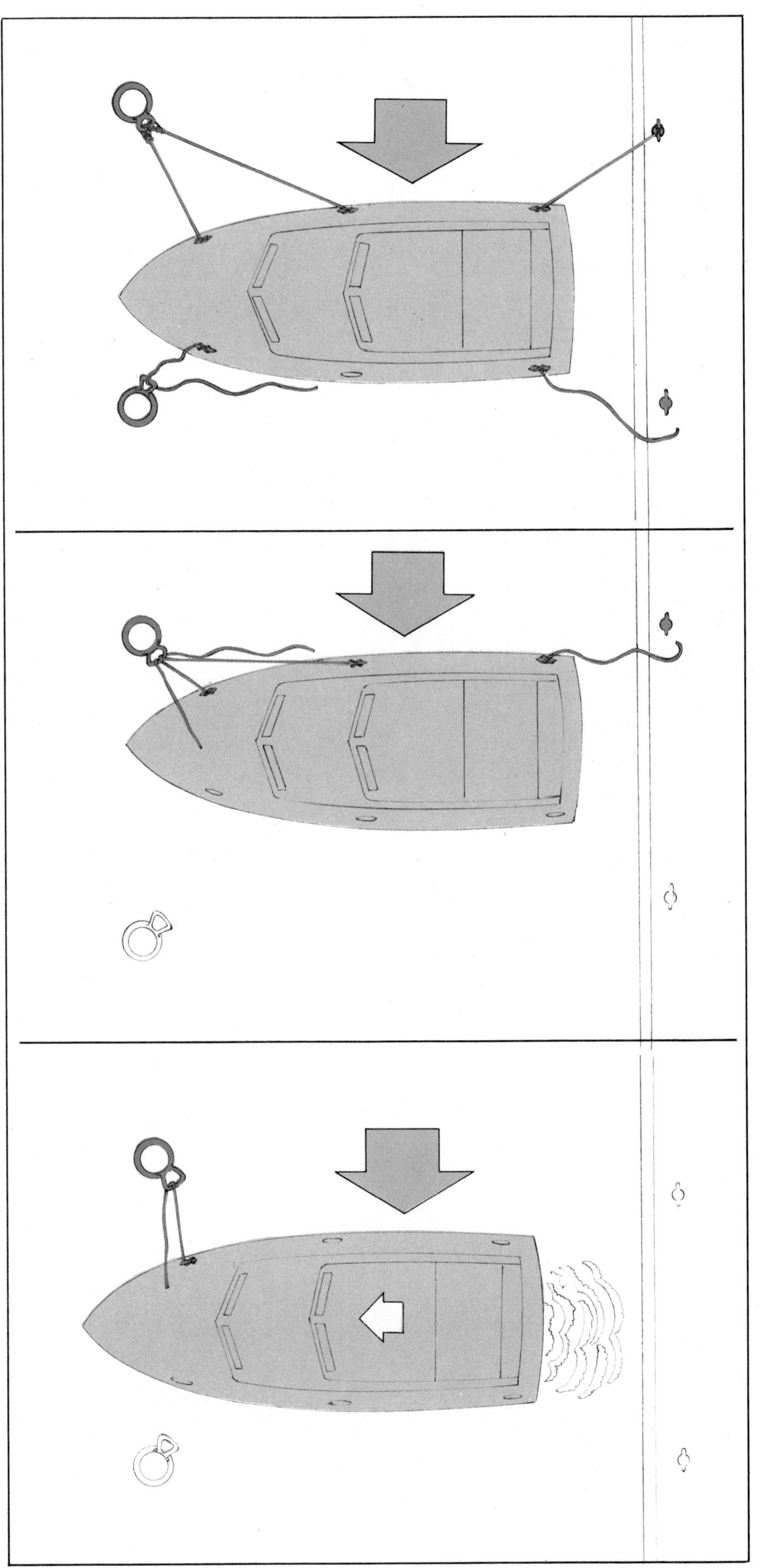

When leaving a slip, precise timing in the release of lines is more important than when getting away from a dock—particularly if, as here, the wind (or current) is abeam. First, ease off on the upwind lines, but do not release them entirely. The boat will drift to leeward, allowing the crew to cast off the lines from the downwind piling and cleat.

Next, start the engine, but leave the clutch in neutral. Haul the boat up to windward and double the bow line. Then cast off the stern line and the spring, in that order. If the boat begins to drift toward the dock, keep it off with short, intermittent bursts of power—making certain that all cast-off lines are safely aboard, out of the way of the propeller.

Alert the crew to stand by to fend off if necessary, and put the engine slow ahead. If the wind is gusty or the current running hard, snub the bow line briefly to assist the bow to turn into them. In calmer weather, simply slip the bow line free as the boat passes by.

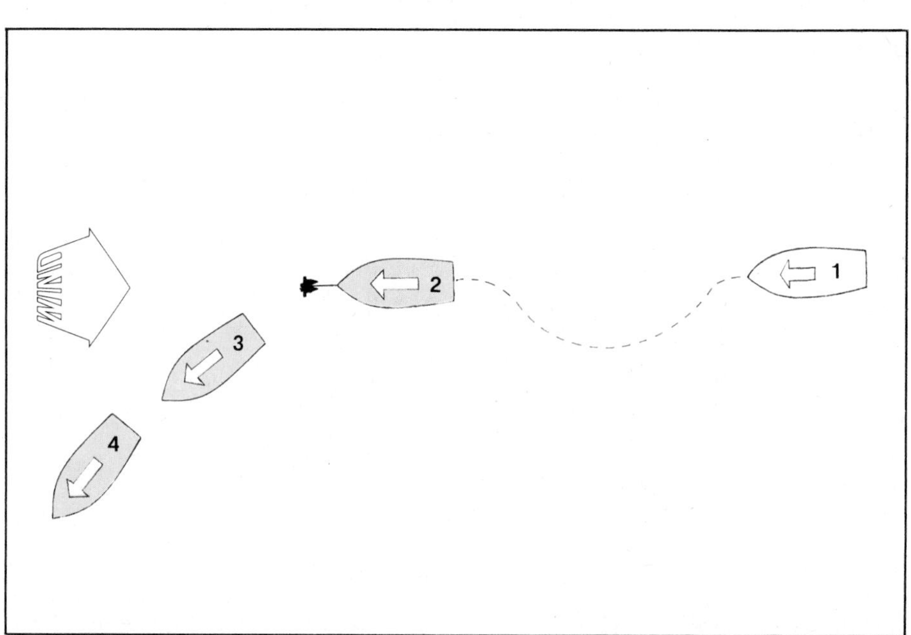

1 *In this diagram of a boat weighing anchor under sail, the hull outline at far right shows the boat's initial position—as it lies head to wind at the end of its anchor rode. The broken line is the boat's path. The shaded hulls correspond to the boat's position in each photograph. To start out, the skipper raises his main, lays the jib to port and bears off to port, gaining enough way to sail up on the anchor as his crew hauls in the rode.*

2 *When the boat's bow is directly over the anchor, the crewman tugs on the rode to break the hook from the bottom and hauls it up to surface level. The helmsman has headed directly back into the wind, and the mainsail is momentarily luffing. Immediately, however, he trims the main and heads off to port to get the vessel sailing again, while the crew prepares to make fast the rode.*

Sailing off the Hook

At least once in every cruising sailor's career will come a time when, as he is about to weigh anchor in a remote harbor, he discovers that his auxiliary engine will not start. In such circumstances, he will have to resort to the classic seaman's maneuver shown here—breaking away the anchor under sail.

To be successful, this maneuver must be carefully planned in advance. The boat must be sailed up to the anchor, arriving head to wind, with the mainsail luffing. But the boat must have enough steerageway so that the helmsman can head off smartly the moment the hook breaks loose. Otherwise he will find himself in irons, drifting backward out of control and in danger of hitting any other vessels that may be anchored nearby. In addition, the anchor must be brought aboard without fouling it in the jib.

The skipper must therefore decide in advance which tack he will sail on, and lay out the jib, loosely furled, on what will be the leeward side, ready to be raised the instant the anchor has been secured at water level. He should start out on the tack away from the direction of the anchor lead; that is, if the rode passes through the starboard bow chock, he should plan to sail off to port. This ensures that the jib and the anchor will be on opposite sides of the foredeck.

3 *Having secured the rode forward, the deckhand raises the jib. The skipper stands by to trim the leeward sheet. The anchor has been heaved just short enough to prevent its flukes banging the topsides when the boat begins to move ahead. For a few moments, the anchor will be allowed to trail in the water to wash off any mud or sand.*

4 *With sails trimmed and the sloop well underway, the crew goes forward to secure the anchor. Lying over the bow, he may plunge the anchor up and down in the water for a final cleaning before making it fast.*

A small dinghy rides on the forward side of a cruising yawl's second stern wave—close enough to keep the dink from veering into the path of a passing vessel, but far enough aft so that it will not skid up and bang the yawl's transom should the larger boat's speed suddenly drop. Poising the dink ahead of the wave's crest has another advantage: the dinghy always coasts downhill, thus reducing its drag on the yawl's forward motion.

Ready to go ashore, the crew of a boat anchored inside a jetty brings the dinghy alongside their cruising boat's quarter, where the topsides are lowest and thus easy for crewmen to slide over. The hand hauling in the painter leans well out over the rail in order to lead the dinghy alongside without letting it graze the topsides. Moreover, he is careful to bring the dinghy up to leeward, where waves will not bang it into the boat.

The Indispensable Dinghy

Every cruising boat should have with it a compact but reasonably seaworthy dinghy, which can be carried aboard on davits *(right)*, chocked to the deck *(below)*, or else trailed astern *(left)*. At anchor in a strange harbor, the dinghy—or dink, as it is often called—may provide the only link to shore. In addition, it is a passport to the leisurely exploration of quiet coves and isolated beaches.

Both trailing and on-board storage have their drawbacks. When towed, a dinghy tends to get in the way during tight maneuvers—tangling with other boats in a crowded channel, or catching around pilings when coming alongside or getting underway from a dock. In such cases, the towline must be shortened and a crew member detailed to keep the dinghy clear of obstructions. On the other hand, if a boat has no stern davits, bringing a dinghy aboard is a cumbersome process unless properly executed *(overleaf)*; and once shipped, it takes up valuable space.

An increasingly popular solution to both towing and on-deck stowage problems is the inflatable dinghy constructed of synthetic-coated nylon *(pages 148-149)*. Light and easy to haul aboard, it can be stowed deflated in a cockpit locker.

The most convenient way to carry a dinghy is with stern davits—but these can only be mounted aboard a substantial vessel like this broad-beamed power cruiser. Small cranes with blocks and tackles, the davits hold the dinghy above water; extra lines leading to the cruiser's stern cleats keep it from swinging.

Since most sailboats have narrow after sections that would make the stern davits impractical, a dinghy must be set in chocks and securely lashed down, usually on the cabin top, as above, or on deck. If the dink is stowed upright, like this one, a cover must be fitted to keep out rain or sea water.

The best method for bringing a dinghy from the water to the deck of a sailboat that lacks davits is to hoist it aboard with a halyard and three-way bridle (right). One leg of the bridle is tied to a lift ring in the dinghy's transom, and the two other legs are tied to the forward thwart supports. The halyard is made fast at the point where the boat's weight will balance on the bridle. As one crew member takes up the halyard, the others guide the dinghy clear of the topsides and over the life lines onto the deck.

Once the dink is on board, the halyard is unhooked from the bridle and the dinghy turned upside down with its rails centered over the deck chocks. It will be secured with canvas straps that cross over the dinghy's bottom and tie down on either side.

At anchor, a dinghy is usually tied astern. But if a contrary wind or current causes the dink to ride up and bump the transom or topsides, mooring it amidships, as here, is a handy solution. The dink is simply hitched fore and aft, and two fenders dropped between it and the cruising boat to prevent contact. This technique is effective only in light winds and quiet seas, however. Should the seas begin to liven, the tender must be secured elsewhere (below) before it tosses its fenders and bangs again against the hull.

In an anchorage where the swinging room is limited and the waters choppy, the dinghy may be set forward of the vessel by tethering it to the anchor rode. This is done by running the cruising boat up on the rode and then tying the dinghy painter to the rode with a rolling hitch near the water's surface. The rode is then paid out until the vessel falls far enough back to clear the tender and re-establish its own safe anchoring scope.

Another way of keeping a troublesome dink from bumping is with the spinnaker pole. The pole is attached to its mast socket—as when rigging the spinnaker—but with its hook fasteners opening downward. The topping lift is then shackled to the pole's outboard end to hold it level, and the pole is lashed to a shroud to keep it from swinging fore and aft. The dinghy's painter is led through the outboard hook and then inboard to a life line. A pull on the trip line attached to the spinnaker hook releases the painter. After dark, an anchor light should be hung on the topping lift to indicate the dink's presence.

With his nine-foot nylon dinghy laid out on the foredeck, a skipper inflates it with a foot pump, a process that takes about five minutes. Like many modern inflatables, this dinghy possesses two separate air chambers for safety reasons: it will float with four persons aboard even if one of the chambers should suffer a puncture and deflate.

The Well-equipped Inflatable

Since their light weight and broad beam make inflatable dinghies hard to row in strong winds or currents, many models can be outfitted with a small outboard mounted aft on a tubular steel bracket that slides into molded rubber beckets. Some dinghies also carry a small dodger forward, to prevent spray from splashing inboard when underway.

Before launching the dinghy, the skipper checks the pressure in both compartments. In normally warm weather, the skin should be taut; if wrinkles are present, he must take a few additional strokes on the foot pump. But when the dinghy is to be kept in the sun on a hot day, it should be left slightly underinflated to allow for expansion inside.

Cautiously making its way into a harbor late at night, a power cruiser employs its searchlight to hunt for an anchorage. Out of courtesy to the sleeping fleet, the operator of the light keeps the beam down low as he sweeps it across the water to find a mooring and to avoid any obstructions.

An invaluable accessory for night sailing is a hand-held, high-intensity searchlight; its 15-foot self-coiling cable plugs into a deck outlet and draws power from the boat's DC electrical system. The lamp has a quartz-iodine filament bulb that puts out three times the candle power of most conventional spotlights—producing a narrow beam that penetrates a mile or more of darkness. Similar lights can also be mounted on a boat's bridge or forward deck and operated either by hand or by control from the steering console.

Night Sailing

Occasionally, any cruising skipper will find himself sailing at night, perhaps to make up lost time in a tight schedule—or perhaps for the sheer adventure of it. Nocturnal trips naturally call for an extra measure of caution and forethought. First, be sure all running lights are in good working order. Stow the day's accumulation of loose gear—cushions, clothing, coffee mugs and anything else that might trip someone up in the dark. Plot the vessel's course in advance, and study charts thoroughly. If the weather looks uncertain, reduce canvas before dark while all hands can still operate efficiently.

Equally important, be certain that a searchlight—either the battery-operated type or, better still, a powerful plug-in version like the one opposite—is on board and that it is functioning properly. A searchlight can be useful in many ways —to spot a mark's identification number, pick a safe course through flotsam-filled waters, enter a harbor or reinforce the message of the running lights in a heavily traveled area *(right)*.

A searchlight must not be overused, however. Paradoxically, in most cases one of the important keys to safe and pleasurable nocturnal trips is to hold down as far as possible on any artificial light, which otherwise can interfere with night vision —the eye's sensitivity to faint black-and-white stimuli. This perceptual power is easily lost; a burst of bright light will produce night blindness for a period of seconds or even minutes, depending on the light's intensity and the individual's eyes. Thus, when a searchlight is necessary, it should be wielded by a crewman who is stationed up forward, and he should be cautioned to keep the beam away from the helmsman. Some light is needed at the helm, of course, in order to illuminate the binnacle or the instrument panel. But the light should be passed through a filter having a red tint, since this color seems to have the least harmful effect on a person's night vision.

Similarly, if the helmsman needs to read a chart he should use a red-filtered flashlight or install a red bulb in an ordinary flashlight—although his night vision will remain even keener if a crew member belowdecks reads the chart for him and communicates instructions by voice.

A crewman aboard a sloop in a highly trafficked sea lane plays his spotlight on the sails every few minutes to announce his vessel's position and establish right of way over approaching powerboats. Because the glare interferes with the helmsman's visual adaptation to darkness, this vital safety measure should be executed very quickly, and only when there is a real hazard of potential collision.

To weather a blow at dockside, double the bow and stern lines. If any of the lines end in an eye splice, place that line on the cleat or bitt first, with the second line belayed securely above. Fix sturdy chafing gear where the lines pass through chocks; rig as many fenders as possible for maximum protection.

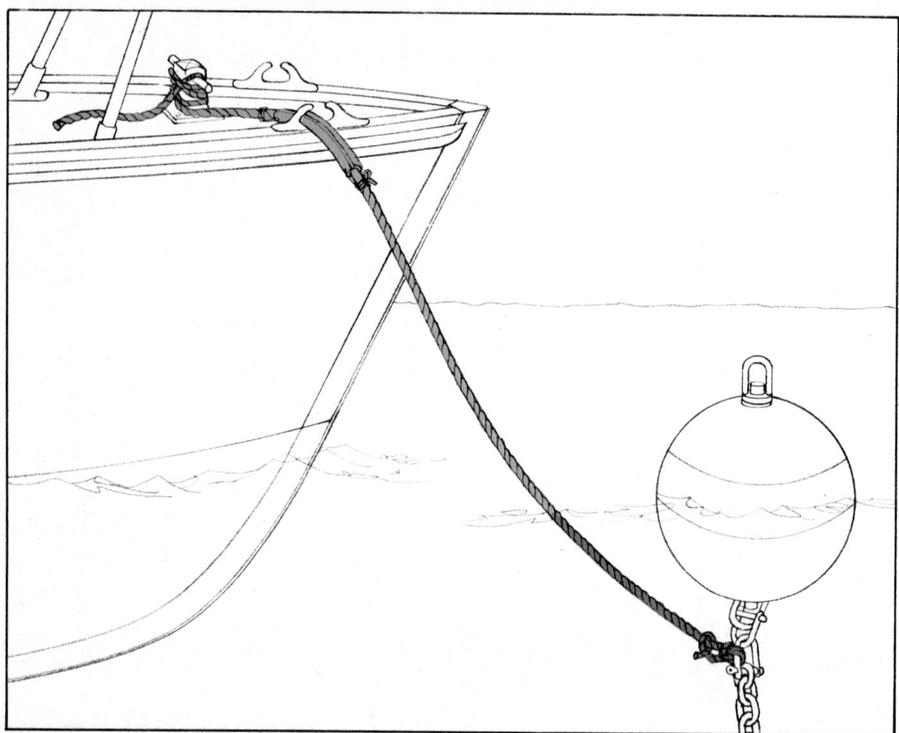

Since the flotation buoy is the weakest link in most moorings, the stress should be put directly on the chain below it when a storm threatens. Reach under the buoy and take two turns with a heavy line through the lower of two shackles underneath. Then make the line fast with a bowline or fisherman's bend.

Getting Set for a Blow

When the Coast Guard weather stations crackle with predictions of heavy winds —34 knots or more—prudent skippers cancel their cruising plans and ride out the blow in a safe harbor. They batten all the hatches and portholes, secure loose gear, and take some sensible precautions against the possibility of the boat's dragging anchor—or, if the boat is made fast to the dock or mooring, against breaking loose and running adrift.

Preparations for an impending storm begin with selecting a well-protected site within the harbor, in the lee of a high land mass or a substantial breakwater. Stay away from a crowded anchorage, if possible, since the least amount of dragging by one boat will bring it down on the next. Find a space that will allow for a generous amount of scope on the anchor rode.

Next, set out the boat's storm anchor. Normally, a 7-to-1 ratio of depth to rode is recommended, but for added safety, let out several more fathoms to make the scope 9 to 1. Then add a second anchor to windward—or even a third—to increase holding power *(right)*. Each extra anchor, run out at an angle from the first, will inhibit the tendency of the bow to veer back and forth, creating stresses that could wrench a single anchor loose from the bottom. In those situations when swinging room is limited, the three-anchor rig shown at near right *(bottom)* will hold the boat in position while still allowing enough scope to prevent dragging.

If the approaching storm catches the boat at a dock or float, double the bow and stern lines to distribute the strain. Make sure the doubled lines are equal in length; if one line is shorter, it will take all the strain and may break. When the vessel is hitched to a guest mooring, ask the harbor master how big the mushroom is and how much tonnage it is designed to handle. Even if the mooring is pronounced adequate, it is wise in a storm to make fast directly to the forged steel fittings on the mooring chain *(left)* rather than to the less sturdy fittings atop the flotation buoy.

Once the boat seems secure in its place, tour the deck and lash down any equipment that might take flight in a high wind. Sails should be laced snugly under their covers, and the covers themselves lashed with extra line in two or three places. The ensign, the burgee and any other flags should be stowed. And the dinghy, which is likely to be swamped in high seas and wind, should be brought aboard and securely strapped down.

Expecting a gale, this skipper has flanked his 20-pound storm anchor with a brace of smaller anchors. The amount of swinging room and expected force of the wind dictate which of the two patterns below he will choose. Since a single deck fitting would probably not be strong enough to stand the pull of his 6.5-ton sloop in this wind, he divides the strain, making fast the center rode to the mast with a fisherman's bend and belaying the others to the mooring bitt on the foredeck.

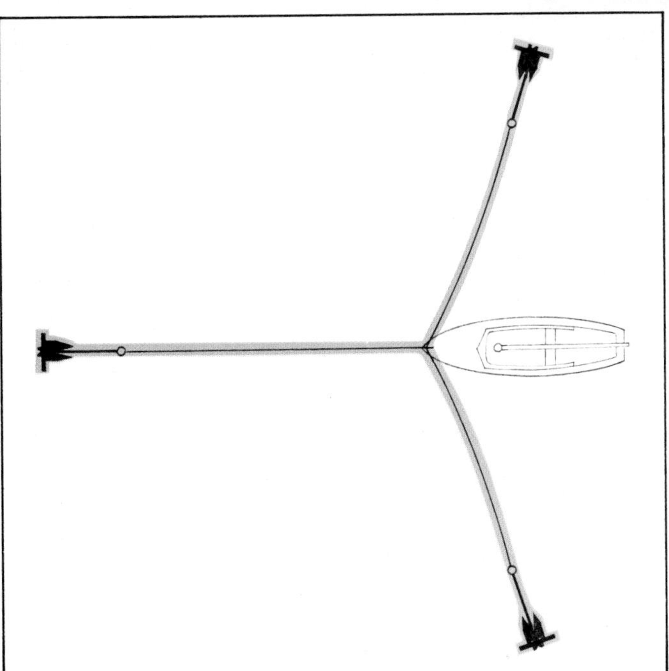

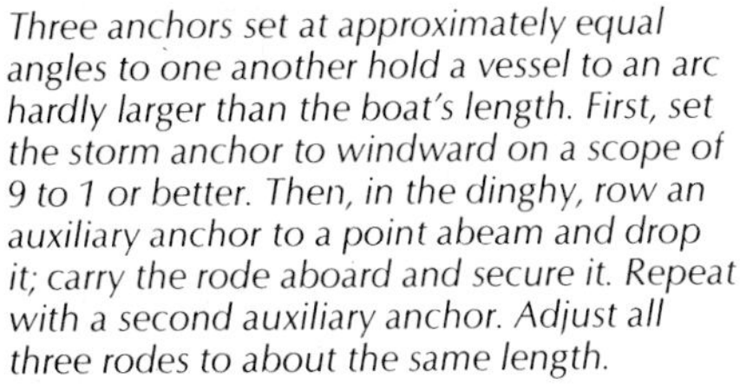

Three anchors set at approximately equal angles to one another hold a vessel to an arc hardly larger than the boat's length. First, set the storm anchor to windward on a scope of 9 to 1 or better. Then, in the dinghy, row an auxiliary anchor to a point abeam and drop it; carry the rode aboard and secure it. Repeat with a second auxiliary anchor. Adjust all three rodes to about the same length.

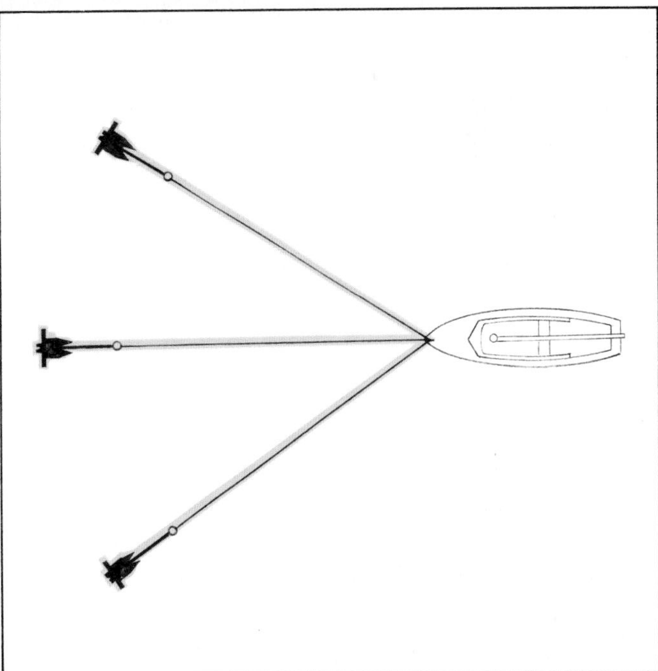

In particularly severe storms—with winds of about 60 knots or more—some skippers set three anchors to windward. The central anchor carries most of the strain. The two flanking anchors relieve some stress and keep the bow from veering back and forth—a phenomenon called horsing. If the wind swings the bow to port, for example, the starboard anchor will quickly bring it back.

The Convivial Raft-Up

An attraction of cruising for the more gregarious yachtsman is the raft-up, or raft, a communal way of mooring that enables sailors at anchor to tie up together so they can move freely from boat to boat in what usually becomes a floating party. In a raft, only one boat needs to be anchored; but it should be the largest one, and its hook should be firmly set.

All boats, power or sail, should approach the raft either upwind or upstream, depending on whether the boats are lying to the wind or the current. A sailboat skipper joining a raft should drop his jib before approaching, since a flapping sail can easily rip on the next boat's rigging; if the wind is at all brisk, he ought to drop his main as well and come alongside under power. The bow line should be heaved to the neighboring boat first, followed by a stern line; the boat can then be hauled in the last few feet. The skippers of both boats should rig a full complement of fenders; even a small swell can bang two rafted boats together. It is also wise to rig spring lines to keep boats aligned across the raft: one spring from the bow of each vessel to the stern of the adjacent boat, and another spring from stern to bow.

If any skipper wants to leave the raft before the party is over, he can do so with a minimum of disruption by using the technique shown opposite, at bottom. And before bedding down for the night, the remaining skippers should break up the entire raft and moor their boats separately—not only to restore peace to the anchorage but because an unexpected squall could wreak havoc among a raft of boats held by a single anchor.

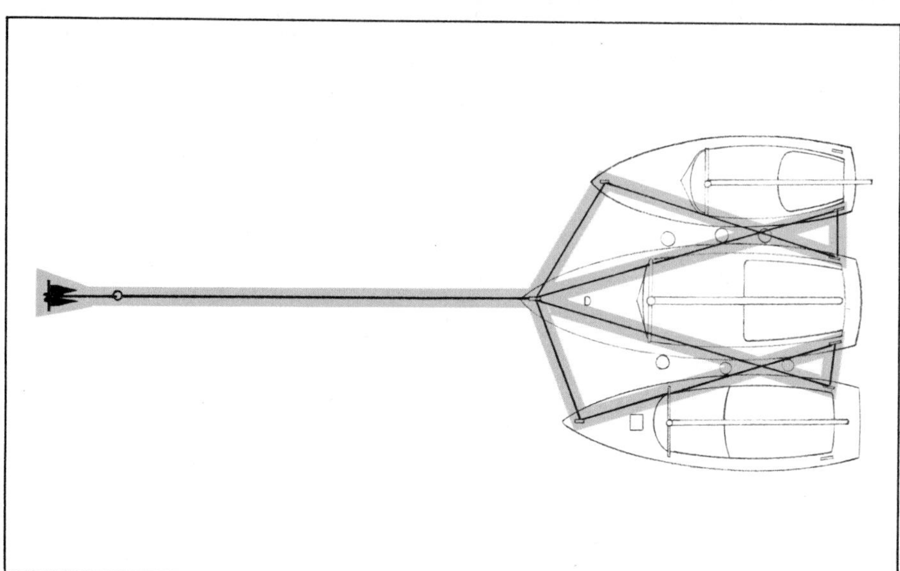

Held by bow, stern and spring lines, three sailboats ride to a single anchor in this small raft-up. The outer boats have taken care to stagger their masts so that their spreaders do not become entangled with those of the center boat when the raft rocks in the wake of passing vessels. Strategically placed fenders provide protection for the topsides.

In a big raft-up like the one above, sailboats moor at one end of the raft and powerboats at the other; boats of approximately the same size are placed adjacent to one another. Since adjoining decks will be roughly the same height in this arrangement, the railing of a boat will be less likely to scrape its neighbors' topsides as the raft rocks. Moreover, boatmen can visit back and forth on the raft with a minimum of clambering.

To extricate an inside boat from a raft without breaking up the entire flotilla, first cast off the spring lines to the adjacent vessels. Then rig a line joining the bows of the two neighboring boats to keep them from drifting apart; run another line to the neighbors' sterns, leading it around the bow of the exiting boat. Cast off the original bow and stern lines, station crew members at either rail to fend off, and back out slowly.

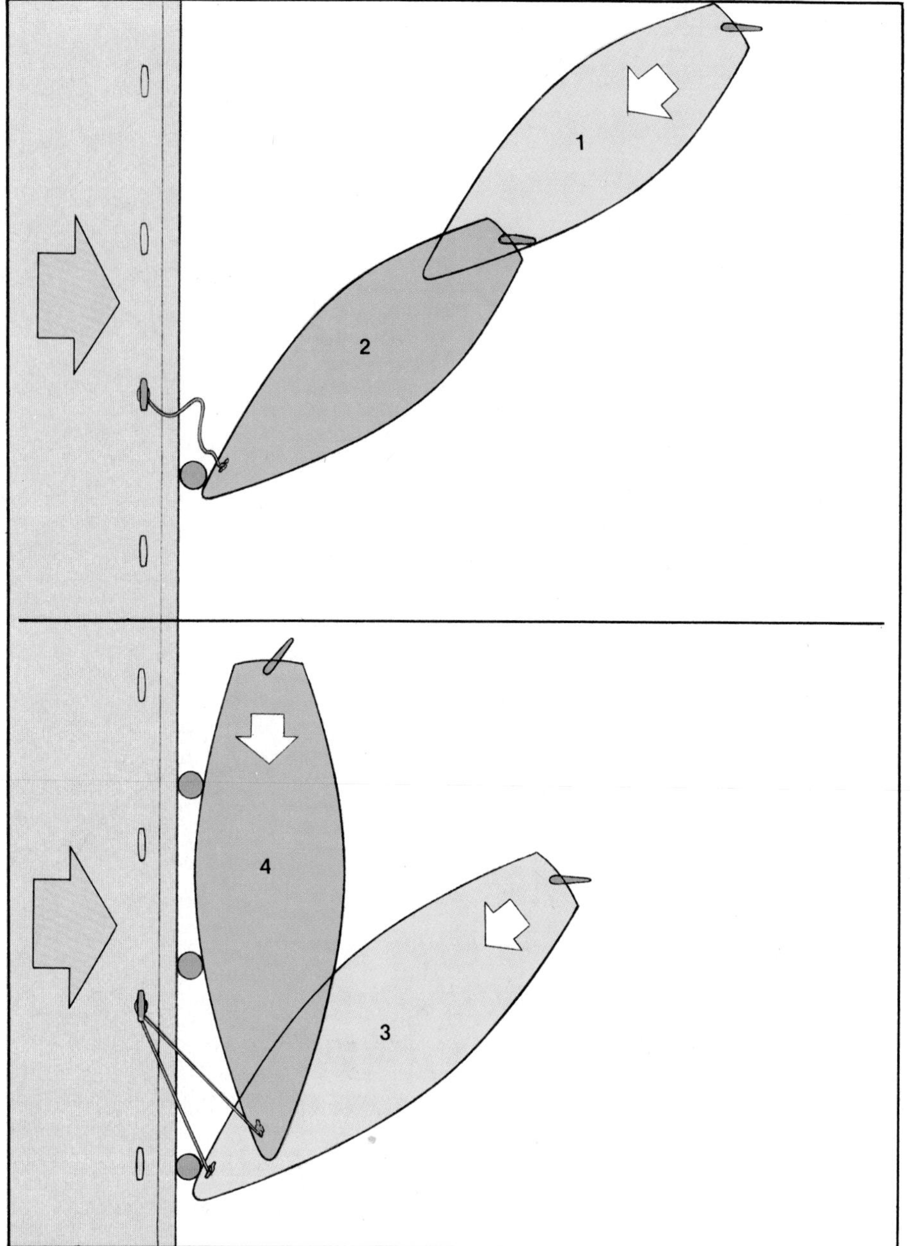

To land at a dock from which the wind or current (blue arrow) is moving off, approach at a 45° angle, with the engine slow ahead and rudder turned away from the dock (1). Ready a bow spring and place a fender at the bow. As the bow reaches the dock (2), secure the spring. Then come ahead slow with rudder still turned (3); the stern will swing in as the bow pivots on the fender. As the boat lies alongside, set out fenders for the topsides (4). Other mooring lines may now be rigged. If the skipper wants to stop only briefly, he can lie alongside under the bow spring alone, using forward power and with the rudder turned, as here, to keep his stern against the dock.

Docking under Duress

Arriving in a strange harbor, the visiting cruiser may have to lie alongside a crowded dock, to moor fore and aft between a pair of pilings or to squeeze into a slip *(pages 158-159)*. Wind and tide can complicate such maneuvers—but an accomplished yachtsman can sometimes turn these forces to advantage *(opposite)*.

Of all these situations, the simplest is the one pictured at left, where the skipper employs a single bow spring to lay himself alongside a dock. Wherever possible, he should come into the dock upwind or upcurrent, and he should scrupulously avoid tying up overnight on a dock's windward side, where, even with fenders out, he could be forced dangerously hard against the bulkhead or pilings.

The maneuvers at right are somewhat trickier. To jockey into a berth between two other vessels, a skipper can usually bring his boat in on a short spring line; but with the wind or current running parallel to the dock, some skippers prefer to dispense with the spring, and use the wind or current to edge their way to dockside under power alone *(opposite, top left)*.

The most difficult mooring situation of all is to tie up bow and stern between two offshore pilings. If the wind or current is running directly in line with the pilings, the boatman heads up to the windward piling and secures his bowline. Next he pays off this line, drifting back until he can reach the leeward piling to make fast his stern line. Then he takes in his bow line until he is midway between the pilings. If the wind or current is moving at even a slight angle, his stern will drift away from the second piling, and he must use the tactic described opposite, at top right.

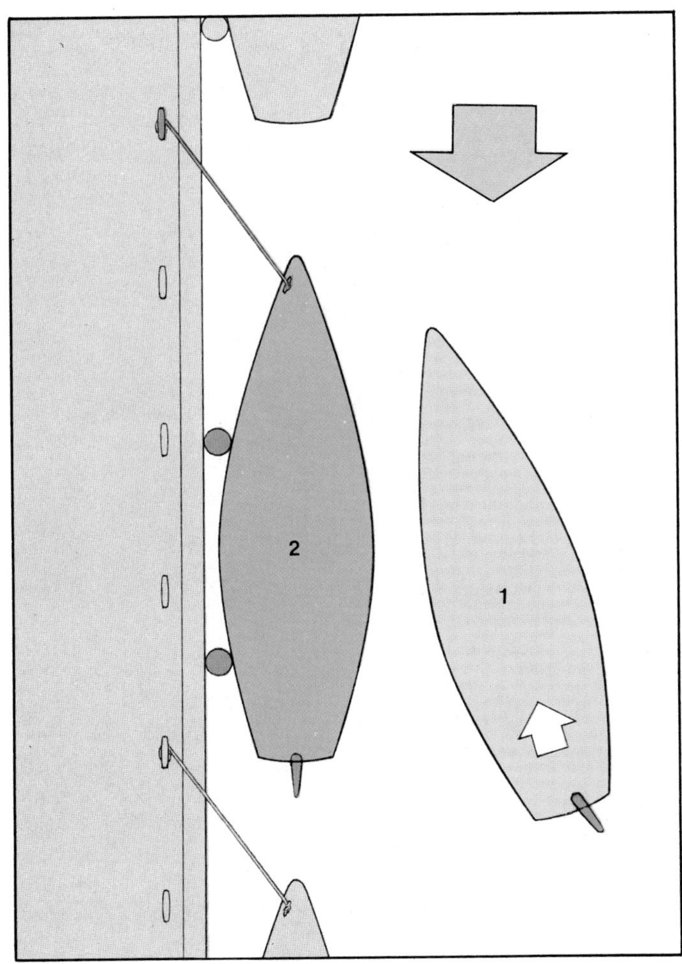

To use wind or current to assist in entering a tight berth, power slow ahead at a slight angle to the dock (1), keeping wind or current on the bow, and applying just enough forward throttle to keep stationary. As the wind or current pushes the bow in toward the dock, give the engine a short burst of power with rudder away from the dock. This will swing the stern in without putting way on. Repeat with intermittent jabs of the throttle until the boat settles neatly in its slot (2).

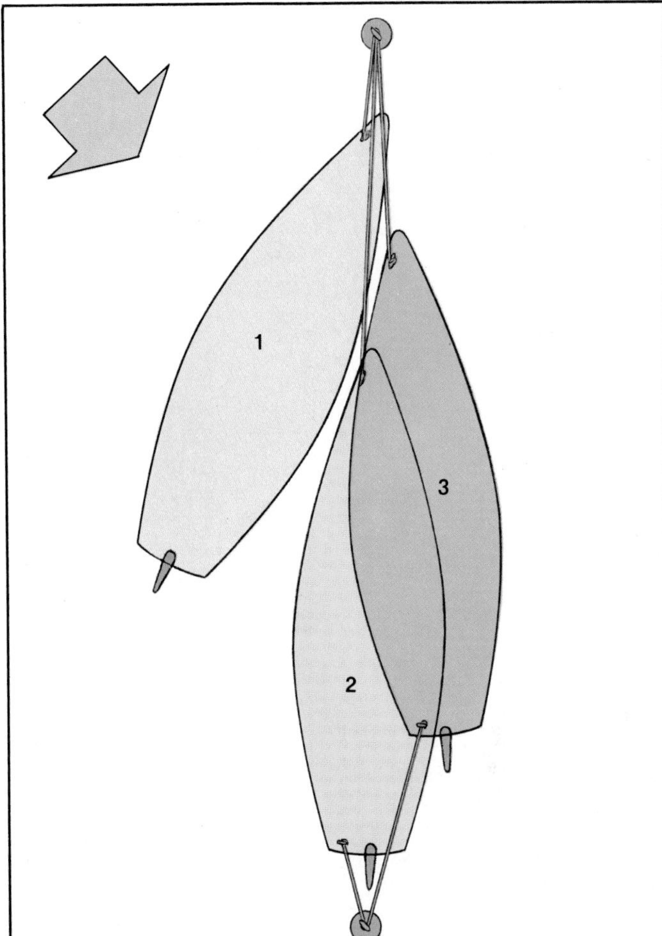

To moor between pilings in a crosswind or a crosscurrent, approach the forward piling from the upwind side, at a slight angle to the wind or current (1). Secure the bow line to the piling, and pay out slowly. As the boat falls back, the wind or current swings the stern toward the after piling (2); now secure the stern line to that piling. Adjust the lines until the boat lies midway between the pilings (3). The same technique is used when tying up fore and aft to mooring buoys.

The All-Purpose Boathook

A valuable aid in any mooring situation is the ship's boathook—a stout pole with a carefully designed business end *(right)*. It can serve a multitude of purposes: to pass lines to a dock, to retrieve them, to pull the boat toward the dock, to fend it off without endangering a boatman's hands, to pick up a mooring, or to control the dinghy when maneuvering between pilings or other boats. To perform these tasks, the boathook's pole should be eight feet or longer. On some modern designs, like the aluminum model here, the pole will telescope down to three feet or so for easy stowage; also, the hook fitting may be equipped with a rubber tip for fending. One caution: when fending off, always hold the boathook to one side of the body. Otherwise it could be driven into the chest or stomach when it makes contact.

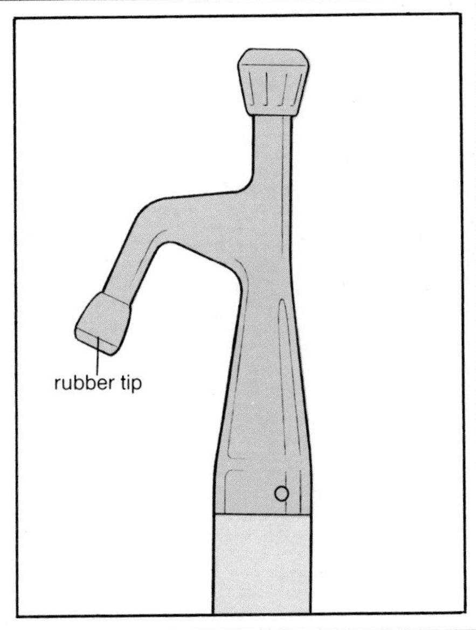

To berth a single-screw cruiser stern first in a narrow slip, this helmsman proceeds along the marina channel until the vessel is abeam the slip's starboard piling. Then he reverses his engine, arresting forward motion, while the bow man drops the bight of a stern spring line over the piling. Meanwhile, the stern man, at the line's other end, prepares to take up slack and snub the spring temporarily.

Throwing the rudder to starboard, the helmsman backs slowly. Because the stern's mobility is restricted by the spring line and the starboard rub rail is hard against the piling, the boat begins to pivot into the slip. (Should current or wind begin to push the transom too close to the port piling, the stern man can take up on the spring line and shorten the turning arc.) Meanwhile, the bow man will set the starboard bow line onto the piling and then lead the port bow line aft.

When the port piling comes within reach, the stern man drops the loop of the port bow line over it. When the boat is in line with the slip, the helmsman will bring the rudder amidships and back the boat in straight while the stern man eases the spring line.

As the boat slides toward the dock, the helmsman halts it with a brief application of forward throttle. The stern man carefully steps ashore and makes the aft lines fast; to keep the transom positioned, he will cross the aft lines, leading the port line to a dock cleat opposite the starboard quarter, and the starboard line to a portside cleat. The bow man secures his forward lines, adjusting them so that the boat lies centered between the pilings and the dock, without touching either.

To avoid the troublesome night music of halyards slatting against the mast, a crew member ties them back with a restraining line attached to a shroud. She uses a short length of line—a shock cord is often substituted—to take up tension until the halyards no longer touch the spar at any point. The line is hitched high enough so that no one will run into it in the dark. After tethering other halyards in similar fashion, she will continue her sound-proofing tour of the deck, checking that the spinnaker pole is firmly seated and that the main sheet is taut enough to hold the main block stationary on its traveler.

Snugging Down at Night

Before sunset—and preferably before the crew turns to dinner—a few steps taken toward bedding down the boat will ensure everyone's comfort and safety through the night. The most crucial one is setting out an anchor light to signal the boat's presence in the hours of darkness. This is required by Coast Guard regulations, which specify that any vessel lying outside a designated anchorage—such as a yacht basin—must carry a white light on the forward section of the boat. On a powerboat, the light is usually mounted on a staff forward; on a sailboat, it is commonly a lamp hung on the headstay about six feet above the deck, as at right. In most waters, the anchor light by law must be bright enough to be seen two miles away on a clear night—and in all directions. The only exception is on the Great Lakes, where a one-mile limit prevails.

With the light properly positioned, the skipper should run through a routine check-out. Most importantly, he should:

(1) Confirm that the anchor is holding by taking several bearings on shore points, then waiting a half hour and taking them again. If the direction of both wind and current have remained steady but the bearings have changed, the anchor is dragging and should be reset.

(2) Inspect to see that the dinghy is riding properly with oars stowed securely.

(3) Check hatches, screens, canvas covers and vents to make sure all are secure.

(4) Secure loose gear or rigging that could blow overboard or flap about noisily. The seemingly harmless pings, thrums and rat-a-tats of shifting deck gear and vibrating rigging can reverberate like clashing cymbals through a cabin when everyone needs sleep after a long day's passage.

Setting the anchor light for the night, one crew member snaps the jib halyard through the light's handle and around the headstay, while the other takes up the slack from near the mast. The line hanging from the bottom of the lamp, called a preventer, will be snubbed to a cleat on deck to keep the light from swinging or riding up the stay. The light shown here runs on batteries, but some skippers use models that plug into a deck outlet, while others rely on kerosene lanterns.

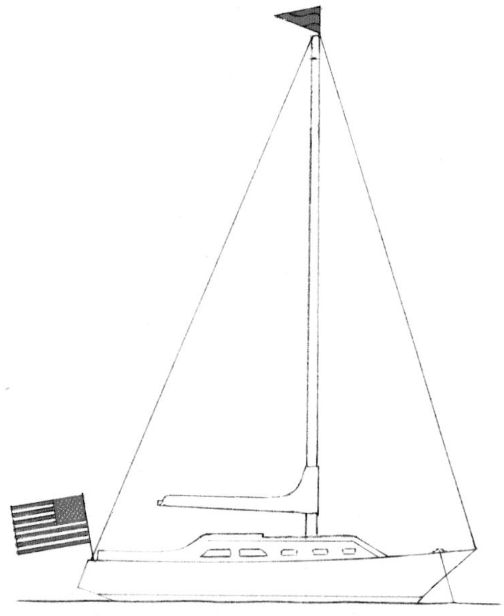

At anchor, a sailboat flies the U.S. ensign on a stern staff, the burgee at the masthead.

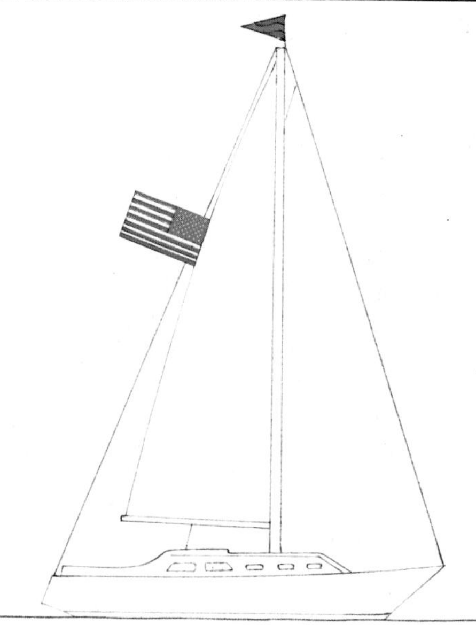

Underway, on a single-masted sailboat, the ensign can fly from the mainsail, two thirds of the way up the leech—or at the stern.

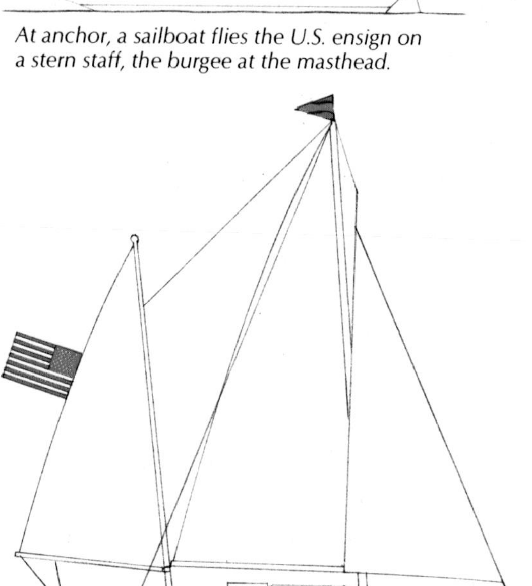

On a two-masted sailboat, the ensign may fly from the leech of the aftermost sail (or from a stern staff), the burgee on the mainmast.

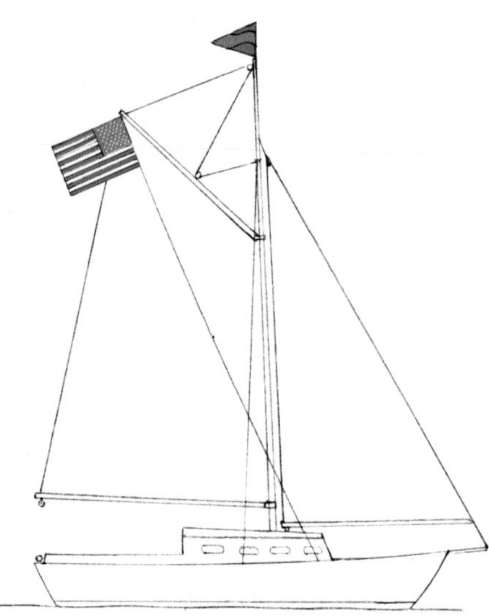

By custom, gaff-rigged boats fly the ensign at the gaff's peak, the burgee at the masthead.

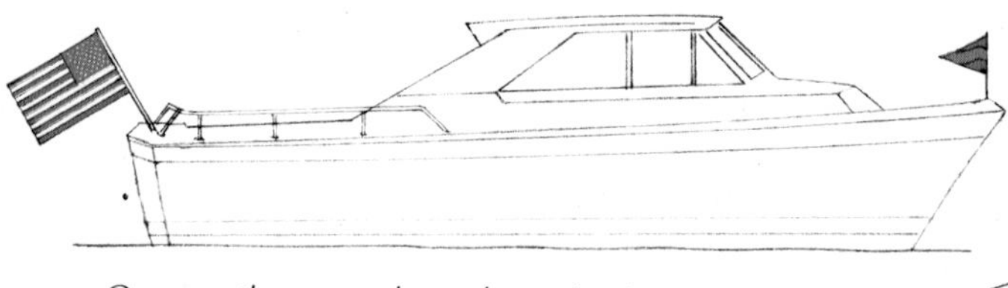

On a mastless powerboat, the ensign is displayed aft; the burgee flies at the bow.

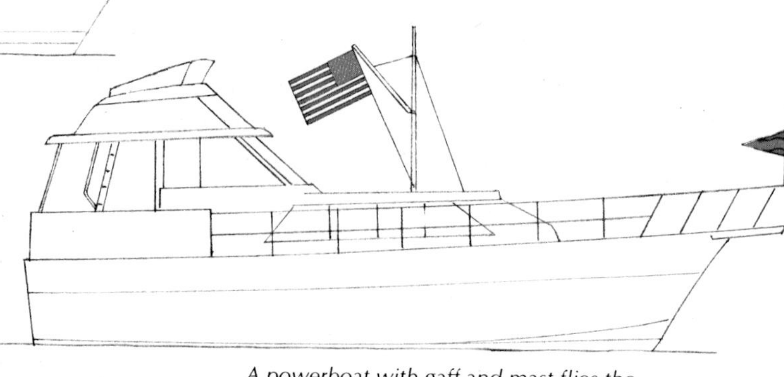

A powerboat with gaff and mast flies the ensign from the gaff, the burgee at the bow.

Showing the Colors

Five thousand years ago, Egyptian vessels flew flags to identify themselves, launching a nautical practice that eventually became so widespread that at one time any unmarked ship on the high seas was considered a pirate. That harsh proviso may no longer apply but most cruising sailors continue to observe custom by displaying a variety of flags for identification. For United States boats, the most important of these is the American flag, whose nautical name is the U.S. ensign. In domestic waters, it may be replaced by the U.S. yacht ensign, bearing 13 stars and an anchor. Another common flag is the burgee, which identifies the yacht club of the boatowner. Although no formal statutes dictate where or when these flags must be flown, most protocol-minded skippers follow an etiquette based on naval usage and yacht-club rulings. At left is a guide to some traditional flag placements on various types of boats.

In foreign waters, the emblem of the territorial power is flown as a courtesy (below); because display customs differ, the boatman should check local practice beforehand. At home or abroad, however, the U.S. ensign always takes the place of honor, and should be flown both at anchor and underway from 8 a.m. until sundown.

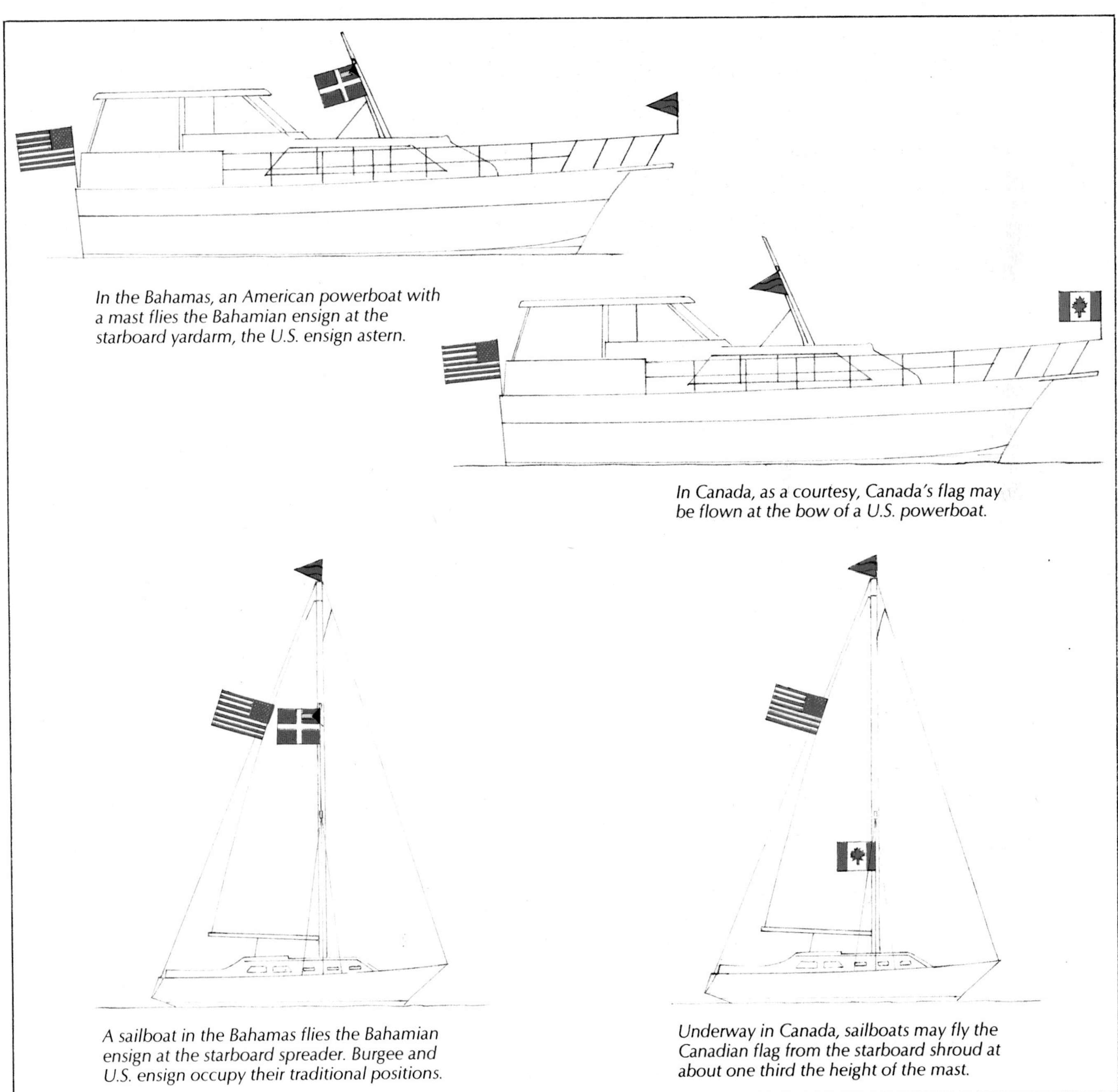

In the Bahamas, an American powerboat with a mast flies the Bahamian ensign at the starboard yardarm, the U.S. ensign astern.

In Canada, as a courtesy, Canada's flag may be flown at the bow of a U.S. powerboat.

A sailboat in the Bahamas flies the Bahamian ensign at the starboard spreader. Burgee and U.S. ensign occupy their traditional positions.

Underway in Canada, sailboats may fly the Canadian flag from the starboard shroud at about one third the height of the mast.

Alfa
Diver down; keep clear

Bravo
Dangerous cargo

Charlie
Yes

Delta
Keep clear

Echo
Altering course to starboard

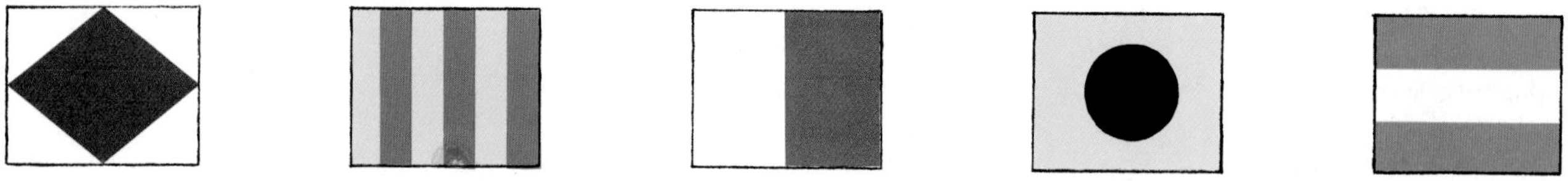

Foxtrot
Disabled

Golf
Want a pilot

Hotel
Pilot on board

India
Altering course to port

Juliett
On fire; keep clear

Kilo
Desire to communicate

Lima
Stop instantly

Mike
I am stopped

November
No

Oscar
Man overboard

Papa
About to sail

Quebec
Request health clearance

Romeo
(No message)

Sierra
Engines going stern

Tango
Keep clear of me

Uniform
Standing into danger

Victor
Require assistance

Whiskey
Require medical help

Xray
Do not carry out your plan

Yankee
Am dragging anchor

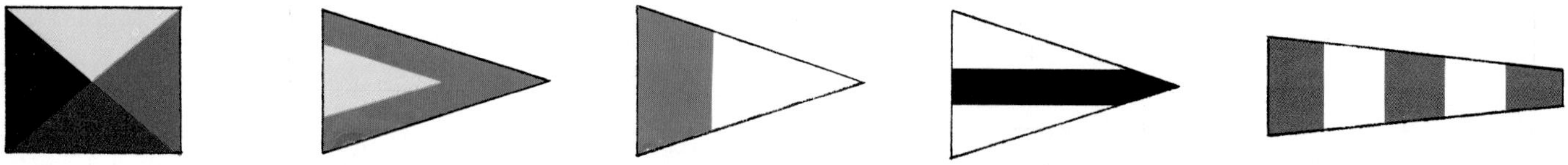

Zulu
Require a tug

1st repeater

2nd repeater

3rd repeater

Answering pennant

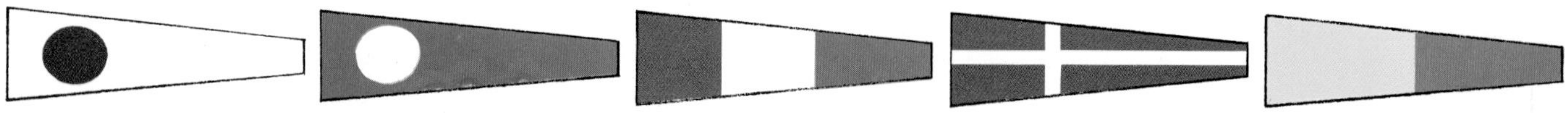

1

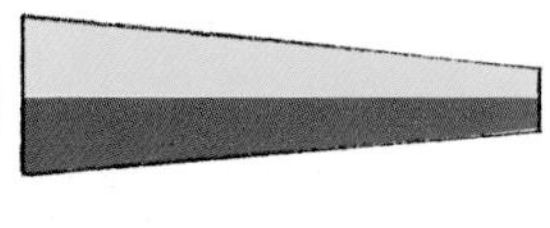

2

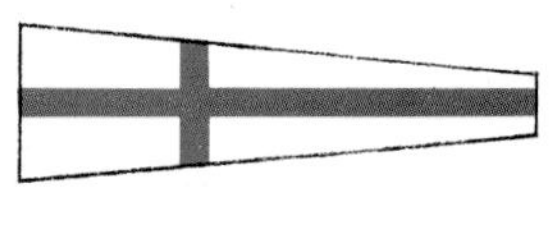

3

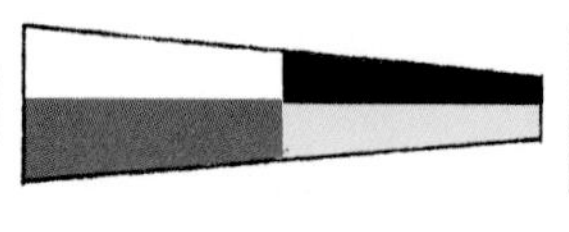

4

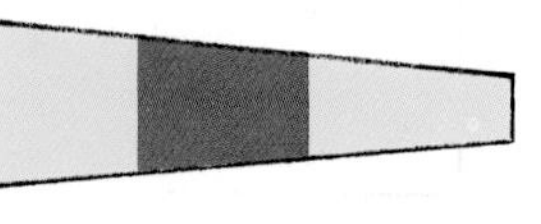

5

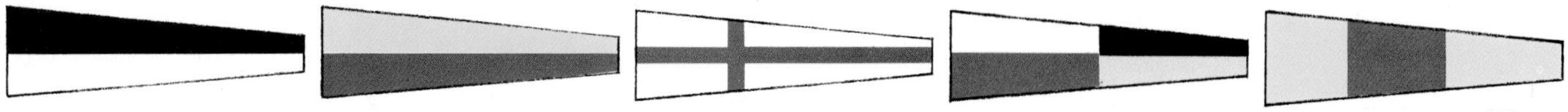

6

7

8

9

0

A Short Course in Signal Reading

Visual signaling by flags, common aboard commercial and naval vessels, is infrequently used for cruising boats, since voice or two-way-radio communication is generally adequate. Nonetheless, skippers should have a knowledge of a few basic signals, such as the ones shown on these pages. Furthermore, understanding the meanings of the international signal flags can add a dimension to cruising in somewhat the same way that familiarity with a foreign language enhances a trip abroad.

The International Code of signals employs 26 alphabetical flags; each one has a distinctive, easily pronounced name like Alfa or Bravo. The flag system also utilizes 10 numerical pennants, three pennants that indicate a repetition of letters or numbers (a number 2 flag hoisted over a repeater pennant would mean 22, for instance), and a flag indicating that an answer is being sent. The Code can get a message across in several ways. Combinations of alphabetical flags spell a word—such as the name of a ship or port—if hoisted beneath the Y and Z flags. An alphabetical flag flying alone carries one of the brief but complete messages listed opposite. And flags flying in pairs (below) carry other standardized messages—some of them extremely urgent.

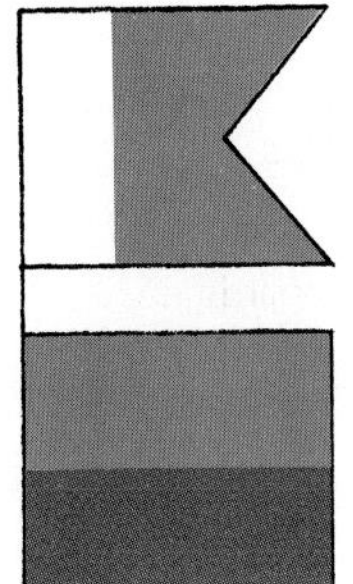

AE Must abandon my vessel

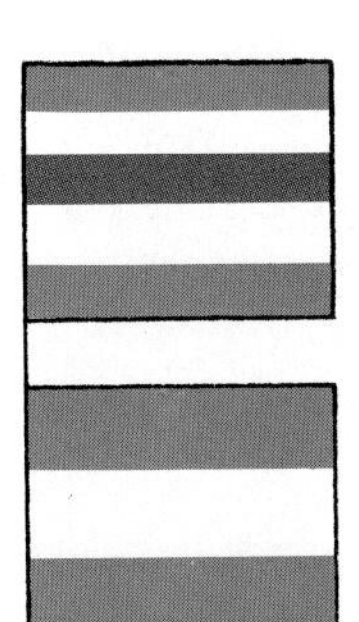

CJ Do you require assistance?

CN Give all possible assistance

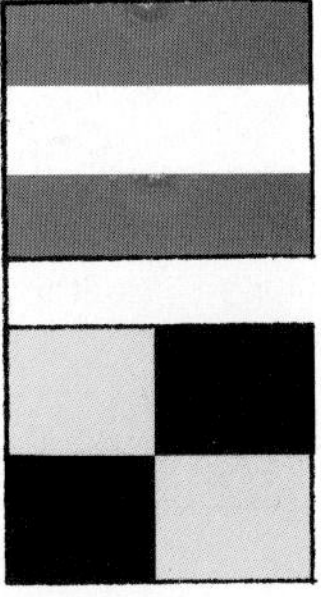

JL You are running the risk of going aground

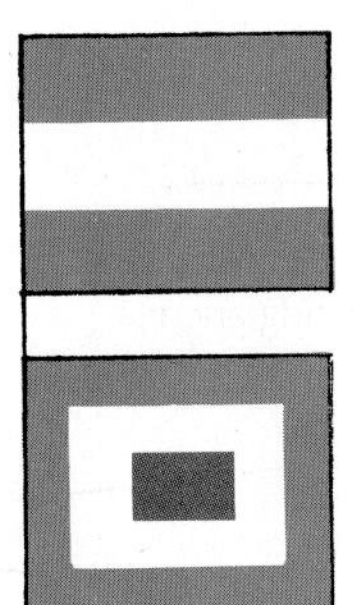

JW Have sprung a leak

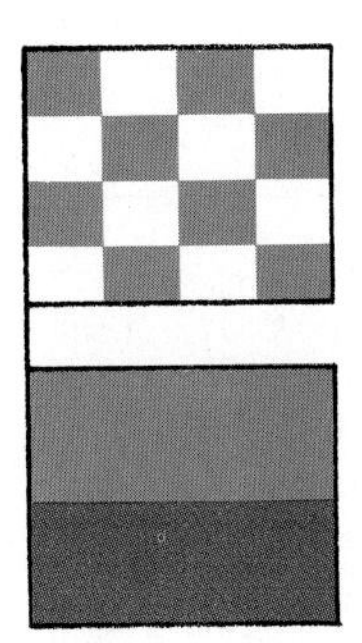

NE Proceed with great caution

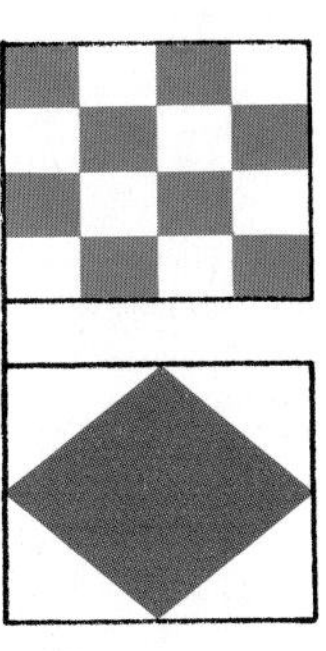

NF You are running into danger

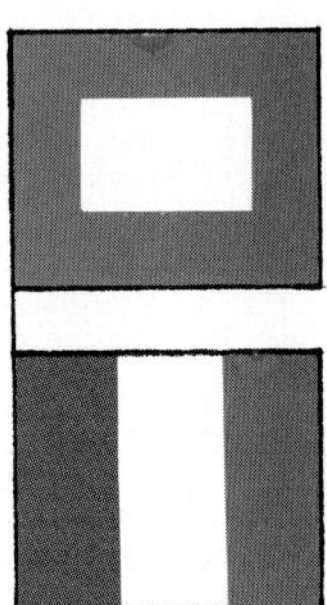

PT What is the state of the tide?

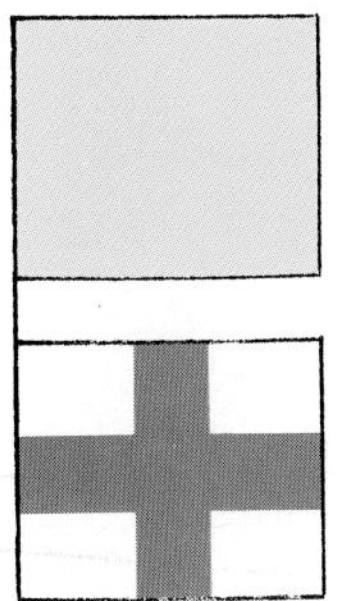

QX Request permission to anchor

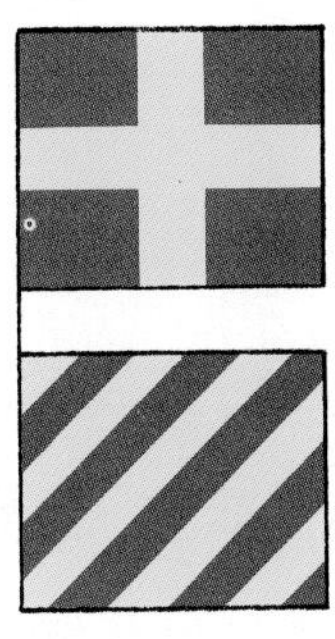

RY Proceed at slow speed when passing me

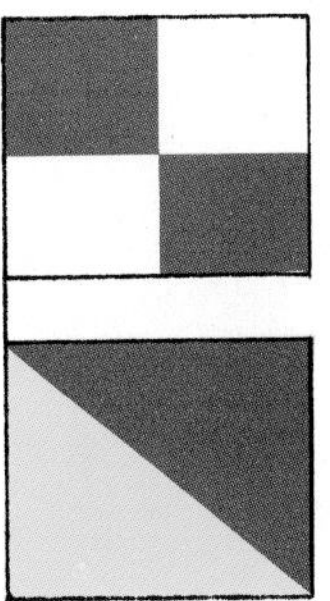

UO Do not enter harbor

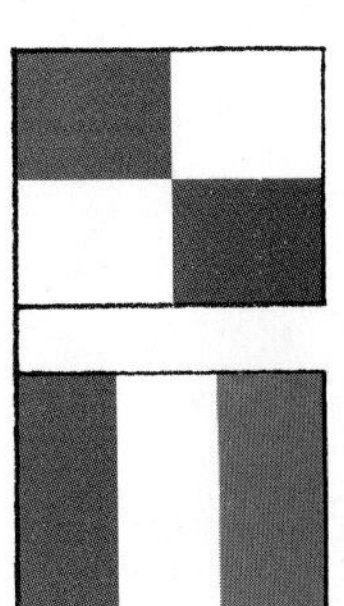

UT Where are you bound for?

A festive display of International Code flags bedecks a ketch in this schematic rendition of the formality called dressing ship. The recommended signal sequence—arrayed on a line weighted at both ends—begins at the water's edge below the bowsprit and extends over the masts and the mizzenmast boom to the waterline aft. The U.S. ensign and club burgee fly at their customary places—on a stern flagstaff and the head of the mainmast, respectively. The head of the mizzenmast carries the private signal of the boat's owner.

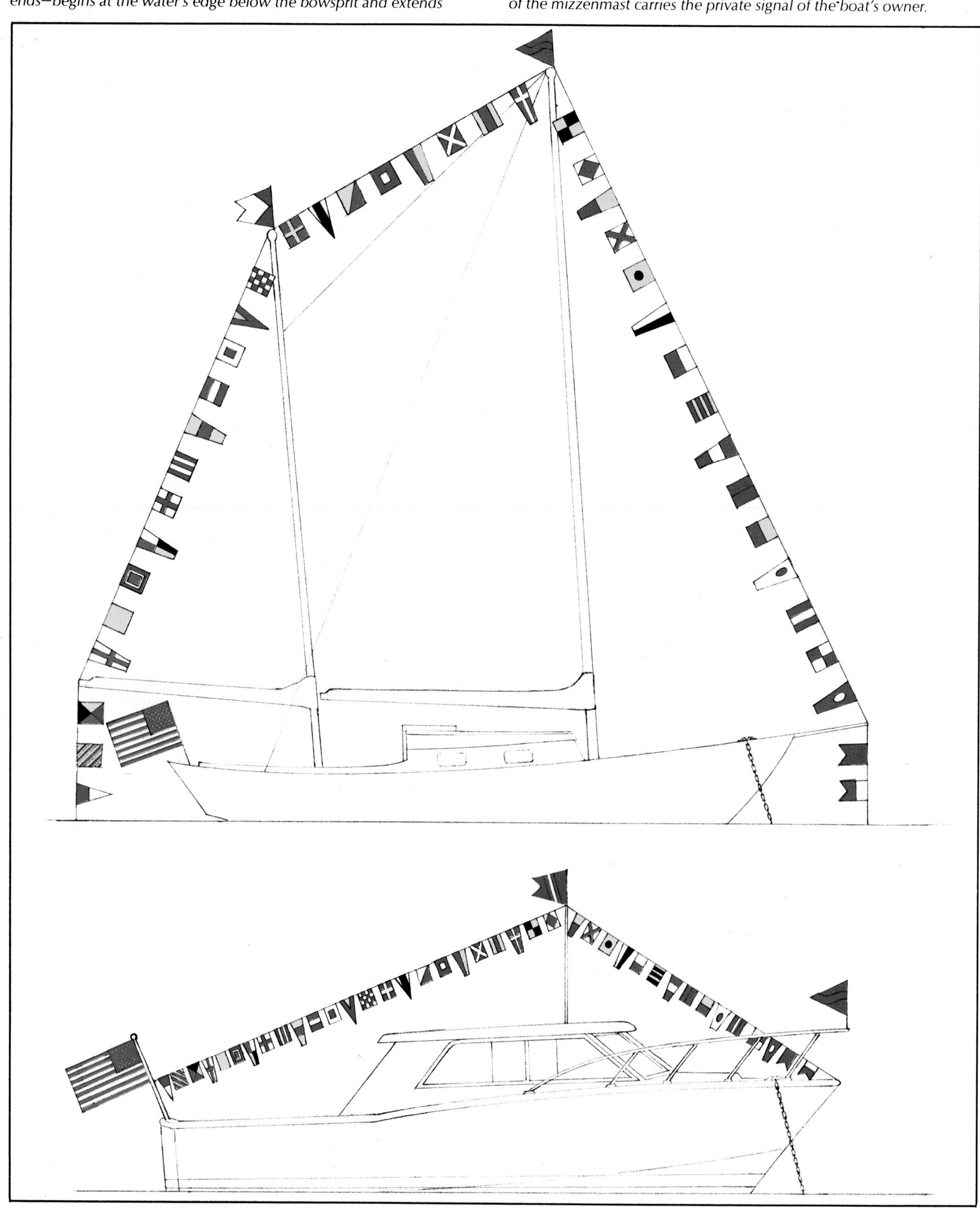

A dressed power cruiser displays the same signal sequence as the ketch at top, but uses smaller flags to fit the entire spectrum of international signals in the available space. (On boats whose size cannot accommodate even the smallest commercially available set of Code flags, the sequence can be arbitrarily shortened.) Here, the short mast that carries the cruiser's anchor light serves to create a showy arch; as on any boat lacking a bowsprit or overhanging bow and stern, the flags do not extend down to the waterline.

Celebrations and Signals

Many cruising skippers carry a set of international signal flags purely for the fun of creating a splendiferous, decorative arch over their boat in honor of a national holiday or a special occasion like a regatta. This custom, called dressing ship, is done only at anchor and only from 8 a.m. until sundown. In order to best show off the contrasting colors and shapes of the signals, some yachtsmen alternate the letters and numerals—a practice originated years ago by the U.S. Navy. One favored sequence runs as follows: A-B-2-U-J-1-K-E-3-G-H-6-I-V-5-F-L-4-D-M-7-P-O-third repeater-R-N-first repeater-S-T-zero-C-X-9-W-Q-8-Z-Y-second repeater. Other flags are not strung with the Code signals, but fly at their usual locations.

However, the basic function of nautical flags is by no means only a shipboard affair. Many yacht clubs have flagstaffs resembling a mast rigged with a gaff and a single yard (below). On such staffs, the gaff is the customary place of honor, and the U.S. ensign flies there, as shown below. The port yardarm is the site of flags of more immediate consequence—signals about the weather that every cruising skipper should heed.

This typical flagstaff—at the Stamford Yacht Club in Connecticut —flies a U.S. ensign at the gaff peak and club burgee at the masthead. A flag betokening the senior officer present—the commodore—is at the starboard yardarm. A small craft advisory is on the port yardarm.

Key Flags to Know

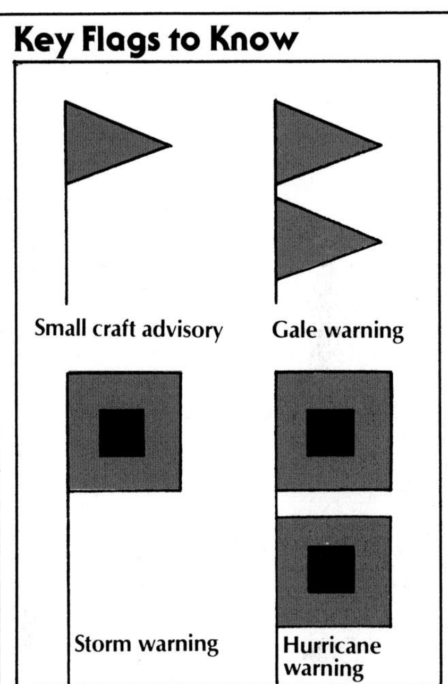

Yacht clubs and Coast Guard stations display these flags to warn of wind danger—the gravest being winds 74 mph and above *(lower right)*.

Glossary

Aft Toward the stern.

Allen wrench An L-shaped hexagonal bar of hardened steel used to drive and remove screws or bolts with hexagonal recessed heads.

Amidships In or near the middle of a boat, either along the longitudinal axis or from side to side.

Athwartships Across the boat.

Auxiliary A boat designed primarily for sailing, but with a supplementary inboard engine.

Bareboat The type of boat charter in which no professional skipper or crew is supplied.

Battens Flexible strips of wood or fiberglass placed in a sail to help the leech retain its proper shape.

Beat To go to windward in a sailboat by sailing alternate legs, with the wind first on one side and then on the other.

Belay To secure a line, usually to a cleat.

Bight An open loop in a rope; a bend in a coastline forming a bay.

Bilge The area of a boat inside the hull and near the bottom—usually beneath floorboards.

Bilge pump A pump used to remove water that collects in the bilge.

Bitt A single or double post fixed on a deck for securing mooring lines and towlines. On a dock, a bitt is more commonly called a bollard.

Block A wood or metal shell enclosing one or more sheaves, through which lines are led.

Bollard A strong metal or wood post on a pier or towboat used to secure docking and towing lines.

Boom A projecting spar used to hold down and extend the foot of a sail.

Bulkhead Any wall in a boat.

Burgee Generically, any swallow-tailed nautical flag; popularly, the identifying signal of a yacht club regardless of shape.

Cabin An enclosed area belowdecks.

Cabin trunk A structure built up above the deck and providing headroom below.

Cast off To let go mooring or docking lines; to remove the turns of a line from a cleat; to untie a knot.

Chafing gear A covering put around a short section of line to reduce wear, or on the rigging to protect the sails.

Chock A metal fitting, usually mounted on or in a boat's rail, to guide hawsers or lines for mooring or towing.

Clevis pin A small cylindrically shaped pin used to close shackles or outhaul fittings, or to fasten a turnbuckle to a chain plate.

Coaming A raised framing around deck openings such as hatches or cockpits to keep water out.

Cockpit A well in the deck, usually aft, where a boat's wheel or tiller is located.

Color An identifying badge, pennant or flag—usually used in the plural.

Companionway A passageway through which a ladder or stairs lead from the deck down to the cabin.

Cutter A sailboat with one mast stepped more than one third of the way aft, capable of carrying two or more sails ahead of the mast; also, a Coast Guard boat.

Dinghy A small rowboat, often a tender to a larger boat; also, any small sailboat.

Ditty bag A bag used by sailors to hold gear needed for repairs on sails or rigging.

Draft The depth a vessel extends below the waterline.

Epoxy glue A resin-based adhesive of exceptional strength and durability, used in patching fiberglass.

Fend off To prevent a moving boat from hitting a dock or other object.

Fid A tapered, pointed wooden tool for insertion between strands of rope while splicing, sometimes having a hole in the blunt end for insertion of rope.

Fiddle A rack or bar used to prevent dishes, pots and other objects from sliding off a counter, table or stove.

Flying bridge A raised platform that affords unobstructed vision for steering and navigation.

Foot To make speed—said of a sailboat.

Foul-weather gear Rain gear worn on board in bad weather, and traditionally called oilskins because in former days cotton jackets and trousers were waterproofed with linseed oil. Modern foul-weather gear is usually of nylon coated with a plastic skin.

Gaff A spar to support and spread the head of a sail of four generally unequal sides. A sail so rigged is gaff-headed.

Gale A range of winds from 28 to 47 knots.

Galley A seagoing kitchen.

Gimbals Pivoted mounts that enable the object they support (a compass, stove, lamp, etc.) to remain level when the boat does not.

Grab rail A securely mounted handhold on or below deck.

Halyard A line used either to hoist or lower a sail.

Hanging locker A closet tall enough for full-length garments.

Hank One of the fittings that attaches the luff of a headsail and a staysail to a stay.

Hatch An opening in the deck giving access below; also, its cover.

Head The forward part of a boat, including the bow and adjacent areas; the uppermost corner of a triangular sail; a seagoing lavatory.

Headstay The foremost stay supporting the mast. The jib is set on the headstay.

Helm The device, usually a tiller or wheel attached or connected to the rudder, by which a boat is steered.

Hurricane A wind of 64 knots or more; a tropical cyclone with extremely high winds.

Intracoastal Waterway The system of inland waterway channels running along the Atlantic and Gulf coasts of the United States from Manasquan Inlet, New Jersey, to the Mexican border in Texas—commonly abbreviated as ICW.

Keel A main structural member, the backbone of the ship running longitudinally along the bottom from stem to stern; also, the vertical downward extension of a sailboat's bottom, usually ballasted, for stability and lateral resistance.

Ketch A boat with a two-masted rig in which the larger, or mainmast, is forward, and the smaller mizzenmast is stepped aft —but forward of the rudder and, usually, of the helm.

Landfall A sighting of or coming to land; also, the land so approached or reached; the land first sighted at the end of a sea voyage.

Lazarette A space for stowage in a boat's stern.

Lead When pronounced "leed," the direction of a line; when pronounced "led," the weight at the end of a line used for taking soundings.

Lead line A line marked off in fathoms and weighted at one end with a lead, used for measuring water depths—also called a sounding line.

Leech The after edge of a sail.

Life lines Safety lines and guardrails rigged around a boat's deck to prevent the crew from being washed overboard.

Locker A chest, cupboard or small compartment for stowing gear.

Log A device for measuring the rate of a ship's motion through the water; also, a ship's journal or written record of the vessel's day-by-day performance, listing speeds, distances traveled, weather conditions, landfalls and other information.

Mainmast Usually, the principal and the heaviest mast of two or more. In yawls and ketches, the forward mast is the mainmast; in schooners and vessels with more than two masts, it is the second mast from forward.

Make fast To secure a line to an object; to doubly secure a cleated—or otherwise tied—line by means of an added hitch.

Marline A two-stranded nautical twine.

Marlinespike A pointed metal tool used in splicing.

Mizzen The sail set on the mizzenmast; the aftermast of a yawl or ketch.

Mizzenmast The aftermast on a yawl or ketch.

Mooring A fixed anchor or weight by which a boat is kept at a permanent berth; the place in which a boat can be moored.

Motor sailer Technically, all craft provided with dual means of propulsion, i.e., sails and motor. The term is most commonly applied to those vessels having a somewhat foreshortened sailing rig and a large motor.

Overhead The interior surface of the cabin roof.

Port The left side of the boat, looking forward; also, a contraction for porthole.

Quarter Either side of a boat's stern; to sail with the wind on the quarter.

Quarter berth Bunk extending along the stern area of a ship's side.

Raw water The water supply pumped into a boat from the body of water in which it is floating, used for engine cooling, toilet flushing, etc.

Reach A course sailed between a beat and a run, with the wind coming more or less at right angles over a boat's side. On a close reach the wind is farther forward; on a broad reach, farther aft.

Rig A noun indicating the arrangement of masts, rigging and sails that distinguishes a vessel by type, for example, ketch, yawl, etc.; also, a verb meaning to prepare a boat or some piece of nautical gear for service.

Rigging The lines or wires fitted to spars and sails for support and control. Standing rigging is made up of the shrouds and stays that provide lateral and longitudinal support to the spars. Running rigging comprises the halyards, sheets, tackles, outhauls and downhauls to put up, take down and adjust sails.

Ripstop tape Nylon spinnaker-cloth with contact adhesive backing, for mending spinnakers and for quick, temporary repairs of other sails.

Rode An anchor line.

Rub rail A strip of wood, sometimes overlaid with metal, extending beyond the topsides of a boat as protection from bumping on docks, piles, etc.

Runabout A small, lightweight motorboat with an open cockpit.

Sail slide A small metal or plastic fitting often used on the forward and lower edges of a mainsail or mizzen to attach it to a track along the appropriate mast and boom. A slide may also be used on the head, luff or foot of a gaff sail.

Sailmaker's palm A stiff leather strap that fits around the hand and contains an inverted metal thimble, used to push a sailmaker's needle through heavy sailcloth —also called a palm thimble or palm.

Schooner A sailboat that generally has two masts (though some have had up to seven). The mainmast is aft of a smaller foremast, and the sails are either jib-headed or gaff-headed.

Scope The ratio between the length of an anchor rode and the depth of the water in which a vessel is anchored.

Sea buoys The first buoys a mariner encounters when approaching a channel or harbor entrance from the sea.

Seacock A shutoff valve attached to through-hull pipes.

Seizing wire All-purpose wire used to bind ropes together or to another object.

Settee berth A long cabin seat that converts into a bunk.

Shackle A U-shaped metal fitting with a cross pin or clevis pin that fits across the opening of the U as a closure.

Shear pin A replaceable pin fixing the propeller to an outboard motor shaft, and designed to break under excess stress.

Sheave The grooved wheel in a block, or in a masthead fitting or elsewhere, over which a rope runs—pronounced "shiv."

Shock cord A cord made of rubber strands bound in woven casing and used for such tasks as stopping sails, lashing a tiller in place overnight, holding halyards away from a metal mast at night, etc.

Shrouds Ropes or wires led from the mast to chain plates at deck level on either side of the mast, and which hold the mast from falling or bending sideways.

Slip A narrow berth for a boat, either at a pier or dock.

Sloop A sailboat with a single mast that is stepped not more than one third of the way aft from the bow. A sloop usually carries only one headsail.

Small craft advisory A warning (either verbal or visual) issued by the Coast Guard or other authority to alert boatmen to potentially hazardous weather or sea conditions.

Snatch block A block hinged on one side and latched on the other so that it can be opened to receive the bight of a line and then closed to hold the line securely.

Snub To quickly check, by cleating or other means, a line that is running out.

Spinnaker A full-bellied, lightweight sail set forward of the mast on a spinnaker pole and carried when a sailboat is reaching or running.

Splice A method of joining together two ends of line or of creating a loop in a line by interweaving the strands.

Spreaders Pairs of horizontal struts attached to each side of the mast and used to hold the shrouds away from the mast, thus giving them a wider purchase.

Spring line A long docking line rigged to limit a boat's fore-and-aft motion, usually run from a boat's stern to a point well forward, and from the bow well aft.

Stanchion An upright metal pole, bolted to the deck, and used to support permanent fixtures such as life lines.

Stay A rope or wire running forward or aft from the mast to support it. The headstay is the foremost stay on which the jib is set; a forestay is aft of the headstay and carries a staysail; the backstay offsets the pull of the headstay.

Storm A range of winds from 48 to 63 knots; the generic term for severe foul weather.

Thimble A grooved round or teardrop-shaped metal or plastic fitting spliced into an eye of rope or wire to prevent chafe and distortion of the eye.

Through-bolt A deck fastening that penetrates the deck and is fastened below with a nut and washer.

Trawler A boat used in trawling, or commercial fishing with a net; a pleasure boat designed along the same lines.

Trim tab A tab device affixed to the lower units of some outboard motors that compensates for the torque produced by the propeller, sometimes made of magnesium to act as a sacrificial anode to help prevent corrosion; a hinged plate attached to the transom of a powerboat to keep the stern from burying when the boat is run at high speeds.

Turnbuckle An adjustable fastening for attaching the standing rigging to the chain plates, and for adjusting the tension on the standing rigging.

Turnbuckle toggle A small fitting, shaped like a shackle, at the bottom of a turnbuckle that fastens it to a chain plate —and allows more freedom of angle for the turnbuckle.

V-berths Twin bunks arranged in a V pattern, and typically placed in the forward part of the boat.

Whip To bind the end of a rope with twine, cord or plastic sealant to keep it from fraying.

Winch A device with a revolving drum, around which a line may be turned in order to provide mechanical advantage in hoisting or hauling.

Yawl A boat with a two-masted rig in which the mizzen, or jigger, is abaft the rudderpost and the helm. The yawl's mizzen is smaller than the ketch's, as well as being placed farther aft.

Bibliography

General

Beiser, Arthur, *The Proper Yacht.* The Macmillan Company, 1970.

Chapman, Charles Frederic, *Piloting, Seamanship and Small Boat Handling.* Motor Boating & Sailing Books, The Hearst Corporation, 1974.

Colgate, Steve, *Manual of Cruising Sailboat Techniques.* Offshore Sailing School, Ltd., 1975.

Heaton, Peter, *Cruising: Sail or Power.* Penguin Books, Inc., 1970.

Henderson, Richard:
The Cruiser's Compendium. Henry Regnery Company, 1973.
Hand, Reef & Steer. Henry Regnery Company, 1965.
Sail and Power. Naval Institute Press, 1973.

Hiscock, Eric C., *Cruising Under Sail.* Oxford University Press, 1972.

International Code of Signals. U.S. Naval Oceanographic Office, 1969.

Kals, W. S., *Practical Boating.* Doubleday & Company, 1969.

Kotsch, William J., *Weather for the Mariner.* Naval Institute Press, 1972.

Rigg, H. K., *Rigg's Handbook of Nautical Etiquette.* Alfred A. Knopf, 1971.

Street, Donald M., Jr., *The Ocean Sailing Yacht.* W. W. Norton & Company, Inc., 1973.

Watson, Ted, *Handling Small Boats Under Power.* Adlard Coles, Ltd., 1971.

Worldwide Yacht Charter & Boat Rental Guide. 18226 Mack Avenue, Grosse Point, Mich. 48236.

Living Afloat

American National Red Cross:
Advanced First Aid & Emergency Care. Doubleday & Company, 1973.
Standard First Aid & Personal Safety. Doubleday & Company, 1975.

Brindze, Ruth, *Seamanship Below Deck.* Harcourt Brace and Company, 1947.

Doherty, Donna Marxer, *The Boatcook.* Seven Seas Press, 1972.

Fuller, Beverly, *Cooking on Your Knees.* David McKay Company, Inc., 1973.

Sheldon, Paul B., *First Aid Afloat.* Yachting Publishing Corporation, 1972.

Winters, Nancy, *Feasting Afloat.* Simon & Schuster, 1972.

Woodward, Nancy Hyden, *The Mariner's Cookbook.* Cornerstone Library, 1969.

Historical

Bunting, William, *Steamers, Schooners, Cutters and Sloops: The Marine Photographs of Nathaniel Stebbins, 1884-1907.* Houghton Mifflin, 1974.

Hofman, Erik, *The Steam Yachts: An Era of Elegance.* John De Graff, Inc., 1970.

Hoyt, Edwin P., *The Goulds: A Social History.* Weybright and Talley, 1969.

Lane, Wheaton J., *Commodore Vanderbilt: An Epic of the Steam Age.* Alfred A. Knopf, 1942.

O'Connor, Richard, *The Scandalous Mr. Bennet.* Doubleday, 1962.

Robinson, William W., *Legendary Yachts: Power and Sail.* Macmillan, 1971.

Where to Buy Charts

Most marine-supply stores carry a full complement of the government charts, tables, light lists and piloting guides needed to navigate local waters. If the boatman finds that the store is out of stock, however, or if he requires charts or other publications for distant areas, he can obtain the necessary materials by writing directly to the appropriate issuing office, as listed below.

1. National Ocean Survey, Distribution Division, C44, 6501 Lafayette Avenue, Riverdale, Maryland 20840. Telephone: (301) 436-6990. Publishes charts for all U.S. coastal areas, the Great Lakes, sections of major rivers; *Coast Pilots,* tide tables, tidal current tables, tidal current charts, *Chart No. 1;* catalogues of NOS charts. Distributes *Notice to Mariners.*

2. Defense Mapping Agency Depot, 5801 Tabor Avenue, Philadelphia, Pennsylvania 19120. Telephone: (215) 697-4262. Issues charts of foreign waters, a chart catalogue and *Notice to Mariners.* Distributes *Chart No. 1.*

3. U.S. Army Corps of Engineers. The district office in each state issues charts and chart lists for inland lakes and waterways.

4. Lake Survey Center, 630 Federal Building, Detroit, Michigan 48226. Publishes charts of the Great Lakes and connecting rivers, Lake Champlain and New York State Canals, and a chart catalogue.

5. Superintendent of Documents, Government Printing Office, Washington, D.C. 20402. Distributes light lists.

6. Hydrographic Chart Distribution, Canadian Hydrographic Service, Surveys and Mapping Building, 615 Booth Street, Ottawa, Ontario, Canada. Distributes Canadian charts and marine publications.

Boating Courses

A prudent step between reading about boating and going afloat is taking a course in boat handling, seamanship and safety. Hundreds of local schools and clubs schedule private classes in all facets of boating. The national organizations listed below provide curricula free or at little cost. Many state and city recreation departments also sponsor public courses.

1. U.S. Power Squadrons. More than 400 local units of this national organization of recreational boatmen present free to the public a 10-lesson course in basic boating safety at least once a year. To its members, the USPS also offers advanced instruction on seamanship and navigation. For information, call your local unit, or national headquarters in New Jersey, toll free, (800) 243-6000.

2. The U.S. Coast Guard. For those who live where other general courses are unavailable, the Coast Guard offers a correspondence "Skipper's Course." Write to the Office of Boating Safety, 400 Seventh Street, SW, Washington, D.C. 20590.

3. The Coast Guard Auxiliary. A volunteer civilian arm of the service, the auxiliary sponsors a number of courses in boating safety for the public. Call one of the 18 district offices or your local group.

4. The American Red Cross. Many local Red Cross chapters periodically conduct small-boat safety classes designed by the national organization.

Acknowledgments

Portions of *Cruising* were written by Peter Swerdloff. The clothing, sports equipment, marine hardware and supplies photographed for Chapter 2 were provided by: Abercrombie & Fitch,.New York, N.Y.; David O. Alber Associates Inc., New York, N.Y.; Brewer's Marine Center, Mamaroneck, N.Y.; The Fulton Supply Co., New York, N.Y.; Goldbergs' Marine Center, New York, N.Y.; Hathaway Reiser and Raymond, Stamford, Conn.; Jensen Marine Division of Bangor Punta Operations, Marlboro, N.J.; LaSalle Automotive Distributors Corp., New York, N.Y.; Liberty Music, New York, N.Y.; Nordiska, New York, N.Y.; Julius Peterson Outboard Division, Nyack, N.Y.; Ratsey and Lapthorn Inc., City Island, N.Y.; Richards Aqualung Center, New York, N.Y.; Universal Motors Division of Medalist Industries, Oshkosh, Wis.; Al Watanabe Marine Service, Mamaroneck, N.Y.; J. H. Westerbeke Corp., Avon, Mass.; Yorkville Inc., North Branford, Conn. For help given in the preparation of this book, the editors also wish to thank the following: John Beattie, Chrysler Corporation, Marysville, Mich.; Dick Bell, Gloucester, Mass.; Mr. and Mrs. Curt Bliven, Seattle, Wash.; William Bouchard, O'Day Yachts, Fall River, Mass.; Linda Briggs, The Moorings, Ltd., New Orleans, La.; Mrs. Edwin H. Burk Jr., Shipmate Stove Division, Richmond Ring Co., Sanderton, Pa.; Bruce Calhoun, Eastsound, Wash.; Tom Chuvet, New York, N.Y.; John A. Cogswell, AMF Paceship Yachts, Waterbury, Conn.; Donald Danilek, Port Washington, N.Y.; John De Graff, Clinton Corners, N.Y.; William Duggen, Fairfield, Conn.; Tina Engelman, Tupperware Home Parties, Orlando, Fla.; Agnew Fisher, Greenwich, Conn.; John C. Flad, Marvel Industries, Dayton, Ohio; Russ Fradkin, New York, N.Y.; Cindy Freeman, Stevens Yachts, Inc., New York, N.Y.; Edwin S. Gaynor, Southport, Conn.; Don Gittens, Flower Hill Estates, N.Y.; Peter and Mary Gray, Scotia, N.Y.; Mr. and Mrs. Kenneth Grunert, The Grunert Co., Osbornville, N.J.; Lou Haufman, Henry Knese Inc., College Point, N.Y.; Tom and Sue Healy, Flamingo Houseboat Rentals, Flamingo, Fla.; Sohei Hori, Librarian, New York Yacht Club, New York, N.Y.; Henry Karlin, Great Neck, N.Y.; Bonnie Knapp, Florida West Coast Charter Service, Clearwater, Fla.; Lieutenant Douglas Kroll, U.S. Coast Guard, Governors Island, N.Y.; Robert B. Kyle Jr., New York, N.Y.; Gerald LaMarque, Nichols Yacht Yard, Mamaroneck, N.Y.; Dottie Land, Fleet Indigo, Treasure Island, Fla.; Elliot Lief, Velcro Corp., New York, N.Y.; Joe and Thea Lucarelli, and family, Rumson, N.J.; Michael Lucia Jr., I.M.P. Boats, Iola, Kans.; Tom McElhatten, Florida West Coast Charter Service, Clearwater, Fla.; Robert A. Massey, Navesink Yacht Sales, Inc., Sea Bright, N.J.; Chappy Miller, Manhasset Bay Yacht Club, Port Washington, N.Y.; Clair Oberly, Clair Yachts, Inc., Long Beach, Calif.; William O'Donovan, King George II Inn, Bristol, Pa.; Brendan J. Palmer, Port Washington, N.Y.; Henry Scheel, Scheel Yachts, Rockland, Me.; Clark Schuler, Imtra Corp., Medford, Mass.; W. L. Scranton, Pearson Yachts, Bristol, R.I.; Norris Shenahan, Chesapeake Bareboat Charters, Oxford, Md.; Daniel M. Shepherd, Thunderbird Boats of Florida, North Miami, Fla.; Elliot Simms, Flagship Yachts, Inc., Port Washington, N.Y.; Irene Smith, Caribbean Sailing Yachts, Ltd., Tenafly, N.J.; Wendell M. Smith, Stamford Yacht Club, Stamford, Conn.; Jack Vincent, American Marine, Ltd., Newport Beach, Calif.

Picture Credits *Credits from left to right are separated by semicolons, from top to bottom by dashes.*

Cover—Enrico Ferorelli. 6,7—David A. Barnes. 9—Bruce Kirby. 12—Chris Caswell. 14—Jack Ward—drawing by Dale Gustafson. 15—Drawing by Ted Giavis—Peter Barlow. 16—Drawing by Ted Giavis—Jim Olive. 17—Drawing by Dale Gustafson—Mike Hirst. 18—Jack Ward—drawing by Jim Whitman Studio. 19—Drawing by Dale Gustafson—Flip Schulke from Black Star. 20—Al Satterwhite from Camera 5—drawing by Dale Gustafson. 21—David A. Barnes—drawing by Jim Whitman Studio. 22,23—John Zimmerman (2)—drawing by Jim Whitman Studio. 24,25—Drawing by Jim Whitman Studio—David A. Barnes (2). 26,27—Henry Groskinsky; Thomas Sennett—drawing by Dale Gustafson. 28,29—Morris Rosenfeld. 30,31—Morris Rosenfeld except top left from *Steam Yachts: An Era of Elegance* by Eric Hofman, John De Graff Inc., courtesy *Rudder,* copied by Paulus Leeser. 32,33—Morris Rosenfeld. 34,35—Reprinted with permission of *Rudder,* © Fawcett Publications Inc., copied by Paulus Leeser. 36,37—*The New York Times;* Wide World. 38—Al Freni. 40,41—National Oceanic and Atmospheric Administration, National Ocean Survey. 42 through 55—Al Freni. 56,57—Al Freni; Gary Miller. 58,59—Eric Schweikardt. 60—Al Freni. 61—Drawing by John Sagan. 64 through 71—Enrico Ferorelli. 72—Ken Kay. 74,75—Ralph Morse except top left Don Hinkle. 76—Ken Kay. 77—Ken Kay, drawing by Fred Wolff. 78,79—Ralph Morse. 80 through 91—Drawings by Fred Wolff. 92 through 99—John Robaton from Camera 5. 100—Al Satterwhite from Camera 5. 102—Robert Perron. 103—Robert Perron—drawing by Nicholas Fasciano. 104,105—Drawings by Nicholas Fasciano. 106 through 109—Drawings by Dale Gustafson. 110,111,112—Drawings by Jim Whitman Studio, photos by James Eisenman. 113—Gary Miller—drawing by Jim Whitman Studio. 114—Drawings by Jim Whitman Studio. 115—Enrico Ferorelli. 116,117—Drawings by Dale Gustafson. 118—Enrico Ferorelli. 119—James Eisenman. 120—Enrico Ferorelli—James Eisenman. 121—Drawings by Jim Whitman Studio. 122,123—Enrico Ferorelli. 124, 125—Enrico Ferorelli, drawing by John Sagan. 126—Enrico Ferorelli—Al Freni. 127 through 133—Enrico Ferorelli. 134—Norman Fortier. 136—Henry Groskinsky—drawing by William G. Teodecki. 137—Drawings by William G. Teodecki. 138, 139—Drawings by Fred Wolff. 140—James Eisenman—drawing by William G. Teodecki. 141—Drawings by William G. Teodecki. 142—Drawing by Nicholas Fasciano—Terry Walker. 143—Terry Walker. 144—Eric Schweikardt. 145—Terry Walker. 146,147—Tomas Sennett. 148—Al Satterwhite from Camera 5. 149—Al Satterwhite from Camera 5—Terry Walker. 150—James Eisenman—drawing by William G. Teodecki. 151—Tomas Sennett. 152—Drawings by Nicholas Fasciano. 153—Henry Groskinsky—drawings by Nicholas Fasciano. 154,155—Stanley Rosenfeld—drawings by Nicholas Fasciano. 156,157—Drawings by Fred Wolff. 158, 159—Stephen Green-Armytage. 160,161—Eric Schweikardt. 162,163—Drawings by John Sagan. 164,165—Drawings by Tesoro & Tesoro, Inc. 166—Drawings by John Sagan. 167—Humphrey Sutton; drawing by Tesoro & Tesoro, Inc.

Index

Page numbers in italics indicate a photograph or drawing of the subject mentioned.

Printed in U.S.A.